Praise for *Predators and Profits*

"As investors across the globe ponder the lessons of the fanciful financial era that appears to have come to a shuddering halt, you can do no better than begin with this remarkable book by Martin Howell. *Predators and Profits* sets a high standard in analyzing just what went wrong during the classic bubble we have just witnessed and presents a thorough, easy-to-navigate compendium that is the definitive study of what went wrong with capitalism."

—John Bogle
Founder
Vanguard Group

"Martin Howell's *Predators and Profits* shows us many of the important reasons why we are in the worst bear market since the 1930s. Well-written and researched, it is must reading for anyone interested in preventing the predators from looting their portfolios, or those of millions of other investors, the next time a market fad runs wild."

—David Dreman
Chairman and Chief Investment Officer
Dreman Value Management L.L.C.

"After three lean years on the stock market and countless revelations of the corporate and financial chicanery that underpinned the bubble, making smart investment decisions has become a tough challenge. Martin Howell's book is at once a caustic commentary on the questionable practices of executives, analysts, accountants and assorted cheerleaders of the boom times, and a first-rate guide for investors wanting to stay in the market but steer clear of the predators."

—Romesh Vaitilingam
Co-author
Dean LeBaron's Treasury of Investment Wisdom

Predators and Profits

100+ Ways for Investors to Protect Their Nest Eggs

Martin Howell

REUTERS

Published by **Prentice Hall**

A Cataloging-in-Publication data record of this book can be obtained from the Library of Congress.

Executive Editor: *Jim Boyd*
Production Supervisor: *Faye Gemmellaro*
Marketing Manager: *John Pierce*
Manufacturing Manager: *Alexis Heydt-Long*
Developmental Editor: *Jennifer Blackwell*
Editorial Assistant: *Linda Ramagnano*
Cover Design Director: *Jerry Votta*
Cover Designer: *Nina Scuderi*

Reuters:
Executive Editor: *Stephen Jukes*
Coordinating Editor: *Peter Millership*
Text Editor: *Giles Elgood*
Commercial Manager: *Alisa Bowen*

© 2003 Reuters
Published by Pearson Education, Inc.
Publishing as Reuters Prentice Hall
Upper Saddle River, NJ 07458

Reuters Prentice Hall offers excellent discounts on this book when ordered in quantity for bulk purchases or special sales.

For more information, please contact U.S. Corporate and Government Sales: 1-800-382-3419, corpsales@pearsontechgroup.com. For sales outside of the United States, please contact International Sales: 1-317-581-3793, international@pearsontechgroup.com.

Printed in the United States of America

1st printing

ISBN 0-13-140244-7

Pearson Education Ltd.
Pearson Education Australia Pty, Ltd.
Pearson Education Singapore, Pte. Ltd.
Pearson Education North Asia, Ltd.
Pearson Education Canada, Ltd.
Pearson Educación de Mexico, S.A. de C.V.
Pearson Education—Japan
Pearson Education Malaysia, Pte. Ltd.

For my wonderful daughters
Mary-Louise and Fionnuala

Contents

2 Pipedreams and Big Lies   19

3 The Superstar CEO: Celebrities, Showmen, and Destroyers   35

4   Jets, Parachutes, and Stealth Wealth: Pay for Performance or Pay for Plundering   55

5   Caffeine Badly Needed: Sleepy, Inept, and Tainted Boards   79

6   Growing Mushrooms: The Art of the Opaque, Sneaky, and Buried   99

7   Culture of Greed: Sports Stadiums, Shooting the Messenger, and Rank and Yank   **117**

8   Earnings Tricks and Games: Manipulating the Numbers and "Creative" Fraud   129

9 Goosing, Stuffing, and Faking: Tricks of the Trade to Drive Revenue Up and Costs Down   151

10 Beyond Their Means: Balance Sheet Clues That May Stop You from Losing Your Shirt   167

11 Snakes and Ladders: Spinning, Flipping, and Walking through Wall Street's Walls 181

12 At the Scene of the Crime: Funds Became Part of the Happy Conspiracy 197

13 Where Were the Auditors? Counting Fictitious Beans   215

Foreword
What Went Wrong
with Capitalism?

It was more than 150 years ago that the poet and journalist Charles Mackay coined the phrase "the extraordinary popular delusions and the madness of crowds." Today, as global investors ponder the painful lessons of the stock market boom and bust, Mackay's phrase rings truer than ever. Every age, he argued in his classic study of 1841, had its peculiar folly, scheme, or fantasy into which even otherwise rational investors plunge, "spurred on by the love of gain, the necessity of excitement, or the mere force of imitation."

Predators and Profits catalogues those very follies and examines just what went wrong with capitalism during the classic bubble we have just witnessed—a bubble that is right up there with the tulip mania in Holland in the 1630s, the great South-Sea Bubble of 1710–1720, and the Great Crash of the New York Stock Exchange in 1929–1933.

This most recent epidemic of high hopes, faulty finances, and pervasive greed by the corporate, financial, and auditing communities, as well as by investors themselves, found its roots in a fundamental perversion of our capitalist system.

A contemporary journalist, William Pfaff, writing in *The International Herald Tribune* in 2002, described what happened as "a pathological mutation in capitalism." The classic system—owners' capitalism—was based on a dedication to serving the interests of the corporation's owners in maximizing the return on their capital investment. But a new system developed—managers' capitalism—in which, he concluded, "the corporation came to be run to profit its managers, in complicity if not conspiracy with accountants and the managers of other corporations."

How did this happen? "Because the markets had so diffused corporate ownership that no responsible owner exists. This is morally unacceptable, but also a corruption of capitalism itself."

Scraping the Barrel

More times than I care to count, I've heard business and financial leaders argue that things are not as bad as they seem, that the problem lies in "just a few bad apples." But while only a tiny minority of those leaders have been implicated in criminal behavior, I'm afraid that the barrel itself—the very structure of our system—is bad. While that may seem a harsh indictment, I believe it is a fair one. Indeed, Martin Howell lists no fewer than 175 (!) "red flags," each describing a particular shortcoming in our recent business, financial, and investment practices.

I have witnessed many of them right before my own eyes.

It is now clear that our capitalist system—as all systems sometimes do—has experienced a profound failure, a failure with a whole variety of causes, each interacting and reinforcing the other: the stock market mania driven by the idea that we were in a new era; the notion that our corporations were trees that could grow to the sky and beyond; the rise of the imperial chief executive officer; the failure of our gatekeepers, the auditors, regulators, legislators, and the boards of directors who forgot to whom they owed their duties; the change in our financial institutions from being stock owners to being stock traders; the promotional hyperbole of Wall Street; the frenzied excitement of the media; and of course the eager members of the investing public, reveling in the easy wealth that seemed like a cornucopia, at least while it lasted. It was this happy conspiracy that drove business standards down even as it drove stock prices up.

Perception vs. Reality

Yet when stock prices are allowed to slip away from their moorings of corporate value, a day of reckoning is never far away. The price of a stock is perception, but the value of a corporation is reality. And when perception soars far above reality, the gap must inevitably be reconciled in favor of reality. Given the nature of competitive capitalism, it was impossible for managers to build corporate value at the rapid rate at which the stock market bubble inflated. Over the long term, earnings of U.S. corporations have grown at an annual rate of about 6 percent, and they did just that during the great bull market of 1982–2000. Yet, the total return on the U.S. stock market soared to almost 20 percent per year. The bear market is now reconciling that gap.

Martin Howell is one of the few observers to note that mutual fund managers played a major role in the happy conspiracy, accurately describing them as "far from innocent spectators . . . (who) played the role of sirens luring investors onto the rocks." The biggest failure of the funds was the metamorphosis from an own-a-stock industry to a rent-a-stock industry, focusing on the momentary precision of short-term stock prices rather than the eternal vagueness of long-term intrinsic corporate value.

Yet mutual fund managers could hardly have been ignorant of what was going on in corporate America. Even before the stock market bubble burst, the industry's well-educated, highly trained, experienced professional analysts and portfolio managers must have been poring over company fiscal statements; evaluating corporate plans; and measuring the extent to which long-term corporate goals were being achieved, how cash flow compared with reported earnings, and the extent to which those ever-fallacious "pro forma" earnings diverged from the reality. Yet few, if any, voices were raised. Somehow our professional investors either didn't understand, or understood but ignored, the house of cards that the stock market had become. And we have yet to accept our responsibility for that abject failure.

Moral and Ethical Standards

Already lots has happened in the areas of legislation, regulation, and corporate governance to return us to our roots. But I am convinced that we will not get there until we eschew managers' capitalism in favor of owners' capitalism. It is the stockholders themselves who bear the ultimate responsibility for corporate governance. If they don't care, who on earth should?

As investing has become institutionalized, stockholders now have the real—as compared with the theoretical—power to exercise their will. Once stocks were owned largely by a diffuse and inchoate group of individual investors. Today the ownership of stocks is concentrated among a remarkably small group of institutions whose potential power is truly awesome. The 100 largest managers of pension funds and mutual funds now represent the ownership of nearly one-half of all U.S. equities: absolute control over corporate America. They must begin to exercise it and exercise it responsibly.

Already we have begun to reform corporate governance and are undertaking the task of turning America's capital development process away from speculation and toward enterprise. But there's even more at stake than improving the practices of governance and investing. We must also establish a higher set of principles. America's founding fathers believed in high moral standards, in a just society, and in the virtuous conduct of our affairs, beliefs that shaped the very character of our nation.

Character Counts

If character counts—and I have absolutely no doubt that character does count—the ethical failings of today's business and financial model, the financial manipulation of corporate America, the willingness of those of us in the field of investment management to accept practices that we know are wrong, the conformity that keeps us silent, and the selfishness that lets our greed overwhelm our reason all erode the character we will require in the years ahead, more than ever in the wake of this great bear market and the investor disenchantment it reflects. The motivations of those who seek the rewards of commerce and finance struck no less a man than Adam Smith as "something grand and beautiful and noble, well worth the toil and anxiety." It is high time we can earn the right again to apply those words to our business and financial leaders—and mean them.

In his first press conference after his nomination to serve as chairman of the U.S. Securities and Exchange Commission, Wall Street veteran William H. Donaldson described his highest priority. It was, he said, "to restore the confidence of investors in the integrity of the financial markets."

With respect, I believe he was wrong. His highest priority should be "to restore the integrity of the financial markets." Once that task is accomplished—insofar as it ever can be accomplished—investor confidence will automatically follow.

John C. Bogle
March 1, 2003
Valley Forge, Pennsylvania

Introduction
Raw Greed
and Red Flags

"Two gladiators are standing next to the door.... We have a lion or horse with a chariot for the shock value.... Big ice sculpture of David, lots of shellfish and caviar at his feet. A waiter is pouring Stoli vodka into his back so it comes out his penis into a crystal glass.... Everyone is nicely buzzed, LDK gets up and has a toast for K.... A huge cake is brought out with the waiters in togas singing.... HBK (Happy Birthday Karen) is displayed on a mountain, fireworks coming from both ends of the golf course in sync with music...."

—from an outline by event planners for the 40th birthday party of Karen Kozlowski, second wife of Tyco International's then CEO Dennis Kozlowski (LDK in the above), in June 2001 in Sardinia

When Tyco's then Chief Executive Officer Dennis Kozlowski held this $2.1 million soiree for his wife and a few dozen friends, it typified an era of corporate greed that had turned many executives into modern-day emperors. The Internet bust had only been the trailer for the main movie featuring business leaders who allegedly used large companies as their personal piggy banks to be looted at will. Many investors were ruined by a combination of hype, deception, and ignorance—their lives destroyed when they lost pension funds and other investments. This book will show you more than 170 ways to avoid the CEOs who cheat and deceive, the Wall Street bankers who promote investments they know are bad, the boards who have been bought off, the see-no-evil accountants, and those members of the media who seem to be in on everything but may know nothing.

If the corporate scandals of 2001–2002 needed a poster boy, then Kozlowski fit the bill. He had everything. His company had grown phenomenally, mainly through acquisitions. Big investors, Wall Street bankers, and award-winning analysts were fawning all over him. He had earned the nickname Deal-a-Day-Dennis, and at the time of the party he had just completed perhaps his most audacious takeover, the $9.5 billion acquisition of finance company CIT Group, a deal that promised to turn Tyco into a true conglomerate along the lines of General Electric Co. (GE). *BusinessWeek* named Tyco as the best performing company in the spring of 2001, and a Reuters survey of analysts at brokerages conducted by Tempest Consultants put the company first in 7 out of 15 categories, including transparency and quality of financial reporting and disclosure. And, if that wasn't enough, his philanthropic work was earning him widespread recognition, including awards and honorary degrees. Life was sweet for the son of a second-generation Polish-American from New Jersey. If anyone might have felt entitled to host a lavish party in the summer of 2001, it was Dennis Kozlowski.

But it was the shareholders of his company, which makes everything from coat hangers to fire alarms to undersea cables, who were paying. Kozlowski had been systematically looting the company's coffers, in addition to pocketing hundreds of millions of dollars of compensation, while he was CEO, according to indictments and lawsuits in September 2002 by the Manhattan district attorney's office, the Securities and Exchange Commission (SEC), and Tyco itself. He allegedly used the company as his personal cash dispenser and got it to pay for everything from a $6,000 shower curtain to a $2,200 wastebasket as part of a $14 million furnishings and improvements bill for his $16.8 million New York apartment, which was also paid for by the company, regulators said. There were also yachts, fine art, jewelery, and vacation estates. Kozlowski and Tyco's former chief financial officer, Mark Swartz, pleaded not guilty to charges that they stole $170 million from the company and obtained a further $430 million through fraudulent stock sales. Kozlowski is due to go to trial in the autumn of 2003, with up to 30 years in prison and potentially massive fines awaiting him if convicted.

While the Enron collapse grabbed more headlines, its roots were more complicated. If there was plundering at the Houston-based energy trader, it was done through Byzantine financial vehicles and transactions, and unraveling those has already taken prosecutors, regulators, the company itself, and bankruptcy court investigators many months. At Tyco, if the prosecution's case is correct, Kozlowski put his snout straight into the trough without the need for complex financial structures. Tyco apparently typified an era when deal-junkie CEOs rode the wave of easy money to drive their profits and share prices to new highs whatever the longer-term costs, receiving a rapturous reception from many major investors and Wall Street securities analysts.

But, with both Enron and Tyco, there were some lonely voices expressing concern about the way the two companies were managed and their financial health. In this book, a number of those voices share their views, suggesting ways in which mainstream investors can spot trouble ahead and avoid losing their shirts.

How to Use This Book

Altogether, I have talked with more than 50 leading investors, short sellers, former regulators, independent analysts, shareholder rights activists, and leading financial figures to create a road map for investors trying to prevent executives more interested in personal compensation than corporate management from destroying the value of their nest eggs. Among those I have spoken with are former Federal Reserve Chairman Paul Volcker, three former SEC chairmen (David Ruder, Richard Breeden, and Arthur Levitt), and New York Attorney General Eliot Spitzer. I have also spoken with renowned money management figures such as Legg Mason's Bill Miller, Vanguard founder John Bogle, TIAA-CREF's just retired head John Biggs, and renowned short sellers such as James Chanos and David Tice. (Short sellers borrow stock and then sell it in the expectation that they will be able to buy it back at a much lower price and take the difference as profit.)

This is a book of warnings, alarm bells, and cautionary tales. It is based around a system of red flags—with three flags next to particular behavior by a company signaling highest risk, two indicating strong risk, and one standing for moderate risk. Also, at the end of many of the sections, I have given notes on how to find the information that I've discussed.

Certainly, this is more of a how-not-to book than a how-to book. If you see everything through rose-colored spectacles, believe the Dow Jones industrial average is heading to 36,000 early this century, and don't hear out the arguments of grizzly bears, this may not be the book for you. To be a good investor, you need to temper optimism with common sense, with proportion, with a large dose of skepticism, and even with occasional cynicism.

I am not telling you to avoid investing in stocks altogether, to hide cash under the mattress, or to sell your house and head for the hills. A red flag on one beach shouldn't stop you from swimming on the next beach where the waves are less threatening, and if you swim in the water when there is a red flag flying, it doesn't always mean you will be dragged under or eaten by sharks. For example, one red flag I will cover later is the sale by executives of their own company's stock. My calling it a red flag doesn't mean that every time you see such a sale you should ditch the investment. If everything else—the company's financial condition, board and management quality, and growth prospects—appears fine, then it may pay to stay put. But, when the inside selling is accompanied by shocks, such as the sudden resignation of the CEO, then it is the equivalent of seeing a shark's fin 50 yards away and heading straight for you.

Readers should take particular note when they see a company that displays five or six of the warnings, especially of the two- or three-flag kind. This was certainly the case with Enron, which had impenetrable accounts, heavy sales of stock by executives, some ominous financial question marks arising from what was disclosed, a compromised board, resignations of senior executives, indications of arrogance at the top, and highly questionable business strategies. All this could have been gleaned from public documents or statements. In Tyco's case, there was also plenty to worry about. Among the warning signs were an SEC inquiry in 2000, a short seller's public warning, a serial acquisition policy that made it very difficult to discern how healthy the businesses really were, and a sudden, inexplicable change in strategy.

Sometimes, just one aspect of corporate structure or behavior creates a stench that should deter all but the most foolhardy. An example was the absolute dominance of the Rigas family at cable TV company Adelphia Communications Corp., which was among the companies that imploded as massive levels of alleged fraud began to surface.

Far from an Exact Science

There are no absolutes in this game. Experts say in the chapter on boards that it is best to avoid those dominated by families and those with long-serving, elderly directors who have business dealings with the companies on whose boards they serve. And yet, this applies to Warren Buffett's Berkshire Hathaway Inc., widely regarded as one of the most successful American companies of the past 40 years. The seven-member Berkshire board includes Chairman and CEO Buffett, his wife Susan, his son Howard, and Buffett's long-time managerial colleague, Vice Chairman Charlie Munger. Some of the other board members have long-term business links to the company. The majority are either more than 70 years old or about to reach that age.

Despite these and other warning signals, Buffett is seen as a key figure driving recent reforms in the American boardroom and trying to get the accounting profession back on track. Buffett is no Rigas. He has pushed hard for companies to expense stock options, which has been one of the major controversies of recent years, and he has condemned excessive compensation of executives. He is also widely regarded as one of the few at the top of the heap who really tells it as it is, admits mistakes, doesn't seek to spin or hype, and doesn't drive Berkshire's short-term profits and share price. Buffett, who says he considers the ice cream produced by Berkshire's Dairy Queen company to be one of his favorite treats, has taken just a $100,000 annual salary for 21 years. There is no reckless or wasteful extravagance. It is one of those exceptions to the rule.

In this book, I do not just focus on executives who looted companies; I also examine corporate leaders with a record of hyping their business prospects, a poor history of disclosure, or a habit of ignoring shareholders' interests. These are hardly crimes. They will not be hauled off in handcuffs at dawn for being tardy about filing a document or for downplaying a major debt problem. However, I argue that anyone who deliberately misleads investors by telling them that a product is going to be a hit when he or she knows it could easily flop, who buries a threat to the health of a corporation, who ignores the wishes of the owners of a company, or who manipulates a board to get more than a fair share of a company's profits deserves his or her own place in a rogues' gallery.

This book has distinct elements. Most of the chapters have an introductory essay on the particular topic being addressed and a second section that details the relevant red alerts. There is also a glossary at the back of the book that explains some of the colorful vocabulary used in this era of corporate skullduggery.

There are two extreme attitudes in investing: one is to put all your trust in reputable chief executives to deliver on their promises and thereby avoid spending time looking beyond the headline earnings numbers. Many investors did this for years by buying into some large successful companies. If GE said earnings would grow at least 15 percent, that's what they did, and there was no need to worry about debt levels, cash flow, pension costs, derivatives, or anything complicated like that. Indeed, GE encouraged this attitude by disclosing only what it had to.

Then there is the other extreme, exemplified by 61-year-old money manager Robert Olstein, who trusted management once early in his career, was lied to, and saw the investments of friends, family, and clients crash. He vowed never again to listen to CEO spin. "We don't talk to management and we don't care what management does," Olstein told Reuters. "No management has ever told us that something is wrong with the company and we should bail out," said the manager of the $1.5 billion Olstein Financial Alert Fund, which has succeeded by focusing on tearing apart financial statements and has therefore avoided investing in many horror stories.

This book tries to take a path between these two views. It starts by looking at some simple investment wisdom that, if followed, might keep even a fool and his or her money united, and it then heads straight into an examination of disclosure policies, the executive suite, and the boardroom—before we shake down the accounts. I have focused as much on how to avoid high-risk CEOs, uncritical boards, dubious fads, and corrupt Wall Street practices as I have on detecting accounting fraud in financial statements. For the Main Street investor lacking the time and expertise to comb through the footnotes of financial documents, the earliest signals of bad news often come from a pattern of behavior by executives rather than a detailed look at a cash-flow statement. Some go so far as to say that looking at the latter for shenanigans can be a waste of time. "You are not going to find financial fraud looking at the numbers—if it got past the auditors it is probably going to get past you," said Michael Young, the outside legal counsel to the American Institute of Certified Public Accountants and the author of a book on accounting fraud. "Often there will be very logical explanations to numerical anomalies," Young continued.

Certainly, when a fraud involves the transfer of large amounts of money from one part of the accounts to another, as was the case with much of the alleged $9 billion-plus fraud at telecommunications company WorldCom, it becomes very difficult to spot from outside. A much earlier alert to ditch the stock would have been the disclosure in the company's annual financial statements filed in March 2001 that the board had agreed to loan then CEO Bernie Ebbers up to $100 million and guarantee loans for even more to help cover a margin call he was facing over purchases of the company's stock. It should have been clear to shareholders at that stage that this was a company prepared to act recklessly, in this case by bailing out its top executive.

How Many Bad Apples? A Handful, a Barrel, or an Orchard?

When I started work on this book in the spring of 2002, it looked like the various investigations into the Enron collapse by Congress, the Securities and Exchange Commission, and the Department of Justice were going to destroy the energy trader's auditors Andersen, probably lead to some prosecutions of Enron management, and prompt some modest tightening of various regulations. However, there was little sign of meaningful reform. The big accounting firms, in particular, appeared to have enough support in Congress to prevent tough new rules from being brought in to govern their behavior.

Well, Andersen was convicted and did disintegrate. Then, throughout the summer, there was revelation after revelation about alleged wrongdoing at a series of large companies, including the disclosure of the alleged massive WorldCom fraud. At the same time, there were continued investigations into corruption on Wall Street, including the use of tainted research, the allocation of shares in initial public offers to get investment banking business, and the role the major banks and brokerages may have played in Enron's manipulation of its balance sheet.

Media and home products entrepreneur Martha Stewart, known to some as the doyenne of domesticity, perhaps illustrated the zeitgeist best. She was under congressional and then Department of Justice investigation amid allegations of insider trading in the stock of biotechnology company ImClone Systems, which had been run by her friend Samuel Waksal. Stewart declined to talk about the issue, and shares in her company, Martha Stewart Living Omnimedia, at one stage lost almost three-quarters of their value.

Every day brought a new scandal, another chief executive sitting stone-faced—but never, it seemed, shamefaced—in front of congressional inquisitors, or another accountant who couldn't say why he or she hadn't been able to detect billions of dollars transferred to one account from another—who apparently took so little interest in the task that he or she never compared his client company with rivals in the industry and asked about glaring discrepancies. Then, the events known in the United States as "perp walks" (when arrested, alleged perpetrators are marched in front of the cameras) began, with executives from Enron, Tyco, Adelphia, WorldCom, and ImClone all providing the photo opportunities. Most of the alleged perpetrators were handcuffed to improve the images. In one memorable moment, Stewart was quizzed about her problems while chopping cabbage during a regular spot on CBS' *The Early Show*. "I want to focus on my salad," she said. Stewart, who also said she expected to be "exonerated of any ridiculousness," stopped the appearances soon after that.

But more important than such examples of the spirit of the times were a sliding stock market and sinking investor confidence. Altogether, $8 trillion of market value was wiped out in the two-and-a-half years following the market's March 2000 peaks, and both the Dow Jones industrial average and the S&P 500 index reached their lowest levels for five years in October 2002. Attempts to rally in the following few months failed dismally. It was no longer a question of a few bad apples but fears that half the barrel was rotten. President Bush was forced to go to Wall Street to promise a crackdown on corporate crooks in the summer of 2002, but the measures he proposed weren't enough once news of the WorldCom scandal broke.

Congress rushed through a tougher law, the Sarbanes-Oxley Act. It created a new accounting regulator, banned auditors from providing many consulting services to a company whose books they examined, forbade most loans to company executives and directors, speeded up disclosure of some information, introduced longer prison terms for securities fraud, and forced top management to certify to the fairness and accuracy of their company's financial statements. The New York Stock Exchange weighed in with new corporate governance guidelines demanding companies appoint more independent directors, requiring directors to meet without executives present, and providing shareholders with voting power over equity-based compensation. Still, there were a number of signs at the end of 2002 and in the first few months of 2003 that reforms could be stymied. This delay in the pace of reform was partly due to a Republican success in mid-term elections, which gave the party control of the Senate (to add to the House and the White House) and suggested that voters were more interested in Bush's tackling of post-September 11 issues and Iraq than in the economy and corporate crime.

And queries about corporate behavior weren't just being levied at discredited telecom, Internet, and energy trading companies.

The veracity of earnings figures produced by some of America's biggest and best-respected corporations, such as GE and IBM, and particularly their ability to meet or beat Wall Street expectations, was increasingly questioned. Critics suggested they massaged the figures from one quarter to the next through the use of accounting sleight of hand, charges that both companies denied. When combined with the uncertainty surrounding war with Iraq and the likelihood of further attacks on the United States and other Western targets, it was enough to undermine an already sputtering economic recovery.

The practices and policies of the business and financial gods of the previous decade were being questioned. Among them was GE's now former CEO Jack Welch, who faced not only criticism of his record of smooth growth in earnings but also disclosures about munificent post-retirement perks during the start of divorce proceedings by his wife. Following days of negative publicity, Welch announced that he was giving up most of the company benefits.

Even the respected Federal Reserve Chairman Alan Greenspan had his reputation undermined. Stung by suggestions that he should have done more to prevent a stock market bubble by raising interest rates sooner, Greenspan said there was little the Fed could do to identify and fight such problems. Yet, on the day Greenspan was knighted by Britain's Queen Elizabeth, one commentator suggested that the "Order of the Bubble" might be more appropriate.

Certainly, we should never forget that the greed, fraud, and corruption of the past few years were fed by the easy, cheap money available in the late 1990s. Half-brained ideas for Internet start-ups received funding from venture capitalists, banks, and ordinary investors. Banks and debt markets threw good money after bad in funding dozens of new telecommunications ventures—even as some observers were warning of a glut in capacity. No one cared about when a company might be able to make a profit—it was all a race to gain control of Internet real estate or future telecommunications traffic, whatever the cost. Business plans and cost controls were an inconvenience. Performance was measured in eyeballs and miles of cable, not cash.

Many believe the excesses were greater than anything seen in the insider trading scandals of the 1980s junk bond-financed takeover craze. They were comparable to the 1920s speculative conflagration that led to the 1929 stock market crash, and to some of the bubbles of previous centuries, including the Dutch tulip mania of the late 1630s that saw the prices of tulip bulbs climbing into the stratosphere, or the South Sea stock bubble that burst in Britain in 1720. "I don't think we have ever seen anything, even the tulip craze, like the end of the last bull market," said John Gutfreund, former head of Salomon Brothers. As for the Internet revolution, terrific things happened in terms of technology, but mispricing and valuations were just crazy. The wider level of stock ownership in the United States in the past 20 years, particularly through pension plans and mutual funds, means that this bust has hurt a wide cross-section of the population. The greed was also deeper than in some of the other scandals of the past 50 years. It involved more than just CEOs and Wall Street, with accountants, lawyers, venture capitalists, fund managers, and consultants all wanting a bigger piece of the pie.

The extent of the partying during the boom means that the hangover may last beyond a couple of years. "I would be astonished if things were over in a year because of the appreciating excesses," said James Grant, the publisher of the newsletter *Grant's Interest Rate Observer* and one of the lone figures who said the good times could not last through much of the 1990s. "I think the recrimination will be somewhat proportionate to the loss and to the betrayal preceding it. My guess is that the recovery from this particular great bubble is going to be protracted and painful and there will be periods of ferocious bear market rallies followed by more disenchantment, more broken hearts, more loss."

Many of the veteran investors and former regulators I spoke with for this book voiced a deep disenchantment with the level of greed and the loss of values exposed in corporate America by the boom and bust. "You have a definite feeling in the past few years that ethical standards did deteriorate in many aspects of life, including the financial markets," said former Fed Chairman Volcker. "There was not that feeling of caution that keeps people in line, whether it is good ethics or good morality or just fright—the fright component diminished and the greed component increased," Volcker added.

The contrast between the images of greedy executives treating public companies as their own playthings and the rescue workers who died when the World Trade Center collapsed after the September 11 attacks clearly hit home with many people. There were pictures of selfishness, avarice, and cowardice on the one hand, and selflessness, generosity, and heroism on the other. Some commentators even suggested that Osama bin Laden hadn't done as much as Enron Chairman Kenneth Lay to damage the American economic system.

One of the problems with being able to spread the blame for the scandals across so many industries, professions, regulators, and individuals is that it has given an excuse for many of the culpable to point at others and say it was everybody's fault. It was, as Vanguard's former head John Bogle likes to put it, "the happy conspiracy." *Money* magazine even apportioned the blame for the disaster in its October 1, 2002, issue, awarding corporate executives 17 percent, stock options grants 16 percent, Wall Street 14 percent, individual investors 14 percent, accountants 12 percent, politicians 10 percent, the mutual fund industry 8 percent, the media 7 percent, and Osama bin Laden 2 percent. Certainly, smaller investors who were suckered in by dreams of overnight riches can't be excused completely. According to Bill

Fleckenstein, a short seller who is head of Seattle-based Fleckenstein Capital, during the mania, the attitude of the public was as follows: "We don't care if you lie to us, in fact we love it, just don't get caught."

No More Heroes Anymore: Twisted and Conflicted Ties

There are few clean-cut heroes in all this. Few on Wall Street or in big business didn't benefit from some of the crazier aspects of the 1990s stock market boom. There are few who can really say they have no skeletons in the closet or conflicts that could still dog them. Investors should question just about everything and everyone.

Indeed, as investors seek evidence of a clean-up in business attitudes, one less than hopeful sign is that many in positions of influence —whether in Washington or corporate America—show little understanding when they either face a conflict of interest or have created a perception that one may exist. The clearest example was Harvey Pitt, who met privately with former clients and others who were under investigation when he was chairman of the SEC for a tumultuous period beginning in the late summer of 2001. Pitt first put his foot in his mouth in October of that year, days after Enron had started to unravel, by telling an audience of auditors that the SEC would henceforth be a kinder and gentler place for accountants. It was a remark that would dog him for the next year as his critics accused him of being soft on accounting firms and some other former clients because he used to work for them.

Eventually, Pitt's decisive vote that pushed through the controversial appointment of former CIA and FBI Director William Webster as head of a new regulatory board for accountants proved to be the final straw. He supported Webster after the accountants had objected to another candidate, former head of the TIAA-CREF pension fund system John Biggs, because he was seen as too much of a reformer. But Pitt and key SEC officials failed to tell the other four SEC commissioners that Webster had been chairman of the audit committee at a failed Internet venture that was both the subject of a fraud investigatons and had fired its auditors after they raised questions about the lack of internal controls. Pitt, the SEC's chief accountant Robert Herdman, and Webster all resigned in the resulting controversy, leaving both the SEC and the fledgling accounting board in turmoil at the end of 2002.

I began this introduction with Dennis Kozlowski, and I'll end it with him. A victim of his reign as the head of Tyco was one of the world's foremost advocates of strong corporate governance, Robert Monks, who had once served on the company's board and had once described Kozlowski as the best CEO in America. Tyco and Kozlowski even donated $4 million to endow a professorship in corporate governance in Monks' name at Britain's Cambridge University. Monks said in October 2002 that he was sad about Kozlowski's indictment. "I was glad that Dennis was willing to put up money for the professorship—I'm just terribly embarrassed and sorry the way things seem to have worked out for him, and for Tyco, and for its shareholders." When a figure like Monks—who has been naming and shaming bad corporate leaders for many years—can have his reputation besmirched by someone like Kozlowski, it shows how vigilant ordinary investors have to be.

Acknowledgments

Iwould like to thank everybody who helped me to write this book. Top of that list have to be my family and friends, who either had to do without me altogether, or, when I was around, had to put up with someone who could be distant and grumpy. "You never write, you never ring," was the headline of one typical email I received from a friend. This book is dedicated to my two wonderful daughters, Mary-Louise and Fionnuala, who had to do without their Dad for much of their 2002 summer holidays. I also want to thank their mother Perry for being so patient and understanding.

Additionally, I want to thank all those at Reuters who believed in this project and helped me to see it completed, particularly Americas Editor David Schlesinger, who supported the idea from the day I brought it to him, Global Head of News Stephen Jukes, News Editor Bernd Debusmann, Equities News Editor Betty Wong, and all my fellow managers for equities news in the United States who had to take on an extra workload in my absence, in particular Daniel Burns. Although the vast majority of this book is based on interviews and other research, I also borrowed at times from my Reuters colleagues. I originally wanted to include their names in the text but in the editing process those were mainly removed to make it flow more smoothly. The following deserve special mention for contributions from interviews, stories, editing suggestions, reading the proofs, or simply ideas: Peter Millership, Dick Satran, Alisa Bowen, Janie Gabbett, Ed Tobin, Deepa Babington, Tim McLaughlin, Bill Rigby, Chelsea Emery, Dan Sorid, Jonathan Stempel, Herb Lash, Bryson Hull, Karen Padley, Ian Driscoll, Siobhan Kennedy, Caroline Humer, Jed Seltzer, Brian Kelleher, Jamie Paton, Paul Thomasch, Dena Aubin, Brooke McDonald, Lesley Norton, Anna Driver, Andrew Mitchell, Brendan Intindola, Haitham Haddadin, Eric Auchard, Rans Pierson, Jack Doran, Greg Cresci, Lauren Weber, Dane Hamilton, Arindam Nag, Svea Herbst, Julie Macintosh, Brian Kelleher, and Jack Reerink. My friend QQ, who helped on the transcripts and some other key parts of the project, deserves a special mention. Apologies to those who should have been on this list but were left off because of my forgetfulness. I also want to thank all the people whom I interviewed for this book, who so cheerfully gave of their precious time.

The material in this book is drawn from a combination of first-hand reporting—mainly interviews by the author—and reports by other Reuters journalists, contemporary newspaper and magazine stories, company filings and news releases, academic studies, and books. Wherever practical I have tried to indicate the sources for the material I have used. Any opinions that are not attributed to sources are my own and are not necessarily those of Reuters or Prentice Hall. Any errors are also my responsibility.

Finally, I want to thank Jim Boyd at Prentice Hall for being so understanding and helpful throughout, particularly when he was getting stonewalled on his gentle inquiries about progress, and Giles Elgood at Reuters for his fine editing.

Martin Howell
New York
March 2003

1

Sages and Charlatans: Avoiding the Fads, the Buzz, the Rip-Offs, and the Merely Dumb

"You could step into the store and see what's going on. Are people buying, are there a lot of people? And then when you see the CEO and he says there are a lot of people coming into the stores, you have to compare the two. And if you know that there aren't a lot of people, then you know there is something fishy."

—Patrick Gallimore, 14, who attends a stock market education program at the
Dr. Gladstone H. Atwell Middle School 61 in Brooklyn, New York

Soon after I moved to New York, in 1999, I met a Chinese woman who had saved every cent to come and study in the United States. Hers was typical of the resourceful immigrant stories on which this city lives and breathes. But it soon became a cautionary tale from which I will show how investors can learn important lessons about the nature of risk.

Altogether, my friend had managed to scrimp together more than $20,000 to pay tuition fees, and eventually she hoped to get a green card and a well-paying professional job. In the meantime, she worked

1

in a Chinatown restaurant for poverty wages and tips. Her savings and income were enough to see her through school and give her independence. But, despite the hardships of combining full-time classes with work, my friend, who is in her mid-30s, was happy because she had the chance to fulfill a dream.

That was until she heard of Globix Corp. Staff from the web-hosting company, which has its headquarters on the edge of Chinatown, would sometimes come into the restaurant in a celebratory mood. It was near the height of the Internet bubble at the end of 1999, and Globix stock had gone through the roof. To my innocent friend it seemed like a no-brainer. She didn't really understand what these guys did on the Internet, but it sounded smart, they sounded smart, and their headquarters building was impressive. Everyone seemed to be making money out of the stock market, and this was her chance to finance her studies without having to work so hard.

She spent more than half her savings buying Globix stock at about $40 a share toward the end of 1999, and it soared to a high of $67.44 in February 2000. She had a paper profit and this seemed like good reason to celebrate, though she didn't have as much reason as the company's then CEO had. Around that time, Marc H. Bell sold about a third of his interest in Globix, much of which he had gotten from generous stock option grants, for more than $120 million.

A lot of people can fill in what happened next.

The Internet bubble's rupture in March 2000 made investors realize that Globix and companies like it carried a lot of risk for precious little reward. Globix was burdened with a high debt load and a big repayment bill, it had expensive real estate, its world of dot-com clients was imploding, competition had increased, and projections for growth in the web-hosting services market were looking wildly overoptimistic. The stock never touched its February high again, and by the end of that year it had sunk below $5 per share. My friend, who had also invested a smaller amount of money in another technology dud, hung on through the collapse in the hope that the stocks would recover, but they never did, and most of her savings were wiped out. The last I heard, she was struggling to put her life back together in the hopes of pursuing her dream. Eventually, Globix, which declined to comment for this book, saying it was inappropriate given a change in management, went into bankruptcy, virtually wiping out any remaining value in its then-existing common shares. While the company did emerge from bankruptcy in 2002, it still failed to file annual and quarterly results on time, and Bell, who had become the company's chairman, quit in December 2002.

Bell told *The Wall Street Journal* in March 2001 that he sold the Globix shares because his wife wanted him to save some money for the twins they were expecting. "Who knew?" Bell was quoted as saying. "Everyone was talking about Nasdaq and a 20,000 Dow. I just had good timing." As did the twins, it seems. They were born in April 2001. Bell did not respond to emails seeking comment.

Clearly, my friend went wrong in just about every way. She listened to advice from people without checking out their credibility. She didn't even begin to know the meaning of risk, let alone think of diversifying it. She invested in something she hadn't a clue about. And, as for price, she had no perception of what was a good price and what was a rip-off. She wasn't dumb. She just hadn't learned any of the age-old lessons in the often-brutal ways of financial markets.

In this chapter, I intend to take you through some of those lessons. This is the timeless first line of defense against the deceptive, the crooked, and the egomaniacal. Subsequent chapters will build on many of the themes touched on here.

Red Flag 1

If You Can't Understand, Don't Invest

The sage of Omaha, legendary investor Warren Buffett, has always urged investors to define what they don't understand—and steer clear of it. "Paradoxically, when dumb money acknowledges its limitations, it ceases to be dumb," he wrote in a shareholders' letter in 1993. His comment was in reference to the man on the street who did better than the professional investor by putting his money in a fund based on a benchmark stock index. And, in 1999, at the height of the Internet stocks craze, Buffett explained why Berkshire Hathaway didn't own any technology shares by saying that he had "no insights into which participants in the tech field possess a truly durable competitive advantage." He added, "Predicting the long-term economics of companies that operate in fast-changing industries is simply far beyond our perimeter."

Former Securities and Exchange Commission Chairman Arthur Levitt has similarly simple advice for investors who don't understand a company's financial statements. "If management and the statements they produce can't adequately interpret what they mean or what the company is all about to an investor or the investor's adviser, then the investor should simply pass it up," he said in an interview.

Red Flag 2

Friends and Family Don't Like a Company's Products

Two thumbs down from your nearest and dearest is a signal to heed. There are, after all, many products made by publicly traded companies that we not only understand but test on a daily basis. One-time Fidelity Magellan fund manager Peter Lynch says that investors should try to kick the tires before stumping up any cash. That may mean visiting a store, staying in a hotel, talking to friends who work for a company, or noticing which cars are becoming popular.

I know, for example, that US Airways was hit hard by the September 11 attacks—and not just for a month or two afterward. I was surprised it took until the following August to file for bankruptcy, and if anyone had asked me about investing in the company's shares, I would have said no. Why was I so certain? I fly regularly from New York to Boston to see my kids, and for about eight months after September 11, the planes were half empty and the tickets cheaper even after flights had been cut. By the summer of 2002, the airline had more passengers, but the ticket prices were still lower than they had been a year earlier, and some of the abandoned flights hadn't returned. My own experience told me—faster than any financial statements could indicate—that US Airways must have been hemorrhaging badly.

In a similar vein, why was I not surprised that Microsoft's MSN Internet service was losing dial-up customers in the fourth quarter of 2002? Because when I canceled my service around the end of the year, I had to wait a long time to get an MSN representative on the phone, and while apologizing he told me that they were getting a lot of cancellations all at once.

Of course, you can take this to ridiculous lengths. The lack of powdered chocolate to sprinkle on my cappuccino at Starbucks four days in a row is not reason enough to launch a full-scale probe of its financial statements. However, my willingness to buy its stored value cards soon after they were released late in 2001 was an indication of something going on. It turned out that many other customers were buying the cards, and their success helped to drive the coffee chain's share price up about 30 percent in the next few months.

This is not rocket science: We can all do this. It's all useful information that can help investment decisions, though you must always look at a company's accounts as well.

Red Flag 3

A Product or Company Is Hyped by Wall Street, the Media, and Others

It is best to avoid the buzz unless you can see the beehive and smell the honey. The only real reason to risk getting attacked by bees is to get hold of their honey, and too often in recent corporate times it ain't been there. The unwary investor has ended up following the noise and getting severely stung, only to find that the hive hasn't yet been built. There was lots of risk and little chance of reward all along.

James J. Cramer, the former hedge fund manager and now media commentator, gives us a summary of how Wall Street insiders can help create the buzz and end up with a pot of honey for themselves. In his book *Confessions of a Street Addict*, Cramer describes how he went into business with his wife Karen, whom he dubbed the "trading goddess," and how they pioneered a money-making formula for getting the kind of analysts' calls on stocks that they wanted to help them make a profit:

> We developed a style that consisted of figuring out what would be hot, what would be the next big buzz. We became merchants of the buzz, getting long stocks and then

schmoozing with analysts about what we saw and heard that was positive.

The aim, in Cramer's words, was to "liquidate the stock into the buzz for a handsome profit." The only problem is that many ordinary investors could end up holding the stock that analysts were promoting and Cramer and others were liquidating. The mom and pop investors would then be left wondering why it had sunk.

Red Flag 4

On Wall Street, the Game Is Usually Rigged Against the Small Investor

If you are not part of the Wall Street in-crowd, then you must remember that the odds are almost always deliberately stacked against you.

This was most obvious during the IPO (initial public offerings of stock) boom of the late 1990s, when investment banks and brokers hyped new stocks so that their prices rose to artificially high levels. In some cases, inflated prices were achieved by forcing those getting an allocation of hot IPOs to guarantee to buy the stocks at higher prices once they started trading—a process called laddering. Sometimes, high prices were achieved through biased research reports that urged investors to buy. Those who knew what was going on got out near the top of the market, and those who thought that the demand was real and bought after the stocks had climbed got killed.

For example, Wall Street brokerages will almost always let their top clients know about their analysts' major stock recommendations before they tell the media. That keeps the clients sweet and keeps the commission dollars rolling in from trading they do through the brokerage. So, when a small investor learns through television, radio, or Internet reports that a brokerage has stuck a strong buy label on Blah-blah Tech Inc., he or she is well behind an institutional investor who has been trading on that information for minutes, hours, or sometimes even days.

In his book *Trading With The Enemy,* which describes working for Cramer's hedge fund, Nicholas Maier explains how the system worked. "Joe helped me to make money and I was expected to return the favor," he wrote of a Smith, Barney analyst who tipped him off about a recommendation change. Maier would get the information ahead of a wider announcement—provided any trading that resulted was done with the analyst's brokerage.

According to John Gutfreund, the man who was once dubbed "the King of Wall Street," money decides everything there. "I have come to the conclusion now, which I should have done a long time ago, that Wall Street is the ultimate home of mercenaries. There is nobody who cares about the company, the loyalty. They care about the money," said Gutfreund, who quit as chairman and chief executive of Salomon Brothers in 1991 as a result of a Treasury bond bid-rigging scandal.

And mercenaries will only work for you until you are no longer the highest bidder for their services. In *Confessions of a Street Addict*, Cramer indicates that he was able to excel in such conditions—he had large commissions to hand out to the brokers. "If you do a massive amount of commission business, analysts will return your calls, brokers will work for you, and you will get plenty of ideas to make money," he recalls his wife telling him.

The spate of reforms to Wall Street practices, whether by the regulators, or by the securities firms themselves, is unlikely to ever make the playing field level. Remember that many experts say that small investors will always lose out because they don't have the connections, the information, the skills, or the time. "They are trying to compete with highly paid professionals and they wonder why it is so dangerous," said Christopher Mahoney, chairman of the credit policy committee at credit rating agency Moody's Investors Service. "It is extremely dangerous."

Red Flag 5

The Motivation of an Adviser Making a Recommendation Is Suspect

If you are thinking of engaging a broker or adviser to help handle your investing, you should first read about Frank Gruttadauria. He is a former SG Cowen and Lehman Brothers star broker who bilked more than $50 million from his clients in Cleveland, Ohio, over 15 years.

Gruttadauria, who was sentenced to seven years in prison in November 2002, got his employers to send client account statements to post office boxes he operated. This allowed him to then send bogus statements out to clients, overestimating their value by an aggregate of more than $270 million, while allegedly siphoning off their money. It meant that Samuel Glazer, the co-founder of coffee percolator maker Mr. Coffee, received monthly statements from Lehman showing he had $24 million in bonds when he really only had $15,000 left, according to *The Plain Dealer* newspaper in Cleveland, Ohio. The broker himself sent the FBI a letter indicating that he could hardly believe he avoided detection for so long. Remember, this wasn't a stock manipulating boiler room in New Jersey. Gruttadauria worked for major investment banks for a long time.

When dealing with your money and Wall Street, be suspicious and trust nobody. That's harsh advice, but many believe the days are long gone when analysts and brokers on Wall Street had only their clients' interests at heart.

"I went on the Street in 1973, bright-eyed and bushy-tailed, worked for a great firm, high levels of integrity, your word was your bond and I was a customers' man—but now there are no customers' men anymore—it's corrupt," said Herbert Denton, president of Providence Capital, a money manager that aggressively promotes shareholder rights.

In 2002, investors filed a record 7,704 new arbitration claims against brokers with the National Association of Securities Dealers, up 39 percent from two years earlier, alleging such misdemeanors as misrepresenting investments and conducting excessive trades to generate fees and commissions, which is known as churning. So, despite all the noise about risk controls and compliance systems, and all the huffing and puffing about disciplinary action and monitoring by the New York Stock Exchange, the SEC, and the National Association of Securities Dealers, the only regulator who is going to guarantee your investments won't be hived off to a broker's Cayman Islands account is staring back at you in the mirror every morning.

Martin Whitman, the 78-year-old manager of the Third Avenue Funds group, had this to say: "Ever since I have been in business, which is over 50 years, the public has always been taken to the cleaners with one thing or other, some type of promotion. And is that going to end? No!"

Note

Be suspicious; check the backgrounds of brokers and advisers through regulators. See Appendix A.

Red Flag 6

Price Means Everything: A Great Company's Stock May Be Too Expensive

James Grant, the founder and publisher of the newsletter *Grant's Interest Rate Observer*, says that the most important three words in the financial lexicon are "at a price." He continues, "Nothing is true unmodified by that phrase, as trite as it seems." There are times, he says, when even an investment that has a strong stench can be worth it—provided that there is a no-strings-attached giveaway price. Conversely, even the best and most ethically managed company in the world should be left alone if the price of its securities is too high. Grant says he would invest in a company with an egomaniac at the helm if the price was right and its prospects were strong. "There are times when you are paid to make a leap of faith as an investor—but unless you are paid, don't leap."

Investors weren't paid to leap during the Internet-telecom craziness, but they did, lemming-like. A key measurement of how expensive a stock is—the ratio of its share price to the profits per share the company is producing—was often ignored. Instead of the more normal range of about 10–20 for this price-to-earnings (p/e) ratio, many technology companies were trading in the hundreds and even thousands. Many didn't even qualify to have a p/e ratio, as they had no earnings and little prospect of them.

Some top investors can see value in scandal-damaged companies such as Tyco. "We don't say in most cases is there a fraud here? But in the case of something like Tyco, this is part of the analysis," said Bill Miller, whose main fund at Legg Mason has beaten the S&P 500 for 12 successive years. "If they are monkeying with the numbers, if we cannot trust the numbers, how much of the value could they have destroyed, and what could we salvage from this thing?"

> **Note**
>
> Compare price-to-earnings and other ratios with those of similar companies, with the average for the industry, and with the whole market. It is easy enough to do this through services such as *www.reuters.com* and *www.valueline.com*.

Red Flag 7

Don't Get Caught Out by the Latest Fad; It Probably Won't Last

Consider the rise and fall of the collapsible scooter. I bought one early in the summer of 2000 before most people in America had cottoned on to the dorkiest form of transport since the pogo stick. Within weeks of my venturing forth for the first time on the streets of Martha's Vineyard and New York City with my kick-powered gadget from hell, it seemed everyone was buying one and it was the coolest item to possess. Technology companies were buying them by the score for their staffs to zip around campuses or warehouses, and adolescents were holding scooter wheelie competitions.

Within about three months it was over. Some blamed it on the dot-com market crash, and some said highly publicized accidents had turned parents off. Others just remembered how silly they had felt when riding the damned things.

Desperate attempts by the retailers, distributors, and manufacturers to keep the craze going, introducing, for example, features such as motors, suspension, and flashing lights made no difference. From prices around $100 at the height of the craze, many scooters are now selling for $20–30. Bicycle maker Huffy Corp. had initially benefited from the scooter fad and saw its shares more than triple in price, but it then watched them lose most of the gains.

To a short seller like David Tice, the scooter craze was typical of a toy fad that has limited shelf life. "If it is a kid's product and it just skyrockets, those tend not to have long legs," he said.

So, if a company is relying on fashion or fad, be wary. People are fickle, and one year's success story can become the next year's failure.

Red Flag 8

If You See Major Funds Are Shunning a Stock, There's Usually Good Reason

Always check who the big shareholders are in a company in which you are thinking of investing, and compare the list to those for its competitors in the industry. If, for example, you find that none of the major telecom funds are invested in a telecommunications company, that is a warning sign. The chances that you have found a gem that they haven't already scrutinized and discarded as a fake are slim. Providence Capital President Herbert Denton said the absence of big funds is one of the key signs he uses to understand whether a company has problems. For example, mid-sized drug maker ICN Pharmaceuticals Inc. had little overlap in shareholdings with other similar-sized companies in the industry. "The folks that know the industry are saying 'not this one,'" said Denton.

A cloud surrounded the company's founder and former Chairman and CEO Milan Panic, a former Yugoslav prime minister who had controlled ICN with an iron fist. Disgruntled shareholders had cited Panic's costly settlement of sexual harassment suits he faced from employees, a felony fraud plea in which the company had agreed to pay a $5.6 million fine, and a civil suit from the SEC over allegedly fraudulent statements by Panic and the company. The latter was settled by the company with a payment of $1 million and Panic through a payment of $500,000, without either admitting or denying the charges, in November 2002. Panic has consistently denied any wrongdoing, though he finally quit as chairman and CEO in June 2002 after losing a battle for control of the board with shareholders advised by Denton.

If the top shareholder list of a company seems to contain only institutions known for running index funds, that can also be a negative, as it shows that only those who have to own the stock so that their funds match index weightings are on board. The discretionary money has gone elsewhere. The flip side, of course, is that if everybody in the investing world is in a stock, your chances of getting it for a bargain price are limited.

Note

Check company reports and sites such as *www.firstcall.com*'s ShareWatch Web. One site for professional investors, and therefore too expensive for most of us, is *www.bigdough.com*.

Red Flag 9

Avoid Companies That Are Too Reliant on One or Two of Anything

If a company is too heavily dependent on any one aspect of its business, then it can be high risk. The one aspect could be one product, one huge customer, or one major supplier. Or, perhaps the whole company has been built around its founder's name and reputation.

The company that epitomizes the latter problem is media and home products concern Martha Stewart Living Omnimedia. In the first nine months of 2002, its shares lost more than half their value, due mainly to news of insider trading probes into its Chairman and CEO Martha Stewart and her transactions in biotechnology company ImClone Systems Inc. The news led to speculation that she might be indicted and would have to step down from the company.

Stewart, whose magazines, TV shows, and products target homemakers, is such a dominant force that there were questions over whether the company could survive without her. Investors began to realize that Stewart was the company and that there were no meaningful plans for succession, an impression the company had done little to counter. At the time of this writing, in February 2003, it was still unclear whether Stewart would face charges.

Earlier in 2002, investors had also lost some confidence in Stewart's company because the discount retailer that sells almost all its home products, Kmart, had filed for bankruptcy protection and had begun to close stores as it sought to restructure. Early in 2003, it announced further store closures. Again, there were too many eggs in one basket.

So, always ask yourself whether a particular investment is so dependent on one individual that it could sink in value if that person falls under a bus or gets hauled off to jail. Do the same for suppliers, customers, and even whole nations. For example, if you know that a computer maker is becoming increasingly reliant on China as a production source, ask yourself what would happen if there were a major political eruption in that country. You should avoid being surprised. Remember, the crowd is often shortsighted and blind to risk.

> **Note**
>
> Check company filings and media reports for information about customers, suppliers, and distributors.

Red Flag 10

Diversify or Bust: Too Much Money in One Stock May Ruin You

This is just about the oldest advice in the book, and I am not going to spend long on it. Most people know by now that to concentrate all their money in only a few stocks is extremely risky, though clearly an Enron or a WorldCom was needed to get this harsh message through to some. A number of Enron and WorldCom staff, for example, held all or most of their investment dollars and pension funds in the companies' stocks. Well, that was an awful lot of trust they put in Enron or WorldCom management, a trust that was, as we know, betrayed.

So, the lesson is to diversify your equity investments so that they are not all in high-risk technology or telecommunications companies, or in the shares of the entity you work for. You can do far worse than buying an index fund, especially if you have little time to watch over your investments or to comb through lists of mutual funds. An index fund will rise and fall in line with the stock market average it is tied to, but the fees are usually significantly lower than for a stock-picking fund.

You should also have a significant percentage of your funds in other assets, such as real estate, cash, and bonds. That way you can limit your losses in a bear market of the kind we have seen in recent years. This is particularly the case when you are within a few years of retirement.

Ejecting at the 11th Hour

If an investor still hasn't ditched a stock by the time the events outlined in the following red flags have come to pass, then it may be too late for a graceful exit. I have given all these warnings three flags.

Red Flag 11

A Company Files for Chapter 11 Bankruptcy Protection

Stockholders almost always get wiped out when a company declares bankruptcy because debt holders get paid off first. This requirement often means that when a company goes into liquidation, there is nothing left with which to pay stockholders. When a company reorganizes under Chapter 11, the creditors will often end up owning most of the equity, leaving the previous stockholders with a much smaller stake, or even no stake at all. So, if you own shares in a company and there is speculation that it is going into bankruptcy, it is probably best to bail out. Waiting until an announcement of a bankruptcy filing to sell your shares will be leaving it too late. The speed with which companies such as Enron Corp. and Kmart Corp. went into bankruptcy in December 2001–January 2002 caught many investors by surprise, though in both cases there was enough time to get out if people had taken note of some of the warning signals detailed in this book.

> **Note**
>
> The bond market often provides an early signal of bankruptcy risk. See Chapter 10.

Red Flag 12

The SEC Launches a Full-Scale Probe into Possible Securities Fraud

Given that the authorities are often late on the scene—well after others have suspected that the books are being cooked—this red flag is a bit like the shark warning sign that is put up when you have already waded into deep water. Companies do survive investigations by the SEC, Congress, and the Department of Justice; however, a securities fraud probe usually takes many months (if not years), and during this time, the company's shares may not see any gains.

A regulator's investigation is also usually symptomatic of much deeper problems. Copier maker Xerox, for example, agreed to pay a $10 million penalty to the SEC in 2002 and to accept an injunction for violations of antifraud, reporting, and record-keeping provisions of securities laws, but the company did not admit or deny allegations made in a complaint by the regulator. Much worse than this punishment was its subsequent need to restate financial results for four years. SEC Director of Enforcement Stephen Cutler said the company "used its accounting to burnish and distort."

Such probes also tend to increase the amount of civil litigation brought against a company by investors. To stay with a stock through this, you really have to have faith, and it may not be logical faith.

> **Note**
>
> Official announcements can be found on the SEC's website: *www.sec.gov.*

Red Flag 13

The CEO or Another Top Company Official Is Arrested

It is also generally too late for investors to protect themselves against a corporate mugging when they hear that a top executive has been arrested. Usually, the company concerned and its stock have collapsed by the time law enforcement officers have cuffed another one-time high-flier in his New York apartment in the early hours of the morning. For example, members of the Rigas family were arrested on securities fraud charges about a month after their Adelphia Communications cable company filed for bankruptcy protection in the summer of 2002. Tyco's share price dropped 27 percent the day it was revealed that CEO Dennis Kozlowski had quit because he was about to be indicted on the first charges he faced, which were for alleged tax evasion on art purchases (the more serious charges were filed some weeks later). By that time, though, the company's stock was already worth less than half its value at the beginning of 2002.

Red Flag 14

A Company's Shares Are Delisted by a Stock Market Such As the NYSE

Exchanges such as the New York Stock Exchange don't like to delist stocks because listing fees are a critical source of revenue. So, when the day finally comes, it usually means that the company being delisted has either committed some terrible misdemeanor or its stock has sunk below $1 and stayed there for a long time, resisting any attempts to resuscitate it. Either way, investors who have stuck with it have almost certainly lost out. The NYSE can issue a delisting warning if a stock is below an average of $1 for 30 days, after which the company usually has about six months to persuade the exchange that it can get the price back above that level. The exchange can also delist a stock for breaching other listing rules, though this happens much less often. The Nasdaq stock market allows a company 180 days to get its stock back above the $1 mark if it has been below for 30 consecutive days; that is double the 90 days that applied before the September 11 attacks.

Red Flag 15

A Company Does a Reverse Stock Split to Remain Listed

A reverse stock split is often a last desperate attempt by a company seeking to prevent a market from delisting its stock, and it often fails. This strategy is like shuffling the deck chairs on the Titanic, as Noah Blackstein, vice president and portfolio manager at the Dynamic Power America Fund, told Reuters when AT&T Corp. announced a reverse stock split in April 2002. Companies that use the method are almost certainly already in deep trouble, with a share price already down a long way. For example, in December 2002, telecom equipment maker Lucent Technologies announced plans for a reverse stock split of anything from 1-for-10, 1-for-20, 1-for-30, or 1-for-40 by February 2004. Its shares fell about 8 percent the day after the announcement to reach $1.74, and at that stage had lost more than 97 percent in about three years.

> **Note**
>
> If a stock heads close to or below $1, consider delisting to be a possibility.

Red Flag 16

A Company Is Facing a Large Number of Class-Action Lawsuits

If the class-action lawyers are circling a company like vultures, then the stock has probably already been shot to pieces. The lawsuits tend to be reactive, so it may be too late to see this as a signal that will save you much money. Even so, as an eleventh-hour alarm, it should be heeded.

> **Note**
>
> There are web sites that specialize in analysis of class-action filings, such as the Stanford Law School/Cornerstone Research site at *http://securities.stanford.edu/index.html.*

Red Flag 17

A Prominent Short Seller Has a Company in His or Her Sights

Investors who hear that a prominent short seller is gunning for a particular company should take heed. Short sellers are far from always right, and their timing can sometimes be askew. But when they do hit the nail on the head, the results can be devastating. We will see later how short sellers were right about Enron and Tyco—months or even years before anyone else. Before you dismiss news that a short seller is hovering or before you believe a company denial, you should do your own research to see whether the short seller's story stands up to scrutiny.

You can follow what short sellers are doing by examining the data issued by major U.S. stock markets every month, although the figures are about a month old. Monitor short sellers' actions on both individual stocks and the market as a whole. A rise in the percentage of short positions on an exchange or in a stock may indicate that sentiment is turning bearish.

> **Note**
>
> You can get the latest monthly report for the New York Stock Exchange by going to *www.nyse.com* and selecting the press room area. For Nasdaq companies, visit *www.marketdata.nasdaq.com.*

2

Pipedreams
and Big Lies

"What we are constantly exchanging, over the incredible network of wires, are quotations, orders, bluffs, fibs, lies, and nonsense"

—Fred Schwed Jr., *Where Are the Customers' Yachts*, 1940

James Chanos makes a living by exposing the big lie. Discovering tall tales and grand deceptions is what make the short seller's day, allowing him to bet against a company or an entire industry in the expectation that it will come crashing down. If you find the big lie in one area, then related areas are often in jeopardy, advises Chanos, who is founder and president of Kynikos Associates in New York.

The technology and telecommunications world has been an especially happy hunting ground for Chanos and other short sellers in recent years. Combine the big lie with investors' greed and easy money from lenders, and suddenly you have the perfect catalyst for disasters at companies such as WorldCom and Global Crossing.

Whether companies were based on the Internet, fiber-optic cable, wireless services, or were based on the so-called convergence of all three, the stories were often similar. Wildly hyped projections drove a boom, but demand wasn't as strong as expected while competition was fiercer. Then there was often fiddling with the numbers in a desperate attempt to cover up the truth, followed by capitulation and bankruptcy.

Our plan here is to comb through the wreckage, highlighting some of the lies, risks, and hype behind many pipedreams.

Red Flag 1

When You Find the Big Lie, Everything Else Crumbles Around It

Chanos began sniffing out a big lie when the telecommunications supervisor for the Citigroup Center in midtown Manhattan told him the number of long-distance phone companies offering service there had more than quadrupled inside a few years.

Then, the second-biggest long-distance telecom carrier, WorldCom, indicated in the summer of 2000 that the growth of Internet traffic was slowing. This was happening while Wall Street analysts were issuing bullish reports on the telecom industry, assuming that bandwidth prices would be the same in 2010 as they were in 2000.

It just didn't add up.

Competition was more intense than it had ever been, and the investment banks were basing their earnings and revenue estimates on cuckoo models—it was clear that prices were already dropping 40 percent a year.

Add all this to an examination of company balance sheets and cash flow statements that showed an ugly picture developing, and Chanos was convinced he had found what he needed. "The whole thing was just a chain based on wildly optimistic projections about growth of demand," he said. "We began realizing that with all these networks being built, tremendous price competition was going to ensue. Analysts' projections for revenues, cash flow, and earnings would never be realized—there was just too much capacity," he said.

Over the next 18 months, he says, he placed a series of bets that stocks in phone companies and telecom equipment providers would plunge. It turned out to be Kynikos' most lucrative winning stance of recent times—even given that Chanos had successfully sold Enron stock short from about a year before the energy trader's collapse. "We were probably short at the peak maybe 10–15 companies—suppliers, local service companies, long haul carriers—it really was much more profitable for us than Enron," said Chanos.

The broadband mania had seen many companies pulling up sidewalks to lay millions of miles of fiber-optic cable with the help of banks and bond market investors prepared to lend them billions of dollars. But, they were all doing this just as the Internet bubble was bursting, and the U.S. economy was heading toward recession. Technological advances also meant that the capacity of the fiber to carry data had vastly increased. At the same time, consumers held off on ordering high-speed Internet and cable connections, with the economic downturn only one of the likely reasons. Much of the hype surrounding the future of programming—such as video-on-demand—had remained hype, and there were a lot of complaints about the quality of connections.

A glut of massive proportions had been created. Some estimates suggest that at the end of 2001, 97 percent of the fiber lines that had been laid were dark, which means they weren't equipped to carry voice and data. Those that were lit, or able to transmit, were far from being fully used. As a results, telecom pricing got slammed, debt burdens easily outstripped the ability to pay, declining shares speeded up the crisis, and bankruptcies ensued.

It wasn't just a bunch of cable layers who had tall stories for investors to hang their hats on.

Then media mogul Ted Turner's declaration that agreeing to merge Time Warner with America Online (AOL) gave him as big a high as when he first had sex was among the more justifiable utterances made when the deal was announced on January 10, 2000. At that time, Turner appeared set to make as much as $2.8 billion, so he could be excused some over-excitement. But in the 36 hours after the announcement, the stream of silliness to come out of the mouths of company executives, consultants, investors, analysts, and columnists was quite remarkable, even by the standards of the Internet bubble.

AOL head Steve Case described the deal's opportunities as "endless" and said it would lead to "the reinvention of television." Time Warner CEO Gerald Levin even went as far as to say that "this is not just about big business, this is not just about money," adding, "this is about making a better world for people because we now have the technology and the instruments to do that."

Unfortunately, such comments aren't just for amusement in hindsight.

After all, any investors who believed them enough to put money in either company at that time would have gotten in just before the shares began to sink, and if they had held on for the ride, they would have lost most of their investment.

Look at what's happened since:

Open warfare broke out between the traditional Time Warner fiefdoms and the AOL New Age entrepreneurs. Advertising revenue from the Internet collapsed, and in January 2003, AOL Time Warner announced a net loss of almost $100 billion for 2002, by far the biggest loss in U.S. corporate history. Indeed, some analysts believed at the time of writing that the AOL arm of the group was being given a zero or even negative value by investors. Levin, Case, Turner, and the executive who ran the AOL subsidiary, Robert Pittman, together with a stream of top AOL managers, have departed.

Even if your nonsense-meter was whirring from the start of all this, many others weren't paying attention.

After all, it was in 1999–2001 that European telecom companies were paying half a trillion dollars for licenses, networks, and acquisitions aimed at running the next generation of wireless networks across the region. It was a bid to make Europe the world leader in turning the wireless phone into a portable computer that offered easy access to the Internet—a chance to show the Americans a thing or two about technology. Again, the idea was that people would want to use their phones to download music and movies and the Internet and, if you believed the hype, life itself.

Instead, the aggressive wireless plans turned into a fiasco that left the expansion plans of most of Europe's major telecom carriers in ruins, burdened the carriers with massive debts, and cost a series of CEOs their jobs.

How can these supposedly intelligent corporate elites, with all the consultants and advisers money can buy, mess up so badly? Perhaps their lack of awareness of what makes the often eminently sensible consumer tick is part of the answer.

Note

Read commentary by contrarian analysts who don't follow the crowd.

Red Flag 2

A Whiz-Bang Device Is Loved by Tech-Geeks, but the Masses Are Unenthusiastic

Remember that the technology geeks (some dub them propeller heads) who design many of the exciting devices that flood the market tend to talk to others who are similarly enthused. They don't often talk to normal people like you and me. As a result, they sometimes produce things that might be cute but that we don't need, that we find frustrating to use, or that cost too much. Often, it is a combination of all three.

There are many examples, but one of the best was the introduction of an earlier generation of wireless Internet services on mobile phones in Europe in 2000–2001. A technology known as wireless application protocol (WAP) promised users a stream of entertainment and information on demand and at their fingertips, wherever they were. But when design and technology consultants Nielsen Norman Group gave 20 people WAP phones to use in London in the fall of 2000, it found that at the end of a week almost three-quarters said they wouldn't want to pay for such a phone in the next year. They thought the technology and service left a lot to be desired. Slow connections, uneven quality of information, the tiny screen, and the cost were all cited as problems. The hype hadn't been fulfilled.

Some believe that if the telecom companies had listened to consumers, they may have avoided overpaying for the new generation of wireless licenses by tens of billions of dollars when they were auctioned by European governments.

Of course, that doesn't mean that Internet-capable phones won't take off as their technology and design improve. But much of the time people devising technology don't think enough about who will be the user—partly because there is a certain pride about being on the cutting edge of technology. "In their own culture that they live in day to day, dumbing things down for the typical user is not all that techie," said Pip Coburn, global technology strategist at brokerage UBS Warburg. Coburn says that the key question about a technology that is aimed at the mass market is, "Have you really helped out my mom?" Unfortunately, the answer is often a resounding "No."

According to Fred Hickey, the editor and publisher of the *High-Tech Strategist* newsletter, another wrong assumption about consumers is that they want to use a keyboard to operate all kinds of interactive services on TV. "I said to myself the last thing I am going to do when I finish work is sit there with a keyboard with which I have been dealing all day. I am just going to lay on my couch and watch the sports," he said. "Common sense is important—it really is. What will the everyday man do?"

Note

Talk to non-geeky friends about what they plan on buying.

Red Flag 3

The Technology Is Great, but Its Price Is Too High for the Mainstream

One of the biggest problems during the boom years around the turn of the millennium was that many technology companies seemed to forget that they were competing against other demands on the business and consumer dollar. This was fine for a while when most executives were terrified of being left behind in the race to engage in electronic commerce, and many consumers were jealous when they heard their friends boasting about the latest gizmo. But, as soon as the bubble began to burst, businesses cut their technology budgets and consumers decided that they could manage without the newest gadget or a broadband connection.

To Neilsen Norman's Don Norman, who has written books on the adoption of technology and has been dubbed "the guru of workable technology" by *Newsweek*, faulty pricing is something investors must keep an eye on.

Wireless phones were adopted by the mass market in many countries ahead of the United States because they offered lower prices. In the United States, for example, you still have to pay to receive a call. On the other hand, Americans ate up the Internet much more quickly than many Europeans, partly because Americans got cheaper fixed-price access to the Internet than many people in countries such as the United Kingdom, who often pay per minute while they are surfing the web.

Norman says that many telecom companies have done themselves harm by charging $50 a month and upward for high-speed Internet access in the first few years they were offering it, putting it out of the range of many families and leading to slow take-up. "The pricing schemes are really damaging, and I think a lot of the telecommunications companies are trying to say we spent a huge amount of money on high-speed bandwidth, so we are going to charge to get it back, and what they do is simply discourage usage. It is very shortsighted."

Still, by early 2003, package deals offered by cable companies meant that high-speed Internet access was finally showing signs of breaking into the mass market in the United States.

Red Flag 4

If a Technology Is Said to Transform the World, It Is Being Over-Hyped

When a technology—whether in product or concept form—is said to be going to improve the lot of humanity or something equally fanciful, it is usually best to ignore it and focus on something that is being promoted more realistically.

Technology guru and author George Gilder told *Forbes ASAP* in an interview carried in its August 2000 issue that "optical networks are vital to the fulfillment of the business plans of the Internet economy and the future of world peace and prosperity." He didn't elaborate on how it fitted in with world peace. Terrorists, of course, have always been as close to the cutting edge of technology as any of the rest of us.

"When you have that kind of hyperbole, when the whole world is going to change, you say to yourself, 'Well, is it really?'" said Hickey.

The pipedream promoters have their own language. The buzz words and phrases include convergence, synergies, fully integrated connectivity, seamless integration, all-purpose multi-access portals, cross-pollination, interactivity on a higher plane, cross-platform integration, multiple access, cross promotion, and new media distribution channels. In layman's terms, much of the ballyhoo was about bringing together Internet providers, movie studios, telecom and cable companies, publishers, and record labels and television networks and gaining more customers, more viewers, more listeners—and, most essential of all, more advertisers—than any of the companies in one industry could do on their own. No one has yet managed to achieve this on any scale.

Red Flag 5

Journalists Are Often Wrong in Predicting the Success of a Deal or Product

Investors should understand that journalists can get swept up in any mania as much as anybody else, especially since some of our news sources were off with the new paradigm fairies. Many journalists were themselves wondering in 1998–2000 whether they should be seeking their fortunes in dot-com land, and indeed, some made the switch.

Still, that's no excuse. It is easy to be wise in hindsight, but business journalists generally need to spend more time being self critical and learning from past mistakes (and I certainly don't excuse myself from that process). It is all too easy for us to say we were merely reflecting what was being said and done in the boom, when we should have been more skeptical, viewed the boom in a greater historical context, and exposed conflicts of interest.

For example, any discussion of a technology, such as video-on-demand, should point out past failures around the world. The reader or viewer should also be told, wherever feasible, whether a consultant has business ties with a company he or she is writing or talking about.

At Reuters, for example, we wrote that the AOL Time Warner deal "promises to remake the landscape of how people around the world communicate and are entertained and informed." Of course, there were plenty of analysts and consultants that day who were prepared to declare the deal the most amazing thing.

"There is an explosion of revenue that comes with this interactive exchange over the television, first, but then handheld devices, cellular telephones with TV screens it's not just advertising, it's enhanced e-commerce dollars," we quoted US Bancorp Piper Jaffray analyst Eugene Munster as saying.

Some publications joined in the spirit so much that they took readers on a dream-like journey into the new era's AOL Time Warner land.

USA Today declared that "a new worldwide web of entertainment is in the wings," dominated by AOL Time Warner's interactive reach. In this world, you will be "watching HBO's *The Sopranos,* and you just have to have Tony's pinkie ring. Armed with your remote control, you order it immediately through America Online's interactive shopping link—and you instant message everyone on your Buddy List about the deal. Your cell phone buzzes with the new Madonna single. The TV calls out 'You've Got Mail' when you turn it on. Meanwhile *Time* magazine is on your printer, with its content customized to your tastes," an article in the newspaper predicted.

More than two-and-a-half years later, hardly any of this is yet achievable for most Americans—even if you have Time Warner cable and an AOL Internet connection. More importantly, there remains lots of doubt over whether the consumer really wants it enough to cough up extra cash for such convergence.

Furthermore, the newspaper had unidentified experts saying that they were expecting AOL's then president Bob Pittman to create unforgettable AOL Time Warner brands and generate gobs of advertising and electronic commerce revenue. Pittman quit AOL Time Warner under a cloud in July 2002 after failing to do either of these things. Instead, sinking advertising revenues at the AOL division had driven the company's stock price down more than 80 percent in the previous two-and-a-half years, and the company was just about to become the subject of an SEC investigation concerning aggressive accounting.

> **Note**
>
> Learn to differentiate between journalists who report in-depth and those who merely repeat what they were told by the last person they spoke to.

Red Flag 6

When Money Is Easy to Raise, Be Alert for Companies Doomed to Fail

When venture capitalists are throwing cash at just about anything, such as in 1997–2000, it's time for investors to be skeptical, says Hickey.

"We were in an environment where you didn't have to have a plan to actually make money—all you had to have was an idea, and then they would fund it," he said. The "they" in this case was everyone from the venture capitalists to the investors buying initial public offerings of stock (IPOs). During that period, the few naysayers could hoist a row of red flags and investors would still go swimming with the sharks.

For example, the Center for Financial Research and Analysis, which specializes in detecting accounting gimmicks, warned clients in November 1999 and again in January 2000 that software company Microstrategy Inc. was engaging in dubious revenue-generating transactions and ventures. Yet, the stock climbed from $20 in September 1999 to $333 in March 2000. Then, suddenly, the company disclosed that there were accounting problems, and it had to restate its results for 1997–1999 to record big losses rather than previously reported profits. There was an SEC probe, and the company's three top officials, including CEO Michael Saylor, agreed to disgorge a total of $10 million in profits from stock sales and pay penalties of $350,000 each. The company was also required to change the way it was governed and bring in new financial controls. There was no admission of guilt from any of the officials, but the stock sank to a low of 42 cents in July 2002 before it did a one-for-ten reverse stock split.

"People were just kind of delirious," said short seller Bill Fleckenstein in reference to the dot-com boom period. "It is not that the liars were so persuasive, it is that the people who were lied to were so gullible. Investors in prosperous times should always ask what will happen when the money runs out, the stock and bond market taps are turned off, and the banks get less friendly. You need a company for the hard as well as the good times—not one that folds when things get tough."

Note

The best companies have a clear and conservative strategy for making profits.

Red Flag 7
A Product Is Only Set to Reach a Niche, but Hopes Are Ramped Higher

Investors must try to differentiate between technology that may be sexy but only likely to gain a niche audience and the products that are destined to become ubiquitous. The automobile, the television, and the mobile phone fall into the latter category, but many devices fail to cross that chasm between niche and mass market—or at least in their early versions. Investing in a company structured on making that leap can be a very costly business when the product falls into the ravine.

An example is handheld computer maker Palm Inc., which saw its stock valued at more than $100 per share on its stock market debut in March 2000—just before the market bubble began to pop. A share in the company was trading at around 60 cents in the autumn of 2002 before it did a one-for-20 reverse stock split and the company was dropped from the S&P500. Now this was a company that once hoped to have every school kid, every homemaker, and every delivery guy using a Palm to keep calendars and phone numbers, play games, check sports scores, and so on. As it turned out, the device remained a business tool.

"It didn't cross the chasm," said Coburn. "I think people didn't want to change their lives. The PDA (personal digital assistant)—that's a big change in habit. First off you break down to the people who want more organization in their lives; not everyone wants that. Then the people who have to feel stupid because they have to learn how to use a stylus, then the people who have to tell their husband or wife that they want to spend $300 on the thing."

Eventually, Coburn argues, you end up with a market of 14 million rather than the hundreds of millions who use mobile phones. The Palm systems of this world are only likely to prosper as part of the new generation of Internet-ready mobile phones.

Red Flag 8

First Company to Market May Not Be the One to Succeed with a Product

In technology, the early bird often doesn't catch the worm.

As we have seen, Palm's problems don't mean the end of handheld computers. It is easy to envisage the day when almost everybody has a mobile device that allows us to make phone calls, use the Internet efficiently, play computer games, and take still and video pictures that can be sent immediately to another phone. It is just the investor in us who must understand that we are not there yet.

Look back at the initial problems some technology had in getting adopted when it was new. In 1943, IBM Chairman Thomas Watson said there would be a global market for "maybe five computers."

I remember getting a demonstration of video-on-demand in 1994 in the Hong Kong offices of the then Hongkong Telecom (now part of

Pacific Century CyberWorks). I was convinced that if video-on-demand were going to work anywhere soon, it would be in Hong Kong. The city was seen as an ideal testing ground because people had relatively high incomes and liked gadgets such as mobile phones and the city's high density made putting in fiber-optics and wiring homes cost effective.

The service known as iTV (interactive TV) was launched in 1998, offering instant access to movies and a range of other activities, including shopping, karaoke, and banking. But Hongkong Telecom's bold experiment soon turned into a disaster, with only about 90,000 households subscribing out of more than 1 million who could receive it and with customers paying much less every month than it cost to run the service. In the fall of 2002, iTV, after being moribund for some time, was read the last rites.

Many reasons have been given for the failure. The territory's economy hit a wall after the Asian economic crisis, Hongkong Telecom made a mistake by first wiring poorer housing estates (which were more concentrated and therefore easier) when more affluent communities couldn't get iTV, the movies weren't good enough, and customers couldn't access the Internet and email through the TV. The availability of pirated video-CDs of the latest movies was also a problem.

Eventually, video-on-demand, phones that take pictures, and videophones will appeal to entire families. But it is hard for an investor to decide when that might be and who will be best positioned to take advantage of the market.

Red Flag 9

Technology Becomes Obsolete and Companies Can Easily Burn Up

Warren Buffett and his associate at Berkshire Hathaway, Charlie Munger, have defined their limitations when it comes to technology companies. They want to invest in companies that are likely to be around in 10, 20, or 30 years time. The unforgiving winds that can easily turn last year's technology star into next year's junkyard piece mean that Buffett and Munger find the sector holds little appeal.

Think of some of Berkshire's holdings, such as Coca-Cola Co., Gillette, and Sees Candies. What they have in common is that the odd marketing misstep or other mistake can be rectified without the company's survival being threatened. In his 1996 annual letter to shareholders, Buffett said that he and Munger, as citizens, welcome innovation. As investors, Buffett said, "Our reaction to a fermenting industry is much like our attitude towards space exploration: We applaud the endeavor but prefer to skip the ride."

A technology analyst like Coburn can see the sense in that. "I think he is really smart not to put a lot of his brain cells to work trying to figure tech out.

"I don't think most tech companies have the assets in place to play the game that they are involved in, which is a very high turnover game. Product obsolescence is very quick, so most players are continually trying to stay on a treadmill that is moving very fast, and having a culture inside an organization to do that effectively is a real challenge."

Hickey points to the many casualties that were once the technology icons of previous decades. Very few of the leading technology companies in 1982 still survive on their own two feet, and hardly any of today's major players were around then. "You have to be able to make the transitions. If you are not prepared to cannibalize your own products, if you are trying to protect margins, you are going to fail— that is the history of this thing," he said. "It is different being Procter & Gamble selling soap, or Gillette your razors, year after year as a brand name; you are not likely to go obsolete."

Red Flag 10

Be Wary of Chasing the Prices of IPOs Soon After They Start Trading

Of course, even a cursory study of the original dot-com implosion offers some valuable lessons for investors. The original lie spawned dozens of really dumb Internet companies that had no real hope of ever making a profit but had more money than sense—thanks to massive funding from venture capitalists and then from the investing public through often artificially manipulated IPOs.

These businesses "were not real companies nor likely to be," says Harvard Business School professor D. Quinn Mills in his book *Buy, Lie and Sell High*. "These firms were built to flip—created to take advantage of the bubble, and for no other reason—not to bring an important product to market, not to create a company with a future."

Ordinary investors, though, were told that it was all about a glorious future and the need to act now to grab hold of it. The promoters of these stocks—whether the executives of the companies or Wall Street research department cheerleaders—explained that they needed to get big fast and that by being the so-called "first mover," you could get to own "Internet real estate" and dominate a market.

This effort to become the first mover entailed spending a lot of money on advertising and site development up front—in effect buying the eyeballs of web customers and, if they were lucky, some revenue. There was little or no thought given to how or when profits would flow. Online bookseller Amazon.com was the model used to justify the strategy, even though it was losing money hand over fist.

Former SEC Chairman Richard Breeden compared it to the tulip mania that gripped Europe in the seventeenth century, when people exchanged land, houses, and other valuables for a few tulip bulbs before that bubble collapsed. "There was a broad tulip mania surrounding the IPOs of tech stocks," he said. Parts of Wall Street had become a "massive hype machine" that "went from providing research on stocks to becoming stock touts," he added.

3

The Superstar CEO: Celebrities, Showmen, and Destroyers

"I would like to know if you are on crack? If so, that would explain a lot; if not, you may want to start, because it's going to be a long time before we trust you again."

—written question and advice from an Enron employee to the company's then chairman and CEO Kenneth Lay at a staff meeting on October 23, 2001

To get a job operating a cash register at retailers Wal-Mart or Winn-Dixie, you have to be a person of near unblemished virtue. In her book on the lives of the low-paid, *Nickel and Dimed: On (Not) Getting By in America*, Barbara Ehrenreich writes that applicants for those jobs face both a drugs test and a computer-checked personality test. And, of course, you also need to fill in a full application.

But, to get a job as a chief executive running a major international company, you may not need to go through any of that.

You are probably too important to need a formal resume, you are unlikely to face a psychological evaluation, and background checks may be cursory, so you may not need to worry about the little inaccuracies you provide about your past employment, which universities you attended, and what qualifications you got.

This is something investors should keep in mind when assessing who is running the companies they are considering investing in. "When you are doing senior level assignments, a lot of the information you get is either from the public record or what the individual tells you," said Thomas J. Neff, the chairman of the U.S. operations of executive search firm Spencer Stuart. "I mean these aren't people who have resumes, and sometimes you don't have the luxury of sitting down for a three- or four-hour interview and finding out every little detail going back, and what is most important is what is relevant to running a $6 billion to $7 billion company."

Criminal and SEC checks are possible, but talking to former colleagues is the usual way to check out a candidate's integrity, said Neff.

This laxity may be coming back to haunt companies and the recruitment industry. In the final few months of 2002, several companies were forced to confront executives who had claimed education or qualifications they didn't have. They had widely differing responses, perhaps dictated more by the company's performance at the time than by any ethical considerations. Bausch & Lomb Inc., the maker of eye care products, stuck with its CEO Ronald Zarrella after it was revealed that he didn't have a graduate degree in business from New York University as he claimed in his company biography. However, Veritas Software Corp. fired Chief Financial Officer Kenneth Lonchar when it found that he falsely claimed to have earned a master's degree from Stanford Business School.

The habit reached into the recruitment industry itself when, in January 2003, online job site Monster.com acknowledged that a "misunderstanding" had led its chairman Jeff Taylor to list a type of MBA from Harvard University on his resume when he holds no postgraduate degree and the type of MBA he described does not exist.

I have set out in this chapter to give you a guide to some of the different kinds of top executives—their backgrounds, personality traits, and behavior—that should make you wary of investing in a company. Essentially, investors must ask whether a corporate leader is working mainly for self-aggrandizement or for the good of the company.

You can get a good idea whether certain executives fit into any of the types listed in this chapter by listening to what they say and how they address people at public events (including conference calls) and by closely examining their statements and comments in the media. If you know anybody in the company, however lowly, they can give you some indication of what kind of character runs the shop.

The absence of normal background checks is only one of the ways in which CEOs are sometimes like sports figures and rock stars. As one former showman CEO, Albert Dunlap, said in his autobiography, "I'm a superstar in my field, much like Michael Jordan in basketball and Bruce Springsteen in rock 'n' roll. My pay should be compared to superstars in other fields, not to the average CEO."

It is a comment like this that can even make Howard Rubenstein wonder. The veteran publicist, who was once described by former New York Mayor Rudy Giuliani as "the dean of damage control," has calmly promoted them all—from the aggressive CEO to the high-strung celebrity. His clients have included Rupert Murdoch, Donald Trump, and Michael Jackson.

But when the hard-driving CEO also begins to think he is a celebrity, even Rubenstein is tempted to get judgmental. The celebrity CEO "looks for personal publicity, personal profiles, television appearances ... I think it is all inappropriate," said Rubenstein.

Certainly, 2002 was a year when many people woke up to the realization that more than a handful of top executives saw the companies they ran as personal fiefdoms. They used acquisitions as an opportunity for self-promotion and lashed out when anyone dared to ask whether the emperor had any clothes.

"The biggest problem with the corporation is that we have endowed our CEOs with the power and rank of the pope, and they are not popes—that I can assure you," said John Bogle, who founded and then built the Vanguard Group into the second-biggest mutual funds group in the world.

Nobody is saying we want gray CEOs without vision or that they shouldn't be seeking to earn good money; but, as ever, it is a question of proportion.

Rubenstein's ideal corporate leader has integrity and veracity, knows his or her industry, boasts a great track record, doesn't hide away from investors, and is devoted to the creation of a strong board and the disclosure of information. Unfortunately, in recent years, "too many executives left a distinct impression that all they cared about was their own pocketbooks," he said.

With the departure in 2002 of such showmen CEOs as the autocratic and flamboyant Jean-Marie Messier from French media company Vivendi Universal and Tyco International's Dennis Kozlowski, plenty of pundits were willing to declare an end to the adulation of corporate leaders. Even the record of the only recently deified Jack Welch was questioned. Welch had also shown how human he was by leaving his wife for a journalist early in 2002. Indeed, the *Economist* ran a cover story under the headline "Fallen idols—the overthrow of celebrity CEOs" in May 2002, complete with a picture of a destroyed statue of the former General Electric Co. helmsman. Such declarations can often be proven wrong. In 1993, *Fortune* ran "The King Is Dead" on its cover and declared, "the imperial CEO has had his day."

Rubenstein, possibly best known for his crisis management public relations, has been around too long to believe that there has been an irreversible sea change—after all, he's seen business trends and their disciples come and go since setting up Rubenstein Associates in 1954. "This will have a short-term effect and then the go-go people will be back," he said of the push for reforms and a change in behavior. "In five years you might be back to a different form of greed."

In some ways, the complexities of today's business world, with esoteric financial structures more the norm than the exception, make the visionary salesman CEO, who promotes the big picture rather than the nuts and bolts of a business, more of a cause for concern than in the past.

For Warren Buffett, CEO behavior comes down to much simpler human values. He says that he only goes into business with people whom he likes, trusts, and admires. Indeed, in a 1997 letter to shareholders, he revealed that he goes into business with the sort whom "you would be pleased to see your daughter marry." He added, "we've never succeeded in making a good deal with a bad person."

With such values in mind, let's look at this particular gallery of rogues, fools, and failures. But first a word of caution. Just because the CEO of a company of which you are a shareholder behaves a bit like one of the characters depicted in these categories, it doesn't mean you should automatically sell your shares. You should view the CEO as another piece of the jigsaw rather than as the answer to an entire investment puzzle.

As former SEC Chairman Richard Breeden puts it, "I don't care whether the CEO is the sweetest teddy bear and the most gracious and kind person who will sit on the phone all day long, or whether he is brusque and curt and in a hurry, you still have to look at the financials very, very carefully."

Red Flag 1
The Quitter: When a CEO Leaves without an Explanation

I start with this one because there isn't a bigger, more fluorescent warning light out there than news that a top executive has suddenly quit.

The biggest tip-off to the impending disaster at Enron was the shocking resignation on August 14, 2001, of CEO Jeff Skilling after only six months on the job, citing personal reasons. Remember, this was a man who was associated with Enron's transformation into one of America's apparently most dynamic companies and who was now at the pinnacle of his career.

"We look for any abrupt senior management changes or resignations," said short seller James Chanos. "That is usually a big red flag for us that something is amiss, particularly when it is abrupt and hasn't been telegraphed for quarters or months on end. The succession thing is well thought out and the CEOs and boards spend a lot of their time thinking about that, and when somebody just abruptly leaves for 'personal reasons' a lot of bells ought to be going off."

The mystery over Skilling's departure deepened in subsequent days.

In an interview with *The Wall Street Journal,* he indicated that he quit because of Enron's declining stock price, which he saw as the ultimate score card on his performance—hardly what is usually thought of as a personal reason. Then, he told the paper the final straw came when he visited England following a power plant accident that killed three Enron workers, saying that it had reinforced a sense of how tenuous life is. He told *BusinessWeek*, "There are some things I need to do in my personal life, and I need to do them now." He talked of getting more balance in his life and of the therapeutic value of going out and building a house for someone or cleaning up a park.

It just didn't make sense. Mind you, while Chanos—who was already short of the stock—got the message, many analysts and journalists didn't.

Most Wall Street brokerages kept buy ratings on Enron; indeed, most kept them on until the company was almost in bankruptcy less than four months later. Even the respected "Lex" column in the *Financial Times* said the 10 percent slide in Enron's stock price after the Skilling announcement "looks like an overreaction." The same newspaper's "Avenue of the Americas" column probably summed up the complacency on Wall Street when it quoted one unidentified analyst as saying that Skilling "wants desperately to get a life," adding, "from someone who doesn't have a life, I wish him well."

At the time of writing, the precise circumstances of Skilling's departure are still not known—even more than 18 months later. All we know is that investors who sensed a bad odor then saved themselves a lot of money.

Red Flag 2

When There Is Family Control, the Rights of Others May Be Trampled On

The alleged looting of cable TV company Adelphia by John Rigas and his family is a warning to us all that family control of the boardroom and executive suite should be feared. At 6 a.m. on July 24, 2002, Rigas and his sons Timothy and Michael were arrested on securities, wire, and bank fraud charges and were taken out of their New York apartment in handcuffs. John Rigas had been chairman and CEO, Timothy had been chief financial officer, and Michael had been executive vice president of operations of a company that filed for bankruptcy the previous month amid massive debts and accounting probes.

The Rigas family is alleged to have secretly siphoned off billions of dollars in loans and payments to finance everything from the acquisition of a professional ice hockey team to construction of a golf course on their property and purchases of luxury condos in Colorado, New York City, and Mexico. All together they ended up with control of almost 100 properties or plots of land. They also allegedly used company aircraft to shuttle family members back and forth on a Safari vacation in Africa and allowed John Rigas' daughter Ellen to live rent-free in an Adelphia apartment in Manhattan.

The SEC is also alleging that, along with other Adelphia officials, the three caused the company, which had 5.7 million cable subscribers in 30 states, to fraudulently exclude from its financial statements more than $2.3 billion in bank debt through the use of off-balance sheet affiliates.

Rigas family directors, together with the other defendants, are responsible for one of the largest cases of corporate looting and self-dealing in American corporate history, a separate lawsuit from Adelphia stated. In November 2002, the company's former vice president of finance, James Brown, pleaded guilty to fraud charges, implicating John Rigas and his two sons in the alleged scheme to falsify the company's finances. The Rigas family members have pleaded not guilty to the criminal charges and denied the other allegations.

So, why should we have suspected possible self-dealing?

Well, the first concern should have been that the Rigas family had five seats on a nine-person board. The family also held all the senior executive positions of the company, and other directors were friends and business associates of the founder.

Not only that, but the company's shareholding structure, with different classes of shares, meant that outsiders had little influence. A former Adelphia executive, Tom Cady, told *Fortune* magazine that "decisions were made at the dinner table rather than in a boardroom or somebody's office."

> **Note**
>
> Check proxy statements (SEC filing 14A) for a company's family connections and board memberships.

Red Flag 3

Beware the Worst Combo of All: An Aggressive CEO and a Compliant CFO

Few disagree that the plague of accounting fraud in recent years resulted mainly from desperate attempts to keep earnings growing at an artificially high pace—even when business was deteriorating. If earnings growth fell below Wall Street forecasts, everyone in the executive suite knew that the company's stock price would get hammered. That could not only eventually cost the CEO and other top managers their jobs, but it would also reduce or even eliminate the value of stock options they had been awarded.

This combination of greed and fear means it is difficult for some executives to resist cooking the books. But the likelihood of fraud increases immensely if you have the worst combination in the executive suite—an overbearing, bullying CEO and a compliant, weak chief financial officer. The CEO makes it clear that the figures must meet or beat expectations, while a fawning CFO, fearing he or she will lose his or her job, bends the accounting rules to make his or her master happy. Initially, it starts with a modest manipulation of the numbers— perhaps by booking some revenue before the company can count on receiving it. But, as the pressure builds in successive quarters, the deceptions have to get bigger to cover up a deepening hole.

"An overly aggressive CEO and an overly compliant CFO can operate in tandem to create a 'tone at the top' that all but guarantees some level of financial misreporting," writes attorney Michael R. Young in his book *Accounting Irregularities and Financial Fraud.*

Red Flag 4

The CEO Bullies Everyone

The bully CEO seeks to dominate everything around him or her, including the board, other managers, investors, analysts, and even politicians and the press. Usually things will end badly for the shareholders of a company run by this kind of CEO.

An example was the late British press baron and one-time *New York Daily News* owner Robert Maxwell, who drowned in the sea off the Canary Islands in 1991. Several weeks after his death, it was discovered that Maxwell had stolen about $700 million from his employees' pension plans as he had tried to keep his companies from collapsing under a deepening debt crisis.

In his biography of Maxwell, Roy Greenslade makes it clear that everybody knew of Maxwell's deceitful nature, but banks, brokers, politicians, and others continued to support him until almost the end. "What makes him so fascinating is that everyone knew he was an untrustworthy character. You did not have to work next to him to know he was up to something: he was so transparently a man with a lot to hide," wrote Greenslade, who was editor of Maxwell's flagship *Daily Mirror* newspaper for just over a year. A British Department of Trade report in 1971 on alleged breaches of company law by Maxwell concluded that "he is not in our opinion a person who can be relied on to exercise proper stewardship of a publicly-quoted company." More than 20 years later, one of those inspectors, according to Greenslade, said that it was Maxwell's "capacity to regard the world as his own, which we thought was extremely dangerous."

"Super-ego is a big part of the problem," said Vanguard founder Bogle in reference to the spate of corporate scandals in the United States in 2002. "The power look does nothing for me and the retinue even less—marching around with a whole bunch of people who are carrying bags for you—it's the pomp and circumstance type of leader."

Note

Read several different media interviews and profiles to assess the character of a CEO.

Red Flag 5

The CEO Hypes a Company's Performance and Prospects

This character is going to promise you much more than common sense would suggest can be delivered.

Think of Enron's Jeff Skilling, who told Reuters on his first day in the CEO's chair on February 13, 2001, that "the new vision is going to be from the world's leading energy company to the world's leading company."

The basis for this wild prediction was that Enron's business model for energy trading could be used to trade just about anything. "The application is almost limitless because every single business has, at its heart, markets. So, if we've got a better market model we can participate in a whole lot of different businesses," Skilling said.

It's at this stage that any thinking investor should quickly head for the exit. First, Enron wasn't the world's biggest publicly traded energy company; second, companies that really do become number one do so quietly over many years and without setting boastful targets; and third, the idea that Enron had discovered a better way of trading all commodities was fanciful.

The key is to differentiate between the executive who patiently builds a business day by day and month by month, and one who goes for the big splash and the absurd target. Ask yourself why so few people know who is the CEO of the world's largest retailer, and biggest corporation, Wal-Mart. Perhaps the answer has something to do with how little publicity he seeks. His name, by the way, is Lee Scott Jr.

Red Flag 6

A CEO Is Caught Making Misleading Statements

Hype merchants eventually get caught out.

They can only bluff their way out of a difficult corner for so long. Eventually, the cards have to be laid out on the table. This was demonstrated by Joe Nacchio when he was Qwest Communications International's CEO.

Facing criticism from investors and analysts over Qwest's accounting practices and the sustainability of its earnings growth, Nacchio (according to *The Denver Post*) told a conference that "you all think we cheat and lie and steal, obviously, and therefore you trade us at a discount to what a normal company with great revenue and great growth should be traded." He said at the October 3, 2001, conference that instead of trying to convince his audience he would "just let the numbers speak for themselves on October 31."

Unfortunately, the numbers didn't quite do the trick as the company missed expectations, leaving Nacchio eating humble pie on Halloween. "Some of you will recall that at a recent conference I said the results will speak for themselves. The reality is, they do not speak clearly for themselves without some interpretation given the current economic conditions and the effects of merger and other one-time charges." Nacchio quit in June 2002 amid an SEC probe into alleged accounting trickery and growing concerns about whether the company could avoid bankruptcy given its massive debt load.

Major investment institutions are starting to test what a CEO says against what has been published previously. For example, New Jersey-based money manager David Dreman says that he is now quite prepared to grill a CEO not to get new information but to see whether he or she is being deceptive.

Note

While smaller investors may not get such access to the CEO, anyone can keep a file on a company in which they are investing and compare conference calls and other public comments with past statements. As always, if you smell anything fishy, it may be time to look elsewhere.

Red Flag 7

When a CEO Is Abusive, It May Be a Sign of Major Problems

Former Enron CEO Jeff Skilling's crude verbal assault on a hedge fund manager during a quarterly conference call in April 2001 was taken as an indication by short sellers that the pressure was really getting to top management at Enron. Highfields Capital Management Managing Director Richard Grubman had asked to see Enron's balance sheet—not an unreasonable request given that the energy trader had just issued its first-quarter results without including it in the press release. After all, you can only get a full picture of a company's performance and prospects by checking on its debt obligations. "You're the only financial institution that can't come up with a balance sheet or cash flow statement after earnings," Grubman grumbled on the call. "Well, thank you very much, we appreciate that, asshole," Skilling responded with a laugh.

Later that day, Skilling told Reuters that Grubman was a short seller and he didn't want to give him a platform on the call as it was unfair to Enron shareholders. "I get a little exasperated with that sort of thing, and I want people to know I am exasperated," Skilling explained.

Grubman, though, was at a loss as to why asking for a balance sheet was such an objectionable question and said that Skilling had "some nerve," given that Skilling and his management team had been selling Enron stock near its record highs and the price had dropped by the time of the call. Chanos said that it was after that conference call that Enron perhaps "began to realize that other people had figured out what was going on."

Red Flag 8

A CEO Is Built Up As the New Star Who Is Going to Fix Everything

This type of CEO is often a corporate public relations and media creation. You take a big-name company that is struggling and bring in an outsider whose reputation may be embellished a little by the image people, and, hey, presto—the share price leaps and the recovery has begun. Sometimes, however, the problems are bigger than the Mr. or Ms. Fixit can handle, and the result is that investors face an even bigger letdown.

Take Conseco's decision to hire the former head of GE Capital, Gary Wendt, in 2000 and give him one of the most generous contracts ever known, including an unprecedented $45 million signing bonus. News of his hiring initially helped to drive up the price of shares in the struggling financial services company, which was deeply indebted fol-

lowing an acquisition spree. But the honeymoon didn't last, especially after Conseco's finance subsidiary made a crippling series of bad
loans. Just before the end of 2002, Conseco filed for bankruptcy, the
third-biggest in U.S. corporate history. Wendt had earlier stepped
down as CEO under pressure from creditors—after announcing that
his original turnaround strategy had failed.

Red Flag 9

When Senior Management Includes the Company's Former Auditors

This one doesn't just concern the CEO or CFO but can include the
whole management team—especially anyone having a direct relationship with the outside auditors.

The revolving door that has seen many auditors become top executives in both American and European companies in recent years is
viewed as a dangerous trend. These executives may not only be in a
position to pressure staff at their former accounting firms who are
examining company accounts, diminishing their independence and
skeptical approach, but they also know how to disguise manipulation.

Indeed, it is such a concern that the Sarbanes-Oxley law includes
a ban on an accounting firm carrying out the audit of a public company if one of the top executives was part of the outside audit team in
the previous year. The one-year "cooling off period" is unlikely,
though, to stop the revolving door from turning: An auditor, for
example, could join a company in another position before being promoted to a top slot the following year.

Among the companies badly hurt by accounting scandals where
the revolving door may have been a problem was Enron, which hired
at least three of its top financial executives from its auditor Andersen,
and Waste Management Inc., which had hired many of its finance officials from Andersen.

Note

Check on the backgrounds of senior executives in a company's annual report and
in its proxy statement.

Red Flag 10

When the CEO Is Known Best for Destroying Jobs and Slashing Costs

It's amazing to think that only a few years ago, Albert Dunlap, otherwise known as "Chainsaw Al," was being lauded by parts of the investing community, Wall Street, and the media for his brutal restructuring efforts that always included massive job cuts.

At Scott Paper, which he joined as CEO in April 1994, Dunlap fired more than 11,000 workers, cutting the payroll by 35 percent, and sold off billions of dollars of assets. In the process, he tripled the stock price. Then, before anyone could determine whether the slash and burn strategy would work in the long run, he sold the company off to Kimberly-Clark Corp. in December 1995, in a takeover valued at $9.4 billion.

For a while, he was part of the talk show circuit, bragging that Scott was "the most successful turnaround in the shortest time in the history of corporate America." Dunlap, who liked to be called "Rambo in pinstripes," wrote a book and lectured to MBA students at Harvard and Wharton business schools.

But, if it were always as simple as that, there would be a lot of Al Dunlaps running around.

When he tried to do the same at kitchen appliance maker Sunbeam Corp., where he chopped half its 12,000-strong workforce in 1996–1997, Dunlap failed. The company's board fired him in June 1998, citing its loss of confidence in him and his earnings forecasts.

Sunbeam went into bankruptcy in 2001, and in 2002, the company's accountants (Andersen), insurers for Sunbeam, and Dunlap himself settled a class-action lawsuit by investors alleging fraud. Dunlap, who agreed to pay $15 million of the $141 million settlement, also agreed in September 2002 to pay $500,000 to settle a case brought by the SEC, though he did not admit or deny charges of using inappropriate accounting techniques that hid Sunbeam's financial problems. He was also barred from ever serving as an officer or director of any public company.

> **Note**
>
> Never believe those who promise quick solutions to longstanding problems.

Red Flag 11

A CEO Known Best As a Serial Acquirer Rather Than a Builder

Corporate America is currently littered with the wreckage of serial acquirers who shopped until their companies dropped. Almost all the big investment disasters of recent years can be at least partly blamed on failed acquisition strategies. Enron, WorldCom, Adelphia, Tyco, Vivendi, AT&T, AOL Time Warner ... the list is almost as long as you want to make it.

For example, Tyco made more than 700 acquisitions from 1999–2001, while Ebbers built WorldCom through more than 70 acquisitions. Investors should always ask why a company is spending time, energy, and money in acquiring new businesses rather than growing the ones it already has.

Remember that acquisitions, especially those that use a company's stock as the currency rather than cash, can sometimes be used as a smokescreen to disguise poor performance in other businesses. Acquisition accounting allows plenty of room for artificially creating a picture of strong growth, and U.S. corporate disclosure rules mean that many smaller acquisitions are never even disclosed because they are not considered "material" in size.

The plunge in stock prices after March 2000 caught out a lot of serial acquirers. Suddenly, they could no longer use their shares to finance takeovers, and previous acquisitions become worth a lot less—leading to massive one-time charges that show up in their financial results. With their assets impaired, their debt burdens become increasingly onerous.

Also, remember that negotiating and announcing a deal, complete with references to synergies to be realized, is the easy part. Often, the cultures of the two companies can be very different and clashes can destroy morale. The internal struggle between Time Warner and AOL managers in the years immediately after their merger was announced is an example of this.

Sometimes, the acquirer may be lumbered with an ugly accounting fraud or litigation that wasn't anticipated. HFS Inc.'s merger with CUC International Inc. to become travel services and real estate company Cendant Corp. almost blew the combined entity out of the water when massive accounting fraud was discovered at CUC. Cendant's shares plunged about 80 percent in 1998 when the problems were disclosed.

Red Flag 12

A CEO Who Blames Others for a Company's Ills

Members of management who blame everyone but themselves for a declining share price are not to be trusted. A particular target for the blame game is the short sellers; at other times, it's the media or even the investors and Wall Street. "It is another qualitative red flag, when they start blaming short sellers for their problems. I wish we had the power that these companies claim we do," said Chanos. "It is often a management that wants to divert your attention away from what the short sellers are saying—their point is who is saying it, not what they are saying," he said, adding that if a company's critics were wrong, a company should be able to confidently rest on its accounts and let the figures speak for themselves.

Tyco was the master of the blame game, but it came away battered from a three-year war with short seller David Tice, whose position was vindicated to a large extent when Kozlowski was charged with plundering the company.

Rubenstein says that CEOs should learn from the unsuccessful attempts made by politicians to blame the media for their ills. "Nixon blamed the media—they have all blamed the media. It doesn't work."

Red Flag 13

An Executive with a Dubious History: Beware Repeat Offenders

Investors can't afford to be charitable when an executive has a doubtful history. By avoiding those who have a record that doesn't stand up to scrutiny, you can avoid trouble. There is a reason for the term "repeat offender."

Take Sam Waksal, the colorful former CEO of ImClone Systems. In October 2002, he entered a partial guilty plea to insider trading charges related to large sales he made of the company's stock before news broke in December 2001 about the FDA rejection of the application for the cancer treatment Erbitux. He was due to be sentenced around the time this book was scheduled to be published, in the spring of 2003. ImClone, which is now run by his brother Harlan Waksal, has sued Sam Waksal, claiming that he ordered the destruction of documents that may be important to the government's investigations. He also pleaded guilty in March 2003 to additional charges of evading taxes on $15 million of art purchases.

Yet, only 18 months earlier, it had been so different. Waksal had made a highly favorable impression with the promise of the "miracle" cancer drug and with the very force of his charm.

But there were many alarm bells ringing in Waksal's past that should have prompted anyone with a cautious bone in his or her body to steer well clear.

"It is one thing to have a red flag; it is something else to have fuchsia," said veteran private investigator Jules Kroll in reference to the Waksal brothers. "There were enough warning signals over a long period of time that you would have to be triply alert to looking at everything that you were considering. I would put it in a very high risk category."

Articles in *Vanity Fair* and *The Wall Street Journal* have highlighted major red flags in Sam Waksal's past. These include lawsuits he has faced from business partners and one-time friends and his earlier departure under a cloud from several research institutions for what *The Journal* reported former supervisors and others as saying was misleading (and in one case falsified) scientific work.

Even his brother Harlan was arrested in 1981 at Fort Lauderdale International Airport for possessing a kilo of cocaine. He was sentenced to nine years in prison, but the conviction was overturned on appeal because the search resulted from an illegal seizure without a valid consent, according to published reports.

> **Note**
>
> Check court records through legal web sites such as *www.westlaw.com*.

Red Flag 14

When Executives Buy Homes in Bankruptcy Havens Such As Florida

The "hacienda watch" is an unusual and untested indicator, but anecdotal evidence suggests that it is worth keeping an eye on where top executives are building multi-million dollar homes—especially if there is even a whiff of accounting scandal in their company.

Homes in a few states, including Florida and Texas, have been protected from investors' lawsuits and other civil litigation provided that the owner goes into bankruptcy under so-called homestead exemption laws.

"It really is amazing that somebody can commit a fraud and buy a $10 million or $15 million house down in Florida and have that house protected while investors are being evicted from their homes or have lost all their retirement savings or whatever—there is something wrong with that picture," said Max Berger, an attorney with Bernstein Litowitz Berger & Grossmann LLP, which is representing the lead plaintiff in a massive securities class-action suit against bankrupt telecom group WorldCom.

"I believe the law was originally designed so that people wouldn't be left homeless, but I am sure nobody contemplated the fact that it would protect someone who lives in a mansion on an estate," he said.

WorldCom's former chief financial officer Scott Sullivan is building a $15 million Mediterranean-style mansion in Palm Beach County, Florida. Building plans show that it includes eight bedrooms, eight bathrooms, six Jacuzzis, a games room, a small theater, a 79-foot pool, a domed exercise room, a library, an art gallery, a wine cellar, and a separate wine room.

Sullivan, who has lived in Florida for some time even though WorldCom's headquarters is in Clinton, Mississippi, was charged with securities fraud in the summer of 2002 following revelations about an alleged massive and growing accounting scandal. He pleaded not guilty.

Among others who have homes in Florida are Tyco's former CEO Kozlowski, who has a $29 million exclusive Boca Raton estate called "The Sanctuary," and a group of other current and former executives at the company. Sunbeam's former CEO Dunlap also has a Florida property. Of course, former top Enron figures mostly have properties in and around Houston, the company's home base, that would allow them some protection under the Texas homestead exemption.

4

Jets, Parachutes, and Stealth Wealth: Pay for Performance or Pay for Plundering

"My father taught me that when you play poker and win a hand, put half in your pocket and walk away from the table."

—Vincent Galluccio, former executive at bankrupt telecom group Metromedia Fiber Networks Inc., explaining to *The Wall Street Journal* in an article on August 12, 2002, how he made $27 million out of selling shares in the company, which later filed for bankruptcy protection

In the summer of 2002, Edward Breen appeared poised to become a very rich man. The one-time varsity wrestler had gotten more than just a hero's welcome from desperate investors when he took over as chairman and CEO of troubled conglomerate Tyco International. A rising share price meant that within a month of starting he was looking at the possibility of becoming one of the best-paid managers in America.

Sure, Breen had his work cut out. Tyco, which has operations ranging from undersea fiber-optic cables to diapers, had been dogged for months by questions about its accounting practices and acquisition strategy, alleged looting by its top executives, and the alleged connivance of some of its directors. Its shares had been slammed, it had been forced into a fire sale of some assets, and lenders were making it more difficult and more expensive to borrow money.

Breen's buccaneering predecessor Dennis Kozlowski had resigned on June 3, 2002, the day before he was indicted on tax evasion charges concerning art purchases. Revelations that Kozlowski had allegedly used the company as a private piggy bank continued to mount through the summer, eventually leading to indictments and lawsuits that accused him of plundering the company.

But, if Breen, who had been number two at wireless phone and chip maker Motorola Inc., could get rid of the stench of corruption and recoup just half the market value Tyco had lost since December 2001, he would be looking at annual compensation of well above $50 million, including the value of share and option awards.

Yes, a new broom can have old bristles. The goal of this chapter is to help you find out whether the executives running companies in which they have holdings are providing value for money. The red flags identified are based on excess.

To begin, let's look at the details of Breen's contract.

It is mainly the many different levels of rewards that Breen can receive, rather than any one aspect of his compensation, that make his employment contract so attractive. It is no wonder that Breen, who was once described by an analyst as part rocket scientist and part used car salesman, called the move to Tyco the opportunity of a lifetime.

The first thing on the pay side that Breen had to be excited about was a $3.5 million sign-on (lump-sum) cash bonus. This bonus was in addition to a $1.5 million annual salary (which was slightly lower than Kozlowski's $1.65 million) and a guaranteed first-year bonus of at least $1.5 million. Then, there are the stock options through two grants: 3.35 million as part of the sign-on bonus and 4 million as part of a long-term incentive plan. The dates on which these can be exercised for shares is spread over three years for the sign-on options and five years for the others, with the price set at $10. Now, that was about the price of Tyco's stock the day before Breen's appointment was announced, but in the month afterward, the shares soared to $17. If the Tyco share price were to stay at that level for the following five years, it would mean that Breen would be able to exercise the options and sell the shares at a profit of more than $50 million.

However, if he can get the price to $35, which would still be well behind the $60 it was trading at before the spate of troubles related to strategy, accounting, and the Kozlowski indictments began, Breen would be able to make a $25 profit from each of the options. Breen also received 1.35 million so-called deferred stock units, which are shares he will receive on a deferred basis over the space of five years from the contract date. At the $17 share price, these are worth about $23 million. Altogether, according to compensation research company Equilar, Breen's sign-on pay package was worth about $121 million based on the company's share price early in 2003.

In addition, Breen gets a range of benefits, including life insurance, a generous retirement plan, relocation benefits that included temporary housing and expenses, the use of private jets for himself and his family for business and personal reasons, and, according to the contract, "all perquisites which other senior executives of the company are generally entitled to receive." The last phrase might normally be seen as just boilerplate, but in Tyco's case, it is a little more worrying because of the allegations that Kozlowski spent company money recklessly.

"Breen's contract is not that different from Kozlowski's in terms of what's on offer for him to receive as perquisites and benefits and whatever else," said Paul Hodgson, senior research associate at The Corporate Library, an entity that specializes in corporate governance issues such as executive pay and board performance. "Instead of awarding him a set of guaranteed bonuses and market oriented options, Tyco could have exerted itself to tie his pay to performance in some concrete fashion," he said.

Clearly, the 46-year-old Breen, who is known for his blunt speech, has an impressive background. His departure was seen as a loss to Motorola, he was previously CEO of General Instrument, and he had, according to *The Wall Street Journal*, turned down offers to become CEO at two troubled telecom equipment companies, Lucent Technologies Inc. and Nortel Networks Corp., in the past year. Tyco was in desperate straits and probably had to pay more—particularly in the sign-on bonus—than it would have if it had not been tainted by scandal. Of course, if Tyco were to collapse, Breen would lose out on the stock options and the stock that has been granted to him, though his salary, guaranteed bonus, and sign-on bonus give him plenty of protection. While the initial signs were that Breen may be able to lead the conglomerate from such a fate, few would blame him if he failed to save a company that already had so many self-inflicted wounds, so he would hardly fail to attract another lucrative job offer or two.

All in all, Breen has plenty of reward but little risk. It is a package that shows there hasn't yet been a transformation in corporate America despite all the calls from major investors, politicians, and the chattering classes about the need to rein in greedy executives.

Indeed, it is far from clear that the image of fat cat CEOs cashing in their multi-million dollar stock options at the top of the market while ordinary workers and pensioners lose their retirement income because of fraud can be erased any time soon.

The negative public perception isn't only of people facing securities fraud charges for fiddling the books or taking money from the companies they ran. It is of people such as Oracle CEO Larry Ellison, who pocketed $706 million from exercising long-held stock options and then selling 29 million shares in a single week in January 2001. Ellison, who owns about a quarter of Oracle and says his salary of just $1 in cash means that his interests are entirely aligned with those of the company's shareholders, then watched the software company's shares lose a third of their value in the following few weeks as it said it was going to miss earnings forecasts. Oracle has said there was nothing linking Ellison's sales and the warning about earnings.

The perception is also of Global Crossing's former Chairman Gary Winnick, who sold $735 million in stock in the four years before the telecom network company filed for bankruptcy and, according to published reports, paid $90 million for the former Hilton estate in Bel Air, California. Global Crossing was at the time of writing still facing an SEC probe into its accounting practices, though the *Los Angeles Times* reported at the end of 2002 that federal prosecutors have decided not to file criminal charges against the company or its former executives. Winnick's lawyer has said that his client has done nothing illegal.

It has to be said that executive pay dropped in the United States in 2001 and almost certainly fell again in 2002—mainly because the bear market made stock options far less lucrative. According to various surveys and depending on what measures they used, the drop in 2001 was anything from 2.9 percent to 32 percent, but the size of the compensation is still so large that the declines were unlikely to make investors, the public, and the media more understanding of executive greed. And with stock options awards facing shareholder criticism and loans now effectively banned under the new law, there are signs that companies were busy lifting sign-on bonuses and restricted stock awards in 2002, some compensation experts said.

There are many who shake their heads in disbelief at the size of executive compensation. "How did it come about that a person could reasonably expect to make $100 million as a hired hand?" asks shareholder activist and investor Herbert Denton. "Does anybody really believe that the 500 people who are running the S&P 500 companies are that much better than the next 500 people out there?"

Some highly regarded investment figures are mad about the levels of greed that have been seemingly encouraged by some boards.

"Angry would be an understatement—it makes me angry and disgusted," said Vanguard funds group founder John Bogle, who has been pushing for institutional investors to take a more active role in getting boards to rein in such largesse.

Naming and shaming does have a part to play. Former GE CEO Jack Welch renounced some generous retirement perks—including the use of company jets and a New York City apartment—after his lavish package was revealed in an affidavit filed by his estranged wife Jane in their divorce proceedings. In an article penned for *The Wall Street Journal* on September 16, 2002, Welch defended the benefits, which included country club memberships, dinners at top Manhattan restaurants, and even groceries and toiletries for the apartment, but he said that perceptions matter. "In this environment, I don't want a great company with the highest integrity dragged into a public fight because of my divorce proceedings," he wrote.

Even compensation consultants wonder how some of the executives who say they need massive salaries to survive can relate to the tens of thousands of employees struggling to make much smaller ends meet.

"I have had executives in a room very seriously tell me that they have a $1 million salary and they cannot live on anything less—it is a rock-bottom survival number," said Robin Ferracone, a worldwide partner with Mercer Human Resources Consulting. "It's like, we have lost perspective here." Indeed, Ferracone always asks directors to consider how various aspects of proposed compensation packages will sound to employees, investors, the public, and the media.

Now, here I should warn you that my British roots might mean I don't quite get it. You see, in Britain, anything above about $1 million a year is seen as outrageous and could get an executive a steamrollering by the tabloid press, especially if a company is cutting jobs or paying low wages to staff. The British, and it must be said many Europeans, might like some of the entrepreneurial ways of American business, but they find $50 million salaries difficult to stomach, whatever part of the political spectrum they are from.

There are big global companies in Europe that are a match for some of the biggest in the United States. Think of the banking group HSBC Holdings, which at the end of 2001 had $698.3 billion in assets and achieved a net profit of $4.91 billion for that year. Its Executive Chairman Sir John Bond received a combined salary and bonus of about $2.7 million in 2001.

That is only a quarter of the $11 million in cash received by JP Morgan Chase head William Harrison, which included a $5 million bonus for overseeing Chase Manhattan Corp.'s purchase of J. P. Morgan & Co. If you start to factor in the value of restricted stock and options, the gulf gets wider. And yet, J. P. Morgan's assets were slightly less than HSBC's at the end of 2001, and its net profit was less than half.

When asked what the difference is between covering the beat in the United Kingdom and the United States, Hodgson, who worked for 10 years as a compensation analyst in Britain, said, "Everything has got more zeroes on it basically: I mean it is that simple—you raise everything by the power of 10."

Just to keep this all in perspective, though, it is worth remembering that investors weren't complaining much about executive pay during the bull market. Then, many didn't seem to mind if executives built palaces, partied lavishly, and used the company jet to fly their kids to Disneyland.

"I don't have a violent objection to CEOs who have done extraordinarily well for their company taking big chunks; I think it is too much, but what is too much?" said lawyer and corporate governance expert Ira Millstein. "What I object to is the CEOs who in bad times continued to get well compensated, or who re-priced options or got loans or did whatever. That I object to—I think that's outrageous."

With that view in mind, let's look at the areas that should unsettle investors most.

Red Flag 1

CEO Compensation Is Not Linked Closely with Performance

First, understand that all companies claim they only reward executives based on performance. Now, some are on the level when they say that, but others may be lying.

In the proxy statement that goes out to all shareholders every year before a company's annual meeting, there is a section on executive compensation and a report from the board's compensation committee—these are among the most important sections of any of the company documents and reports issued during the year. They are likely to tell you a lot about the corporate culture and whether independent directors have some control or if executive greed is dominant. According to TIAA-CREF's senior vice president for corporate governance, Peter Clapman, it is the best window an investor has into what goes on in the boardroom. "Executive compensation jumps out at us because it is a quick read as to whether there are problems at a company," he said.

You may see a lot of horrid compensation-speak—but when you understand it, some of this jargon is actually useful. It is important, for example, if a company talks about a "pay positioning strategy" that sets base salary at the 75th percentile of a peer group of companies. This means the starting point for executive pay decisions is above average for the industry, which is a worrying initial declaration.

Ferracone says the only justification is if a company were so much larger than its rivals that pressures on management were of a much higher magnitude. She says that if you see such "above market pay" (another warning phrase) policies, you should ask why. Most companies should be settling for a 50th percentile or even below average comparison. She also says any compensation committee charter or statement should be talking more about performance targets than pay levels. If the focus is on money and rewards rather than on targets and achievements, investors should be concerned.

Of course, if everybody is at the median, then the median numbers go up, which creates its own inflationary spiral, a problem actually exacerbated by increased disclosure. "If you are sitting at the head of one company and you see all three of your competitors are getting $1 million and you are only on $900,000, then you will ask what is the justification for that?" said Hodgson.

In looking at compensation, investors need to look at measurements such as earnings per share growth and share price performance relative to a company's competitors and then compare these measurements with various measures of rewards for the CEO and other top officers. In simple terms, "if pay is going up at the same time a corporation is doing poorly, that is a bad sign," said New York-based compensation consultant Frederic Cook.

A guaranteed bonus is another warning. Investors should ask why, if it is guaranteed, it isn't just put in salary instead of being called a bonus? The same goes for any stock awards that aren't tied to meeting goals.

Note

Read the proxy statement carefully, and when new CEOs or CFOs are named, check the employment agreement that has to be disclosed (usually hidden in the appendices) in the next quarterly or annual filing with the SEC. So, if you want to know how much companies are paying their new CEOs or CFOs, what kind of perks they get, and how much it would cost to get rid of them, look through their subsequent filing of a financial statement. If the SEC insisted on separate and faster filing of this information it would, of course, help investors.

Red Flag 2

When Stock Options Are Handed to Executives Like There's No Tomorrow

The biggest concern about stock options is that they can provide an incentive for executives to cook the books in the short term to get a share price higher.

The manipulation of company accounts—whether through fraud or through questionable but legal means—is only exposed after the executives have exercised their options and cashed in the resulting shares. The share price then slides, hurting ordinary investors who had been under the impression the company was on a strong growth path, while the executives may already be sitting pretty in their Florida homesteads.

The awarding of stock options, which was supposed to align executives' interests with those of shareholders, suddenly took them in the opposite direction. A key problem is that companies have not had to include an estimate of the cost of stock options in their expenses, which led to their being thrown around with no thought for the wider consequences. Some companies are now starting to expense stock options because of the growing controversy, though technology companies are mostly resisting.

Since the unrestrained granting of stock options to executives is suspected to have played a role in some of the blow-ups of the past few years, investors should look to companies that ensure stock options are used as a carefully targeted part of a compensation package.

As we have seen, options grants that can quickly take executives into the mega-million brackets are a concern. There is a big difference between rich rewards for the CEO who has provided shareholders with long-term growth in earnings and share price and the windfall received by one who has just walked through the door.

Companies like Dell Computer reduce some of the risk that options will give executives an immediate high by spreading the vesting of awards over five years. There may also be more options awarded with step-up prices so that the first year they can be exercised at 10 percent above the current share price, the next year at 20 percent, and so on, said Thomas J. Neff, who is U.S. chairman of headhunters Spencer Stuart. "In other words the executives wouldn't have earned the options until the shareholders have already gained on price," he said.

Then, there is the issue of balance. If a large percentage of a company's stock options are being given to executives and other top employees, it is probably less of a healthy sign than if a company makes sure that grants are spread far and wide so that secretaries and factory workers can also have an incentive. For example, in

2001, semiconductor giant Intel Corp. gave its chairman, Andy Grove, only 0.16 percent of the total number of stock options handed out. In contrast, at Tyco, then Chairman and CEO Kozlowski got 4.26 percent.

Still, perhaps the most important question is whether companies place any restrictions on executives to make sure they retain most of the shares that they buy through options rather than—providing the shares have gained—selling them straight away for a big cash profit.

Note

Again, read the proxy statement carefully, particularly the areas on executive compensation and stock options.

Red Flag 3

When Top Executives Own Very Little of Their Company's Stock

If they're not eating their own cooking, you have to wonder how bad the kitchen is.

WorldCom's former chief financial officer Scott Sullivan, for example, clearly didn't like his own menu. By the end of 2001, he owned only about 5,385 shares in the second-biggest U.S. phone company, which in 2002 slid into bankruptcy amid a deepening accounting scandal. Even at its peak 1999 price of $62, those shares would only have been worth $333,870.

This loyalty to shareholders came from an executive who got paid a $10 million retention bonus in 2000, a $2.76 million bonus in 1999, a salary of $600,000 to $700,000 in each of the three years from 1999–2001, and substantial stock option grants—so substantial that he cashed in $35 million in stock from the beginning of 1999. A quick glance at WorldCom's proxy statement might give the impression that Sullivan owned 3,264,438 shares, but the footnote reference shows that this mainly consists of options over 3,259,053 shares.

The overall picture is of an executive who was cashing out of just about every option he received as quickly as he could. Such low share ownership by a top executive—and especially the top financial executive—is about as big a warning sign as you can get. Sullivan was charged with securities fraud after it was revealed that $7.2 billion of WorldCom's costs had been misstated in its accounts (the figure later had to be revised upward).

"The main thing investors should look at is how much stock the executives own," said Cook. "If they don't own any stock and they exercise a lot of options, it means they are selling the stock." A handful of major companies, including banking concerns Citigroup and Bank One, now require that their top executives hold onto at least 75 percent of the shares they obtain as a result of stock grants and stock options. These retention ratios can certainly help to better link the financial interests of executives and stockholders if they both have to eat out of the same pot.

> **Note**
>
> Always read the footnotes—even to compensation and stock ownership tables.

Red Flag 4

If a Company Rewards Failure by Re-Pricing Stock Options

There was a joke in Silicon Valley when the bubble burst that some companies' stock options were so far under water, which means share prices were far below exercise prices, that they should be dubbed depth-charge options. In the view of many major investors, options that are headed to the bottom of the sea should be allowed to drown. After all, the original intent—to provide incentives for management and staff to get the company's performance to a level where the shares would rise—had clearly failed. Unfortunately, the view in some executive suites and boardrooms was different, particularly in technology companies. Divers were sent down to rescue the options, which were then resuscitated by being re-priced or reissued.

Among those to use this salvage operation in recent years were Internet retailer Amazon.com, phone company Sprint Corp., telecom equipment maker Lucent Technologies, and dozens of software and Internet companies.

When companies re-price, they are effectively destroying the link between shareholders' interests and those of management and staff. The shareholders get all the pain; the company insiders get only the opportunity for gain.

Red Flag 5

If a Company Rewards Failure by Lowering Compensation-Linked Targets

It isn't only options that can be a moving target. In April 2001, Coca-Cola Co.'s board gave its boss a break—the kind that makes some shareholders steam. It lowered CEO Douglas Daft's performance targets for earnings growth that had been set only about six months earlier. The shifting of the goalposts followed the company's admission that it wouldn't reach its original targets. That meant Daft would get one million shares even if earnings growth didn't reach the earlier goals. Coca-Cola's compensation committee said in the company's annual proxy statement that the change was merely a realignment with the company's new targets, and while heaping praise on Daft, it said that he will still only achieve significant wealth from the incentive program "in the presence of significant performance."

Hodgson says that any such discretion in the setting of performance targets should make shareholders uncomfortable because it undermines the principle of pay for performance.

Red Flag 6

Executives Making Money for Themselves from Company Business

The scandals at Enron, Tyco, Adelphia, and elsewhere had many common themes, but one of the most pervasive was alleged self-dealing by many executives and directors who appeared to treat the public companies they were supposed to be serving as their own property to be pillaged and looted at will.

The best place to find such questionable arrangements is in a company's proxy statement, usually under a title such as "transactions and legal actions involving management" or "certain transactions," though there are many variations on the theme.

The proxy statement is where you can get some clues about whether there are any business ties that could influence directors to turn a blind eye to malpractice by executives and where you can find out whether there are incestuous relationships with major shareholders, such as the Rigas family that controlled Adelphia. In the cable company's 2001 proxy statement, for example, we could learn that the company was loaning and advancing huge amounts of money to affiliates controlled by the Rigas family and other related parties. As of June 30, 2000, the statement says the total reached $263.1 million. The company was also paying entities owned by the Rigas family $15.9 million primarily for property, plant and equipment, and services in 2000. This is a drop in the ocean compared to the alleged siphoning off of funds by the family, but it was still a warning sign, particularly as there was little explanation about what the payments and loans were for.

Red Flag 7

When a Company Forgives Large Loans Made to Senior Executives

Who would have thought that instead of deadbeat dads we would be talking about deadbeat CEOs? These are the people who have borrowed often massive sums from a company—usually at the kind of low interest rates you or I could only dream of—but then can't pay the money back.

The biggest example is WorldCom's CEO Bernie Ebbers, whose penchant for wearing cowboy boots and jeans to work helped to get him dubbed the "telecom cowboy." He borrowed $408 million from the company in 2000–2001 so that he wouldn't be required to sell WorldCom stock he owned to meet margin requirements from his lenders as the price of those shares sank.

In the past, many companies have forgiven loans to CEOs, especially if they are being pushed out of the company. This happened when toy maker Mattel ousted CEO Jill Barad in 2000. It forgave $7.2 million she had borrowed to buy a home and company stock, and it also covered $3.3 million in tax, according to a proxy statement from the company. Altogether, Barad left with a package worth more than $37 million.

Under the Sarbanes-Oxley corporate reform legislation, companies will no longer be able to hand out loans to their executives except for home improvements or to buy trailer homes, though the Corporate Library's Hodgson says he imagines ways will be found to get around the ban. He estimated at the end of 2002 that more than one-third of the nation's 1,500 largest companies, as measured by market value, have loaned cash to executives, with an average of $10.7 million per loan, and current executive indebtedness of $4.5 billion.

When big loans remain outstanding, there is always a concern that the executives will try to boost the stock price in the short run so they can cash out any options or stock and pay off the debt, said Sean Egan, managing director of credit rating firm Egan-Jones Ratings Co.

Given that there are a lot of outstanding loans still out there, compensation experts also say that investors should be on their guard for companies that forgive loans through the back door, perhaps by increasing an executive's pay when it wasn't warranted by performance. "I am anticipating that we may see some companies paying their executives more in order to pay off loans," said Ferracone. "But that is just loan forgiveness in sheep's clothing."

Red Flag 8

Big Payments Are Made to Executives for Their Work on a Takeover

Executives have often been paid huge sums for their role in takeovers. Some investors believe this gives CEOs an incentive to grow through acquisition rather than take the harder slog needed to develop new products and services.

We saw above that Chase Manhattan Corp. head William Harrison received a $5 million cash bonus in January 2002 for the bank's takeover of J. P. Morgan & Co. Well, that was only the quarter of it. He was due to receive a further $5 million in January 2003 for the same deal and has been awarded 237,164 restricted stock units, which are dependent on getting the bank's share price above $52 by January 2007. This was all on top of his regular salary of $1 million, a bonus of $5 million, and further grants of restricted stock and stock options.

In the bank's proxy statement outlining the payment, the board's compensation and management committee said Harrison's payment was in recognition of his role in structuring and implementing the merger. Some other executives also received big bonuses.

Sometimes, the sweetheart payments are made to directors. One of the most extraordinary was the $10 million Tyco paid to board member Frank Walsh Jr. for a finder's fee as he helped to set up the acquisition of financial services firm CIT Group in 2001. It also gave $10 million to a charity of his choosing.

It wasn't money well spent. Tyco took a big bath on the CIT acquisition and had to sell it in 2002 for about half the price it paid. It turned into a bad deal for Walsh, too, as he was charged with securities fraud for failing to disclose the payments to fellow directors. In December 2002, he was given a conditional discharge and ordered to pay the $20 million back to Tyco and fines of $2.75 million to the authorities.

Red Flag 9

When Boards Hand Out Massive Severance Packages to Failed Executives

Some business leaders say that those who say CEOs are getting paid too much do not understand how vulnerable top executives are in a world that demands short-term returns.

For example, a study by consultants Booz Allen Hamilton showed that CEO turnover in the world's largest 2,500 publicly traded companies increased by 53 percent in 2001 compared with 1995, with the average tenure dropping to 7.3 years from 9.5 years. Even more dramatic, the number of CEOs leaving because of a company's poor financial performance increased 130 percent.

But, what the study didn't show was how much those booted out were getting to sweeten their way.

Anecdotal evidence at least shows that few CEOs quitting major companies go without a check for millions being thrust into their hands. It is probably the one area that has investors, staff, and the public all climbing the wall, as the CEO's failure is often tied in with a collapsing share price and job cuts.

For example, Jacques Nasser received $17.8 million in compensation from Ford Motor Co. in 2001 based on a company-estimated valuation of stock option grants—even though he was ousted in October of that year. Indeed, the value of his package rose 32 percent from 2000, though Ford suffered a staggering $5.45 billion loss in 2001, its first full-year loss since 1992, and its shares sank. The contrast between Nasser's lot and the company's cutting of jobs, health benefits, and bonuses across its operations was stark, to say the least.

One much-lower-level official who needed an armored truck to carry off his booty was Salomon Smith Barney's telecommunications analyst Jack Grubman, who left with $32 million even though his bad calls to buy telecommunications stocks in 1999–2002 may have cost investors billions. He got the money despite a series of government probes of his conflicted activities as an analyst that led him to pay a $15 million penalty and to accept a lifetime ban from the securities industry in December 2002. He tore down the Chinese walls—the barriers that were supposed to prevent deal-hungry investment bankers from influencing their firm's research.

Even the compensation industry thinks that some of this has gone too far. "Some of the severance packages are clearly excessive," said Neff, who blames contract add-ons negotiated over the years for much of the problem.

Note
Check clauses covering departure in executive contracts usually appended to company financial statements filed with the SEC.

Red Flag 10

Executives Retire with Huge Packages, Including Costly Perks

We have already seen the sweet deal that Jack Welch initially got when he retired from GE. Well, some others, who ran much smaller companies, are not that far behind. Take Terence Murray, who had certainly earned a comfortable retirement after building FleetBoston Financial Corp. into the seventh-largest U.S. bank through 80 acquisitions in the two decades he was at the helm. However, the generosity of his retirement gift means that it is likely to be more than just comfortable.

Murray receives an annual pension worth around $5.8 million a year, has the use of a corporate jet for up to 150 hours a year, a car and a driver whenever he wants, home security, an office and secretarial support, plus payment for tax and financial planning services, and some other fringe benefits. Oh, and his wife and guests can fly for free even if he is not with them.

Murray, who stepped down as the Boston-based bank's CEO at the end of 2001 and was due to retire as chairman at the end of 2002, will also be able to make $3.5 million in charitable contributions in his name.

The pension part of the package was more than doubled in size in August 2001, from an original figure of about $2.7 million a year, after the board changed the formula for calculating it. Previously, the calculation had been based on about 60 percent of an average of his annual salary and bonus between 1996–2000; but, after the change, it was based on the average package, including gains from exercising stock options and stock grants, for only the highest three of those five years.

When disclosing the new pension in March 2002, the bank said that it was to reflect Murray's outstanding contribution to Fleet during his long and successful tenure.

Red Flag 11

Companies with Golden Parachutes for Any Kind of Takeover

In 1977, investment banker Martin Siegel invented a takeover defense that many corporate executives have had good reason to thank him for since and many shareholders may wish he had never dreamed up.

The golden parachute is a part of employment contracts for executives that guarantees them an excessive payout in the event of a takeover. "Supposedly, the contracts were intended to deter hostile takeovers by making them more expensive. In practice, they tended to make the officers very rich," wrote James B. Stewart in his book about the insider trading scandals of the 1980s, *Den of Thieves.*

By deterring takeovers, golden parachutes can keep a bad management entrenched and prevent shareholders from getting a higher price for their shares from a bidder. Even if the deal goes through, it will be the shareholders who pay for the executives to take the money and run.

Ferracone says that investors should look at contracts and check whether an executive can walk out with a big fat payout merely because the company has been taken over or whether this can only happen if the executive has been penalized through a reduction in his or her role. She says that under some contracts, CEOs could arrange for buyout funds to take a company private and then fly off with a golden parachute even if they could have kept their jobs.

"You want a double trigger so that not only does the change of control have to happen, but, in addition, something bad has to happen to the executive," she said.

Red Flag 12

If a CEO Is Protected by a Contract Even if Convicted of a Crime

Amazingly, some executives have employment contracts that mean they can't necessarily be fired if convicted of a felony—or, in some cases if they are, it is stipulated that they get a big pay off.

Take, for example, retailer J. C. Penney's Chairman and CEO Allen Questrom. Under his employment contract signed in 2000, Questrom can't be fired "with cause" for any old crime; he has to be "convicted of a felony involving theft or moral turpitude." So, given that the definition of turpitude is "depravity" or "wickedness," an average kind of felony would not be enough. You can imagine the lawyers having a field day with that one.

Investors can only hope that absolution in employment contracts doesn't catch on. Indictment for a felony is one of the reasons usually stipulated in contracts that allows a company to fire an executive for cause, though even then the company still usually allows an executive to resign and depart with a generous package.

Red Flag 13

When a CEO's Perks Are Excessive and Costly

Companies that include Tyco, Vivendi, and Adelphia have been criticized for buying or renting luxury apartments in New York City for their CEOs and other executives—often when their main offices are elsewhere.

Vivendi bought a $17.5 million Park Avenue, New York, pad for Messier when he was CEO, complete with maid's quarters and a wine cellar. "What's wrong with a hotel or a more modest abode," comes the cry from some investors and shareholders' rights experts, especially if it is a question of only a few weeks a year that the executive needs to stay in New York City.

"If it is a company out of town and it is for business purposes and available to any executive to use, I don't see any problem with it, but if it is dedicated to the CEO and his mistress, well that is a whole different matter," said Cook, who was making a general comment rather than one about a particular company.

One of the biggest problems with the housing perks is that they are often kept under wraps, even though SEC rules say that perks worth more than $50,000 should be disclosed.

Red Flag 14

When a Company Pays for Private Jet Travel, Clubs, and Agents' Fees

One of the most remarkable perks is that executives being wooed for a top job will often have a lawyer come in to act like an agent for a sports star, getting some additional benefits for the compensation package in the process—and then the company will agree to pay for the lawyer's fee as part of the deal.

For example, Breen's agreement with Tyco states that the company shall promptly pay the executive's reasonable costs of entering into this agreement, including the reasonable fees and expenses of his counsel and other professionals up to a maximum of $100,000.

Another kind gesture that can frequently be seen in various disclosures is the company's decision to pay for an executive's hiring of a personal financial planner. Again, this is a perk that critics of excessive compensation say is unnecessary given the size of the rest of the packages.

In a quaint reminder of gentler times, some companies still pay their executives' country club or golf club memberships—quaint unless you are a shareholder, that is. In 2000, for example, semiconductor equipment maker Novellus Systems spent $40,279 for a country club membership for Chairman and CEO Richard Hill.

Some companies require that their CEO and his or her family always take company jets for security reasons—even when they are heading off to a ballgame. To some critics of excessive compensation, the security argument isn't valid. They point out that an executive can have personal security with him or her on a commercial airplane and that there is no evidence to suggest that it is safer to fly by private jet.

The corporate jet requirement is unstoppable, it seems. "I can't see it going away," said Hodgson. "But when it is for personal use, it gets iniquitous."

And, of course, a company can go the whole way—in 2001, Apple Computer gave its CEO Steve Jobs his own personal plane worth $90 million for past services.

Red Flag 15

If an Executive Is a Philanthropist with Shareholders' Money

The United States has a great tradition of philanthropy and charitable giving, with the industrial titans in the early years of the twentieth century, such as John D. Rockefeller, Andrew Carnegie, and Henry Ford, all creating great institutions and foundations that to this day bear their names.

One of the "robber barons," Carnegie, once said that "the man who dies ... rich, dies disgraced." After building up a fortune in the steel industry, Carnegie retired in 1901 and devoted his time and money to charitable purposes—in particular the founding of libraries, education, and the arts.

Unfortunately, some of today's tycoons seem to have decided that their idea of philanthropy is to donate the company's money to schools, hospitals, and charitable organizations while making it seem like it came out of their personal pockets and slapping their own names on the projects.

Take Tyco's former top gun Dennis Kozlowski. The company alleges in a lawsuit that he stole company funds to make $43 million in personal donations, using this "philanthropy" to enhance his social standing. Among the beneficiaries were the California International Sailing Association, which got $10 million; his alma mater, New Jersey's Seton Hall University ($1 million); Shackleton Schools ($1 million); Angell Memorial Hospital ($2.5 million); New York Children's Hospital ($1 million); and the Nantucket Conservation Foundation ($1.3 million). "He" also made huge contributions to an arts center and to local charities in Boca Raton, Florida, where Tyco moved many of its key headquarters staff in 1998. Sometimes, there were related naming rights for Kozlowski himself.

"If executives are philanthropists, they ought to be just philanthropists on their own accord and not have it be a special perk," said Ferracone.

Red Flag 16
When Executives Bail Out
of Their Company's Stock

When the top dogs are bailing out of the shares of a company in which you have an investment, you need to know.

One of the warning signs that alerted some investors to possible trouble at Enron and other companies in recent years was the disclosure of large sales of shares by a number of senior executives.

The question is simple: If the company's doing well and going to do even better, why would senior executives want to sell?

"People point out that insiders can sell for lots and lots of reasons and we understand that, but when you suddenly see people who never sold before, or rarely sold, unloading large blocks of stock, and a pattern of it, not just one person but a number of people throughout the executive suite, it is a red flag," said short seller James Chanos.

A *Fortune* survey showed just how massive the insider selling was in companies whose share prices fully reflected the bursting of the bubble between the beginning of 1999 and May 2002. In companies that had at some stage hit a market value of at least $400 million and whose shares had dropped at least 75 percent from their highs, the magazine identified $66 billion of sales by top executives and board members. Of that, $23 billion went to 466 insiders at 25 companies where the executives sold the most. *Fortune* concluded that the not-so-secret dirty secret of the bust was that while many investors were losing their shirts, many of the top dogs "were getting immensely, extraordinarily, obscenely wealthy."

Heavy insider selling by Enron executives when the stock was buoyant in the fall, winter, and spring of 2000–2001 helped to underline concerns Chanos had about the company. He said that it is a question of looking for the abnormal. Transactions that fit in with a program set up by a company for executives to sell a certain number of shares every month may not be of great interest, but something suddenly outside of that pattern can be, Chanos said.

Insider trading data is likely to become an even more important indicator following the introduction of the 2002 Sarbanes-Oxley corporate reform law. Under the legislation, a director or executive of a company, and any shareholder owning more than 10 percent, has to publicly disclose a sale or purchase of stock within two business days after the date of the transaction. Before, such a person only had to do so by the 10th of the month following the trade, which means the data could be as much as 40 days out of date.

"This is definitely going to make the information more powerful in that people will be able to mimic insider behavior a lot closer," said Lon Gerber, director of research at Thomson Lancer Analytics, in reference to investors who try to make trades in line with those of executives in the belief that they have inside knowledge. Thomson Lancer analyzes insider trading activity and identifies deviations from the norm (see *www.thomsonfn.com*).

He said that investors will have to keep a closer eye on the information and analyze it more carefully because instead of one big disclosure around the 10th, there will be a significant number throughout the month.

Thomson Lancer tracks the insider trading performance of the executives and directors of all major companies and ranks their last transaction on a scale of 1–100 according to how prescient their previous actions have been. For example, an executive consistently selling ahead of a decline in the stock price and buying ahead of gains would get top marks.

"We look for those with consistent performance; we want somebody who has repeated success, not done it once or twice," said Gerber. "It is very interesting; there really is a group of insiders that do time their trades better than others."

A quick glance at the performance of some directors on the Thomson web site can be fascinating. For example, in early August 2002—the month his brother Sam Waksal was indicted on insider trading charges—Harlan Waksal had a score of 99 for his last sale in Imclone Systems Inc. shares. Harlan, who replaced his brother as chairman and CEO of Imclone earlier in the year, had a perfect record on sales. Six months after each of six sales stretching back over nine years, the stock was lower. His buying record wasn't quite so stellar—the stock was higher six months later for only three out of his five purchase disclosures.

Of course, this is not some indication that Harlan was trading on the basis of privileged inside knowledge, as was admitted by his brother through his guilty plea to insider trading charges. But, ironically, Harlan's performance was much better than his brother's on this measurement. Sam Waksal only scored 76 for his last recorded sale.

Gerber says that a negative indication is a series of sales when a stock is trading at or near its lows for the year. "Potentially it tells us they don't see a turnaround in the near term," he said.

Thomson also produces a sell-buy ratio for the market as a whole, which can be seen as an indicator of the confidence of corporate America in the direction of stock prices.

Notes

• Watch insider trading sales and purchases closely for patterns, especially now that they are being disclosed more quickly.

• Look for any break in the normal pattern of buying or selling by executives and directors of a company.

• Look for a group of directors selling unusually large amounts of stock at the same time.

• Study the history of their trading. Were they buying or selling at an opportune time in the past?

• If they are selling out when shares are at year-to-date lows, it is a red flag.

• Buying by executives provides no guarantees of performance. Companies still collapse with their executives owning barrows of worthless shares.

• Use the insider trading information as only one indicator. It has to be used in conjunction with an analysis of a company's announcements and financial statements.

• Use market insider trading ratios as another indicator. This indicator is not one to bet the house on, but it is one to keep in mind when making investment decisions.

Note that both Thomson and another service, Vickers Weekly Insider Trading Report, charge for anything but the most basic of research on insider trading. Their more sophisticated slicing and dicing can cost hundreds and even thousands of dollars a year. You can also look at EDGAR Online and Quicken.com for insider trading data, while About.com has articles on insider trading of the legal and illegal varieties.

5

Caffeine Badly Needed: Sleepy, Inept, and Tainted Boards

"The board of directors didn't just fiddle while Enron burned, some of them toasted marshmallows over the flames."

—Senator Joseph Lieberman when he was chairman of the main Senate Governmental Affairs Committee, May 7, 2002

Distinguishing between a good and a bad board is a vital investing skill, though perhaps it is more art than science.

Perhaps what was most worrying about the collapse of Enron Corp. is that on paper it had one of the most experienced and talented boards in America. Its 14 members included a former top U.S. regulator, a leading official from one of the country's best-known fund management groups, a highly distinguished accounting professor, and a former British energy minister, with most of the rest either current or former chief executives of significant companies. OK, it included a couple of cancer specialists from the University of Texas who didn't quite seem to have the background to handle a rapidly growing ener-

79

gy trader and its $100 billion of gross revenue, but at first glance this bunch would stand comparison with just about any U.S. company board in 2001. The board was also at least nominally dominated by "independent" (sometimes known as "outside") directors who didn't work for the company and hadn't been past employees, though some had business ties with Enron that meant their loyalty to shareholders could be questioned.

"It had all the appropriate board committees with people occupying positions on them of apparently spotless pedigrees and having the highest degrees," said Bill Lerach, who is one of the best-known class action lawyers in the United States and who is representing investors seeking damages following the Enron collapse. Before the collapse, Enron could hardly have looked better, he said. "What was wrong with that picture? Nothing. It looked perfect. You have to realize that it doesn't ensure integrity or skepticism. That's why you can't tell, you can't trust."

It is sometimes difficult to tell who will be alert to any wrongdoing and who will go to sleep at the wheel, said veteran corporate governance expert and lawyer Ira Millstein, who has advised many companies, including most recently Walt Disney Co. and Vivendi. "I have been in 50 boardrooms in my career at least, in good times and in bad, and I have seen some of the best names in the world be lousy directors and some of the worst names in the world be terrific directors, because they are independent and they are willing to raise hell when the time comes," he said.

We got a glimpse through the boardroom doors during the U.S. Senate's hearings on the Enron scandal in 2002—and in particular from a report titled "The Role of The Board of Directors in Enron's Collapse" issued that July by the Permanent Subcommittee on Investigations. This should be required reading for directors of all public companies as it starkly lays out how awful a board of seemingly reputable figures can be. This was the group that, for example, didn't probe further when they were told in October 2001 that an employee had sent a letter expressing concern about certain transactions and that this had been discussed with outside legal counsel, according to the report. They didn't get to see the letter until after the disintegration had begun. In the letter to Chairman Kenneth Lay, Enron Vice President Sherron Watkins—who has been dubbed the Enron whistleblower—had highlighted the company's aggressive accounting and alleged improprieties while expressing fear that it was going to "implode in a wave of accounting scandals."

Neither did they bat an eyelid when told on a number of occasions by Andersen partners that Enron's accounting practices were high risk and pushed limits or when they saw a chart that showed the company had moved almost half its $60 billion in assets into entities that weren't on its books, according to the Senate report. They were also prepared to waive the company's code of conduct to allow Chief Financial Officer Andrew Fastow to establish and operate private equity partnerships that transacted business with Enron and then profited at its expense.

It was only when Enron began to unravel in mid-October 2001 that the chairman of Enron's compensation committee, Charles LeMaistre, discovered Fastow had made $90 million from three of these operations. A year earlier, he had asked an Enron official for information about executives' outside income, but when he didn't get what he wanted, he let the matter drop. This was also a board whose compensation committee approved $750 million in bonuses for managers in early 2001 when Enron's entire net income for 2000 had been only $975 million. "Apparently no one on the compensation committee had ever added up the numbers," the report concluded.

It also allowed Lay to use the company like a bank— one that provided him with $7.5 million in lines of credit. He then used this credit like an ATM, repeatedly drawing down the entire amount available and then repaying it with Enron stock. In this way, he not only got $77 million of cash from the company in return for the stock, but he also managed to legally delay reporting share sales by bypassing SEC rules. LeMaistre, who is the 78-year-old president emeritus of the University of Texas M. D. Anderson Cancer Center, told the Senate investigation that it wasn't the committee's responsibility to monitor the credit line. Nor was anybody else responsible for monitoring it. Enron executives became millionaires many times over thanks to the corporate largesse that was built on questionable growth in profits. One such executive, Lou Pai, took away more than $265 million in cash when he left the company in 2000 because he sold shares he received from stock option grants. Lay himself was one of the highest-paid CEOs in the United States, with total compensation of $140 million in 2000, including $123 million from stock options.

And, the directors who oversaw all this were also better paid than most, pulling in about $350,000 each in total compensation in 2000, including cash, stock, and stock options. This is more than double the $138,747 average at the top 200 U.S. public companies.

And for what? Well, each year the board held five regular meetings plus a number of special meetings (in 2000 it had four), with committee meetings usually held the day before a full board meeting. However, these were far from long, drawn out affairs. For example, a crucial special meeting on June 28, 1999, was held by teleconference and only lasted one hour.

This meeting approved the setting up of a controversial special partnership involving Fastow and authorized a stock split, an increase in the shares in the company's stock compensation plan, the purchase of a new corporate jet, and an investment in a Middle Eastern power plant. Fast work. After all, many of us would take almost as long to decide what to see at the local movie theater. The Senate report concludes that discussion concerning the approval of the Fastow partnership, which was a key step towards the company's collapse, appears to have been minimal.

The report says that preparation for board meetings took each director between two hours and two days. The part-time nature of a board seat, albeit on what many would consider a very full wage, was cited by one director, Herbert Winokur Jr., who is CEO of an investment company and on several other boards, as a reason not to expect too much.

He said in testimony before the subcommittee that the Enron affair was a "cautionary reminder of the limits of a director's role." He said that the independent directors could not "be criticized for failing to address or remedy problems that have been concealed from us."

Some of the directors got more than board attendance fees and prestige. A number also had contracts with the company or other business and charitable connections. Lord John Wakeham, a director who was a former British minister, was paid an additional $6,000 a month for consulting services from 1996 onwards, while another board member, John Urquhart, received $493,914 for his consulting work in 2000 alone. Enron director Robert Belfer is a former chairman and CEO of Belco Oil and Gas, which had major business arrangements with Enron, while Winokur was also on the board of the National Tank Co., which sold oilfield equipment and services to

Enron. Enron and Lay had also given large sums of money to the M. D. Anderson Cancer Center, where board members LeMaistre and John Mendelsohn were respectively past and current presidents. Also, a donation was made to George Mason University and its Mercatus Center in Virginia. Enron Director and former Commodity Futures Trading Commission Chairman Wendy Gramm is employed by the Mercatus Center.

So, there you have Enron's meaning of independent. More than half the directors had either direct or indirect financial links to the company or its executive chairman. The shareholders weren't necessarily going to be top priority. The Senate report concluded that "the independence of the Enron board of directors was compromised by financial ties between the company and certain board members." It also said that the board and its audit committee had failed to ensure the independence of Andersen as the company's auditor because the accounting firm had not only been allowed to provide consulting services for Enron but had also taken over the internal audit function. "No board member expressed any concern that Andersen might be auditing its own work, or that Andersen auditors might be reluctant to criticize Andersen consultants" for structures it had been paid millions of dollars to design.

The report makes it clear that the board relied on being spoon-fed by management and by Andersen "with little or no effort to verify the information provided," while readily approving new business ventures and complex transactions and only having weak oversight of company operations. It outlined 16 red flags that should have been signals to the board that something was wrong, going all the way back to early 1999. Yet, right up until the company began to publicly unravel, the directors expressed confidence in its health.

The Enron case goes to show that the government or the stock exchanges can't wave a magic wand and create diligent, skeptical boards through decree. "You can't solve any governance problem through structural means," says Nell Minow of the shareholder rights' web site *TheCorporateLibrary.com*. "You could decide what the definition of independence was and I could subvert it within about 30 seconds," she says. "The fact that somebody qualifies as independent by anybody's definition, and there are many out there, does not mean that he is doing a good job."

Now, all this might sound impossibly gloomy. Individual investors can't be expected to decide whether to support little-known, board-nominated candidates for directorships given that the companies usually provide only very short biographical details about them and little or no justification for why they might do a good job. Don't completely despair. The reforms introduced in Congress and proposed by the New York Stock Exchange should make some difference; they demand that members of board audit, compensation and nomination committees be independent and tighten the definition of independent so that any director having a "material" relationship with the company won't qualify for the status. Independent directors will also have to meet regularly without the CEO being present.

In the rest of this chapter, I am going to present some of the red flags that you should be looking out for when it comes to examining the makeup of a board. These signals are not, on their own, perfect indicators. But, as part of a larger picture, which includes an analysis of the financial statements, they can help you avoid the next Enron or Tyco.

Red Flag 1
Sudden Unexplained Resignation of a Director from a Board

On the same day that biotechnology company ImClone Systems Inc. announced that it was under the scrutiny of the SEC and the Department of Justice, it also revealed that one of its directors, Peter Peterson, had resigned—only three months after joining. It didn't give a reason. The beginnings of a government probe are clearly bad news for any company, but the departure of Peterson should have been an additional warning signal. He is not only chairman of the private equity concern Blackstone Group, but he is also one of the most highly respected figures in business and government circles. A former secretary of commerce in the Nixon administration, he is chairman of the Federal Reserve Bank of New York and chairman of the Council on Foreign Relations.

In an interview in May 2002, Peterson told CNBC "it was very clear to me that, with all the investigations going on, the SEC and the congressional investigation, that I was probably the only unconflicted member because I had not sold stock." He said he didn't want to be "the lone ranger" spending all his time heading an internal investigation into what had gone on.

> **Note**
>
> Read all 8K filings with the SEC by companies in which you have a significant investment. This is where many key events are disclosed.

Red Flag 2

When the Board Rarely Meets

TMP Worldwide, parent of online jobs web site Monster.com, held just one board meeting in 2001 and acted by unanimous written consent on 11 occasions, according to a filing with the SEC. If a board only feels the need to meet once in a year when its earnings are starting to fade, that raises questions about whether the directors have any real involvement in the company's affairs. In the year to February 2003, this company's share price has lost about two-thirds of its value, so it wasn't as if it was delivering the goods for shareholders. Investors should ask where the checks and balances are. Most boards meet at least six times a year. TMP's audit committee met four times in 2001, which is about average, but its compensation committee met only once. TMP's Chairman, CEO, and founder Andrew McKelvey effectively controlled the company through Class B stock that has super-voting power and through his 18.8 percent of the ordinary shares as of March 31, 2002.

> **Note**
>
> Check proxy statements to find out how often a board and its committees meet.

Red Flag 3

When "Independent Board" Means the CEO's Grocer Is a Director

The authorities can only go so far in defining independence, and it really is up to investors, analysts, and the media to point to abuses of the spirit of the recent reforms as much as breaches of the letter of the law. For example, it may be possible for CEOs to get their golf club buddies onto the board and yet still call them independent directors because the company has no "material" business relationship with them. Mind you, getting such board memberships with potentially large fees may seem material to some.

To some cynics, this is a problem that can't be legislated away. "Outside directors are still going to be friends of the chairman and audit committees are going to be buddies, and it (reform) can help at the margin but it is no panacea," said short seller David Tice. It is still important for investors to ask detailed questions about the backgrounds of board members. "Are they in some way related to the CEO? Is it his wife, his accountant, his grocer, his car dealer?" said Herbert Denton, shareholder rights activist and president of investment group Providence Capital. A key issue here is how the nomination committee works. It can be chock full of independent directors, but if it only takes suggestions from the CEO, it makes no difference. A good sign would be the hiring of outside consultants—who report directly to it rather than the CEO—to help in a search for new directors.

Short seller James Chanos says that, invariably, any company he takes an interest in (which would usually be negative) has a board that is dominated by management. "An acquiescent board is almost a given," he said. However, there are signs that boardrooms are getting much less cozy and collegial. John Biggs, the former head of the giant pension fund system TIAA-CREF, says the tone of TIAA-CREF's board meetings changed a lot after the Enron scandal broke, and it has been a difficult but necessary transition. "I have found myself offended by people challenging this or that projection, but my second thought is, wait a minute, this is what we want boards to do," said Biggs, who is also a Boeing director.

Red Flag 4

Boards Lacking Outside Directors Who Are Respected Business Figures

If you find a board that has a smattering of academics, retired politicians, and the kind of people who turn being directors into a full-time occupation and yet has no one who is easily recognizable as a respected business leader, the chances of its being compliant in the face of an aggressive CEO are high.

"You need someone who says 'no, this doesn't cut it for me, we are not waiving the ethics policies,' and it would end right there," said Sarah Teslik, the executive director of the Council of Institutional Investors, referring to the Enron board's decision to breach its ethics policy to allow CFO Fastow to invest in partnerships that had business dealings with the company. "And, if you look at companies where there have been substantial allegations of fraud in the last few years, by and large they did not have boards of stature." Teslik says that when she analyzes a board, she looks to see whether it includes a currently serving CEO of an equivalent-sized company. "It is someone who doesn't have to be on this board for his or her reputation, but on the other hand who would really care about his or her reputation tanking if the company went down," she added.

Investors should keep in mind a comment from one unidentified former board member of scandal-plagued telecommunications group WorldCom when assessing a board's resilience in the face of a dominating CEO. "Never stick your finger in a fan. Never run in front of an 18-wheeler. And never talk to Bernie if you don't have to," the former member was quoted by *The Wall Street Journal* as saying in reference to the company's former CEO Bernie Ebbers.

"What you need are people who are of sufficient stature that being on the board is not the most important thing to them, so they are not afraid to say to the president, 'that was not acceptable, I want another explanation of that at the next meeting or by conference call next week, because I still don't get that,'" said Moody's Investors Service's Credit Policy Committee Head Chris Mahoney.

Millstein said he knows one outside director and audit committee chairman who was crystal clear in his warning to the CEO of one company. "Even before Enron, he told his CEO that if there was a fraud anywhere in the organization that CEO was gone the next day—period," said Millstein, who didn't identify the company. According to Millstein, having outside directors who are prepared to read the riot act like that has an immense impact on a company.

Red Flag 5

Companies in Which the Chairman and the CEO Are the Same Person

This one still applies to most American companies, though there have been signs of some movement toward the system in the United Kingdom, where the jobs are usually separated. The justification for having one executive do both jobs is that there is no doubt who is leading the company and it reduces the potential for clashes. The argument from corporate governance experts is that it means one person sets the agenda and controls the flow of information to the members of the board, which reduces the chances they will be told the bad news until it is too late. In a sense, the CEO is also part of a board that is evaluating himself or herself.

The proposal to split the roles is far from an open and shut case. Some studies have shown that when one person has both roles, company performance is on average better than when the roles are separated. There is also anecdotal evidence that goes both ways. After all, Enron divided the CEO and chairman's role, AOL Time Warner has done the same during the period when it suffered a huge loss in value, and Tyco and Adelphia combined the roles.

But, most agree that having that extra pair of eyes in a senior position can help to prevent a CEO from using the company as a personal bank. "If there is one thing I could change, I would require that the chairman of the board be an outside independent director to establish a governance power base. Because right now we have a system where the chief manager of the corporation is also the chief governor. His power is unchecked," said John Bogle, the founder of the Vanguard group of funds. "I do think it is unequivocally better to have separation."

An increasing number of companies are appointing a lead independent director, and this trend will gather pace now that the New York Stock Exchange has proposed requiring non-management directors to meet regularly without executives present and has called on them to disclose how the presiding director is decided for those sessions.

Red Flag 6

Professional Directors Who Are Keener on Collecting Fees Than Aiding Shareholders

The directors who do nothing but serve on boards can be problematic. I am not talking about retired businessmen but a younger group that has turned it into a profession and serves on many boards. "They are really looking to board membership as a vehicle for income, so if they are on 10 boards it is so they can make $1 million a year," said Millstein. "And they are very chary of being in a disruptive group because if they get to be known as being disruptors they won't be asked to serve on somebody else's board. You have got to use your noodle when you start to look at these directors, some of these people who are allegedly professional directors and serve on many boards. I get a little queasy about them because they are not likely to lead a revolution."

Some professional directors take on so many directorships that they can't possibly give each one adequate attention, especially now that the pressures are increasing for much closer scrutiny. If a company is willing to put up with a director who is on eight or nine other boards, it doesn't say much for its attitude toward boardroom oversight.

Former United States Secretary of Defense Frank Carlucci was at one time on no less than 32 boards, 20 of them for-profit companies and 12 non-profit organizations. *The Washington Post* reported in 1993 that at one stage, he had to call into a board meeting while he was visiting his doctor.

Note

Various online services such as *www.TheCorporateLibrary.com* and *www.Equilar.com* now offer subscription services for checking on directors fees, attendance, board memberships, and related topics.

Red Flag 7

Boards That Have a Large Number of Long-Serving and Elderly Directors

If you take a look at the Enron proxy statement to shareholders in 2001, some questions about the quality of the board come to mind. One such question is why the average age of the independent directors is 62.5. In much of this book, I quote from quite a number of top investors, former regulators, and academics who have their wits about them more than most and yet are in their 70s and 80s. Many of these characters saw the bubble being formed in the late 1990s before the rest of us and were condemned by the cheerleaders of the technology boom as silly curmudgeons.

However, leaving aside renowned figures such as investor Warren Buffett or former Federal Reserve Chairman Paul Volcker, it is worth considering having a retirement age for board members. Three members of the Enron board were in their 70s, and they had powerful positions on board committees. Robert Jaedicke, who was then 72, was chairman of the audit committee and LeMaistre, who was then 77, was chairman of the compensation committee. LeMaistre, 73-year-old John Duncan, 65-year-old Robert Belfer, and 59-year-old Herbert Winokur Jr. joined Lay and Skilling on a six-member executive committee. This is important because all four of these "outside" directors had been on the board for between 16 and 18 years. Some corporate governance specialists say that when directors serve this long on a board, they shouldn't be considered independent because they probably have become close to the management. Indeed, some believe there should be term limits for directorships.

"I think age among directors is an important issue," said former SEC Chairman Richard Breeden. "If you look at a company and it has six directors in their 70s, then that is a bad sign. I also think term limits for directors are a good thing. I don't know what the right number is—8, 10, 15 years, but you have too many people who are 75 and 78 years old and who have been on the board for 20 years, and it is not likely that they are still as questioning and still as willing to dig into the detail as they were 20 years ago."

> **Note**
>
> Check ages and length of service for directors as outlined in the proxy statement.

Red Flag 8

Too Many Academics and Ex-Politicians May Lead to an Uncritical Board

A board packed with academics and former politicians may not necessarily ask the stupid and often not-so-stupid questions needed to be fired at management, corporate governance experts say. Enron had several academics, including Jaedicke, and on the political side, it had Lord Wakeham, a former British energy minister.

"I would say that former government officials and academics tend to do a poor job because they don't know what they don't know and they are so accomplished in their other fields that they don't feel comfortable about saying, 'I am just an imbecile about this, so you have got to explain it to me,'" said Minow.

> **Note**
>
> When assessing the strength of a board, don't be impressed by "names" from government or academia.

Red Flag 9

A Compensation Committee in the CEO's Pocket Lacks Independence

All the requirements for "independent" directors in the world won't make any difference if they are so smitten by their CEO that skepticism goes out the window. Investors should be on their guard if they read comments from the board or one of its committees that deify the CEO. It puts that CEO in a position to milk such sentiment for all it's worth.

Take a look at the compensation committee report from web-based share trading and financial services company E*Trade, which was under fire for paying then Chairman and CEO Christos Cotsakos an $80 million compensation package in 2001, almost half of which was later returned. In a four-page defense of the compensation in the 2002 proxy statement, the committee describes Cotsakos as "one of the visionaries, architects and leading founders of e-commerce and e-finance as well as the company's architect and leader of its guiding principles, strategic matrix and operating model." There is more. Cotsakos, we are told, has "vision, drive and passion," and words such as "unprecedented," and "unique" were tossed around to describe his achievements at the company despite its suffering a big loss and a plunge in its share price.

Arguably, the chairman of the compensation committee. David Hayden, wasn't independent since E*Trade had made a nominal investment in the company he once headed, the loss-making electronic message system provider Critical Path. E*Trade was also a Critical Path customer and Cotsakos had also once sat on the board of Critical Path, which had to restate its financial results for 2000 amid an accounting and insider trading scandal. It will be interesting to see how E*Trade copes without its visionary, as Cotsakos resigned in January 2003 to the relief of some investors. Hayden had already stepped down from the E*Trade board in May 2002.

Note

Read the compensation committee report in a company's proxy statement with a critical eye.

Red Flag 10

Cross-Board Memberships Can Lead to Conflicts of Interest

When CEOs and other directors at two companies have cross membership, it can create perceptions of a conflict of interest, especially if the companies have any kind of business ties. An example was the presence of AT&T Corp. CEO Michael Armstrong on the board of

Citigroup while the banking giant's CEO Sandy Weill was on the AT&T board. New York Attorney General Eliot Spitzer and other regulators looked into whether Weill leant on Jack Grubman, who was the star telecommunications analyst at Citigroup's Salomon Smith Barney investment banking and brokerage unit, to change his recommendation on AT&T to a "buy" in 1999.

The probe ended as part of the settlement announced in December 2002, but which was not formalized at the time of writing, that saw Wall Street investment banks agree to make payments of $1.5 billion, including $400 million by Citigroup, over allegations of tainted research and unfair allocation of IPOs to corporate officers to gain investment banking business.

The investigation into the regulators' probe into the Citigroup–AT&T relationship examined whether this helped Salomon gain lucrative business underwriting one of AT&T's largest stock offerings. Weill has acknowledged asking Grubman to "take a fresh look" at AT&T but denied he had an ulterior motive. However, in one email to an analyst at a money management firm, Grubman boasted that Weill wanted a change in the rating so that he could get Armstrong's help in an internal power struggle against then Citigroup co-chairman John Reed. The analyst also said that Weill was helping Grubman to get his twins into an exclusive New York City nursery school. Citigroup's philanthropic arm donated money to the nursery school. Grubman said later that the reasons he gave for the AT&T recommendation in the email were fabricated.

Cross board membership can be a big problem, said Richard Koppes, former general counsel for the California Public Employees Retirement System (CalPERS). "It is usually you scratch my back, I'll scratch yours—you don't question, I don't question."

Red Flag 11
Directors Who Don't Own Much of Their Company's Stock

When directors own very little of their own company's stock, it says a lot about how they perceive their role and possibly about how they perceive the prospects of the company. Three Enron directors, for example, owned fewer than 6,000 shares of the company by the time it filed its proxy statement in March 2001. John Mendelsohn owned 5,563, Frank Savage 4,005, and Paulo Ferraz Pereira held 3,195. And, these were directors who received options on more than 10,000 shares in 2000 alone.

To feel comfortable with a company, investors should be able to believe that any pain from a share price slide will hit the pockets of the directors, too. The key here is stock ownership, not stock options. You don't want a situation in which directors get so many stock options that they are prepared to overlook aggressive and even fraudulent accounting aimed at keeping the share price up because they want to cash out their stock options at a profit. "If they don't own any stock, that tells you they are there for the wrong reason; they are there for the stipend or the honor; and their interests are not particularly aligned with the shareholders," said Providence Capital's Denton.

> **Note**
>
> Check directors' stock ownership in a company's proxy statement.

Red Flag 12

When a Company Hits Low Points in Corporate Governance Rankings

An increasing number of organizations are compiling tables that rate companies based on how well they are governed. Investors should keep a close eye out for these because if they show that a company has a low rating for corporate governance, it is a red flag.

For example, Institutional Shareholder Services (ISS) says its corporate governance quotient (CGQ) rating would have set off the alarm for an investor owning or thinking of buying stock in cable television company Adelphia Communications. In early 2002, it gave the now-bankrupt and scandal-ridden Adelphia a rating of just 24.4 against companies of about the same market value and 28.0 against its industry peer group, out of 100 maximum in each case. "Clearly in the case of Adelphia and others whose poor governance practices have made recent headlines, the CGQ database would have raised a red flag for an investment manager holding or considering the stock," said Jill Lyons, a vice president at ISS, which is a provider of proxy voting services for companies.

The ISS ratings are based on the following seven main criteria: board structure and composition, charter and bylaw provisions, laws of the state in which it is incorporated, executive and director compensation, financial performance, the level of directors' and executives' stock ownership, and the amount of education available for directors.

Among other rating systems to keep an eye on are those produced by The Corporate Library (*www.thecorporatelibrary.com*) and ratings agency Standard & Poor's Corp. with its corporate governance scores.

BusinessWeek came out with its latest list of the best and worst boards in its October 7, 2002, issue. The eight worst were Apple, now-bankrupt finance company Conseco, retailers Dillard's, Gap, and the bankrupt Kmart, telecom company Qwest, poultry producer Tyson Foods, and copier maker Xerox.

Note

There will be a lot of these rankings and services around in the next few years—but be wary about corporate governance proposals when they pay no heed to whether a stock is performing well. One corporate governance expert recommended shareholders vote against the board re-nomination of Berkshire Hathaway CEO Warren Buffett because of his family's control of the company. Clearly, given Buffett's phenomenal success on behalf of investors, there was room for an exception.

Red Flag 13

Audit Committees That Don't Take Responsibility for Policing Auditors

One glance at the audit committee report in WorldCom's proxy statement issued in March 2002, more than four months before the disclosure of massive fraud at the telecom company, should have been enough to scare its shareholders out of their skins. Here is one lengthy paragraph in full:

> The members of the *audit committee* are not professionally engaged in the practice of auditing or accounting and are not experts in the fields of auditing or accounting, including in respect of auditor independence. Members of the audit committee rely without independent verification on the information provided to them and on the representations made by management and the independent auditors. Accordingly, the audit committee's oversight does not provide an independent basis to determine that management has maintained appropriate accounting and financial reporting principles or appropriate internal control and procedures designed to assure compliance with accounting standards and applicable laws and regulations. Furthermore, the audit committee's considerations and discussions referred to above do not assure that the audit of our financial statements has been carried out in accordance with generally accepted auditing standards, that the financial statements are presented in accordance with generally accepted accounting principles or that our auditors are in fact 'independent.'

So, there you have it. These folks are admitting they are next to useless. The four of them, led by committee chairman Max Bobbitt, can't protect shareholders against fraud, they can't guarantee the accountants aren't in some way tainted, they can't trust management or the auditors, and they really don't understand accounting. In fact, they can't really help at all. Why, one wonders, did they feel they could stay on the board and continue to pull down their fees?

Clearly, lawyers or consultants were very busy spreading the same mantra around corporations, because an almost identical paragraph could be found in the 2002 audit committee report of hundreds of companies, including such prominent entities as insurance behemoth American International Group Inc. (AIG) and investment bank Goldman Sachs Group Inc. The WorldCom board's use of such a statement is in some ways more excusable, because the company was already in serious difficulty when it was issued and its auditor was Arthur Andersen LLP, which was well on the way to disintegrating at that time. However, a company such as AIG was clearly not in financial trouble and its auditor was PricewaterhouseCoopers LLP. Not only that, but its audit committee included some very distinguished political and financial figures, including former World Bank President Barber Conable, former U.S. Trade Representative Carla Hills, and former Chairman of the Nasdaq stock market Frank Zarb.

Contrast WorldCom and AIG with the report issued around the same time from the audit committee at fast-food giant McDonald's Corp. It detailed discussions with auditors Ernst & Young about a range of issues including the clarity and extent of disclosure, the adequacy of internal controls, whether judgments made in the accounts were reasonable, and the impact of off-balance sheet structures.

"At WorldCom, the audit committee basically said we don't really understand this stuff very well and we don't look at it very hard and so maybe you had better not count on us," said The Corporate Library's Minow. "But if you look at McDonald's they say, look, we know you feel nervous about this, so let's explain what our role is. We are not the auditors, we are not the guarantors of the financials, but perhaps you would like to see the steps that we follow to make you feel a little better about the direction we are taking here."

Indeed, under the various reforms introduced by Congress and the stock market bodies, board audit committees are seen as a critical defense against accounting fraud. Audit committee members won't be allowed to have business ties (other than board membership and related fees) with the company, the committees will have the power to hire and oversee auditors, and they can hire outside advisers. They are also required to set up a system to allow company employees who are concerned about questionable accounting policies to voice them. Members of the audit committees are supposed to be financially literate and to produce a written charter outlining the committee's purpose, duties, and responsibilities.

Investors should keep an eye on audit committee membership to ensure that its members really do have the expertise to ask pointed questions about accounting policies. Their experience and training should be disclosed. It would be fine, for example, for retailer Saks Inc. to keep basketball legend Julius Erving, who is better known as

Dr. J., on its audit committee, but the company could perhaps disclose the accountancy training he has received.

> ### Note
>
> Use the examples above as a rough guide to the two extremes in behavior when reading the statements from an audit committee of a company in which you have an investment.

6

Growing Mushrooms: The Art of the Opaque, Sneaky, and Buried

"In 2000 and 1999, Enron entered into transactions with limited partnerships (the related party) whose general partners' managing member is a senior officer of Enron."

—among footnotes to the Enron annual financial statement issued April 2, 2001

In his memoir, Benjamin Graham recalls traveling from New York City overnight in a Pullman berth and then taking a rickety local train on a bitterly cold and snowy morning to attend the annual meeting of Northern Pipeline in Oil City, Pennsylvania. It was 1927.

Graham, who is widely regarded as the father of modern securities analysis and who taught Warren Buffett, wanted to propose that the company sell a huge slab of railroad bonds it owned and distribute the cash to shareholders. The problems he was about to encounter contain lessons for investors three quarters of a century later, as we shall see.

Graham's plan, which would unlock hidden value for the company's shareholders, had already been rejected by Northern Pipeline's president, D. S. Bushnell. But, Graham decided to go straight to the company's shareholders by attending the annual meeting of the small oil pipeline operator. The difficulty was that only the company's employees attended the meeting and it hadn't even published an annual report.

When Graham asked how it was possible to approve a report that wasn't available, Bushnell replied, "We have always handled the matter this way. Those in favor say 'aye.'" Graham didn't let it go, though. He came back the following year with enough support to change the board and eventually got shareholders a rich payout.

Investors today certainly have the opportunity to read annual reports and proxy statements before annual meetings—securities regulations ensure that. The Internet, the growth of business news services, and various disclosure regulations have put a massive amount of information at a small investor's fingertips. Yet, it is clear that the Bushnell spirit lives on in the executive suites of many companies.

The Bushnell attitude can take many forms, and in this chapter I want to give you a guide to some of the most egregious ones, give tips on how you can fight for more (and most importantly, better quality) disclosure, and let you know when it is time to take your money and run.

The transparency, simplicity, and, of course, accuracy of an earnings press release are among the most important indications of how honest a company is with investors. It could be some weeks before you see the full financial statements that corporations have to provide in SEC filings under the law, so the last thing you need is a hyped-up press release in the meantime.

Even under new SEC rules being phased in by 2005, companies will have until 60 days after a year's end to produce their annual statements and 35 days after the end of the quarter for the full quarterly filing. These, by the way, are known as 10Ks and 10Qs, respectively, in SEC jargon.

The safest advice would be to tell investors not to trade off earnings press releases at all but to always wait for the real thing. However, in our trigger-happy world, that wait may be unrealistic.

Reasons for extreme caution, though, include the following.

Red Flag 1
A Press Release That Buries the Net Earnings Figure

The public relations folks, executives, and lawyers don't just bury the net earnings figure accidentally. Understand that they are deliberately trying to draw your attention away from one of the numbers that is harder to manipulate. Often, when the net figures are hidden, they will show a loss or a decline in profit. See Chapter 14 for the Qwest example in 2001.

> **Note**
>
> Be suspicious and don't do anything until you have examined the net profit performance.

Red Flag 2

A Press Release Begins with a Questionable Measurement of Profit

The announcement that starts with a measurement of profit that is not clear, such as "pro forma," "operating," "as reported," "normalized," or "core," should be treated with skepticism. If you are to give these figures credibility, the company has to be immediately frank about what it has taken out to reach the calculation. Too often, companies have stripped away key costs and important one-time losses so that you are left with EEBS, or EESU, earnings excluding bad stuff or earnings excluding screw-ups. A bank doesn't send its customers statements that only highlight the credits—and neither should a publicly traded corporation. While new SEC rules will force companies to match "pro forma" figures to net profit figures, there is no guarantee that the press releases will be much clearer.

> **Note**
>
> Always go to the tables that include net profit figures rather than the text, in which a company can more easily disguise a poor performance.

Red Flag 3

When the Earnings Table Is Produced in a Creative or Confusing Manner

There is a standard format for an earnings table, and when companies don't keep to it, investors should be suspicious that something is being hidden. Look out for the absence of comparable numbers for the year-earlier quarter, the use of non-comparable periods (three months and one week against three months), the absence of a table altogether, or the absence of the bottom-line net profit figures. All these kinds of deviations should put investors on their guard. During the Internet boom, the imaginative accountants and image men used all these tactics and more.

> **Note**
>
> Don't invest in the company's stock until you are satisfied it isn't hiding something.

Red Flag 4

If the Press Release Omits a Cash-Flow Statement or Balance Sheet

Too many companies delay releasing all the key information until filing with the SEC weeks later. Without the balance sheet and cash-flow information, it is virtually impossible for you to detect any possible accounting malpractice, to get a picture of the risk of bankruptcy, or indeed to form any idea of how healthy or sick the business is. Enron's refusal to provide such information led to a clash between then CEO Jeff Skilling and a short seller on a conference call in 2001, as related in Chapter 3.

> **Note**
>
> Wait until you have all the key parts of the accounts—even if you miss a trading opportunity as a result.

Red Flag 5

When the Company Treats One-Time Charges As if They Aren't Real Money

Many companies would like to convince you that there are two kinds of money in the world—the real type that is reported in some kind of operating or recurring profit figure and the one-time losses or charges, often massive, that you are not supposed to worry about.

Even massive write-offs related to share price plunges reflect a real loss of market value. For example, Tyco International bought the finance group CIT for almost $10 billion and sold it for $4.6 billion through an IPO, taking write-downs and losses of almost $7 billion in the process. The same goes for the massive write-downs by AOL Time Warner that led to its 2002 net loss of almost $100 billion as just about everything went wrong after the merger of America Online and Time Warner. Remember, this means that Tyco and AOL Time Warner screwed up. Tyco paid too much for an asset and then managed it so badly that its value plummeted and it suffered losses. AOL Time Warner shareholders suffered tens of billions of dollars of losses as the Internet bubble burst and Internet service America Online's value dropped (some say it's now almost worthless) to only a fraction of its market value at the beginning of 2002. It is as simple as that.

Red Flag 6

The Upbeat Tone of a CEO's Comments Is Not Matched by Performance

When there is a big loss or the profit has slumped and the focus of the executives' comments is all on revenue growth or contract wins in Botswana, investors have to question the company's credibility. If a company has problems, investors want them addressed openly and honestly. You want to know what steps it is taking to overcome them.

Note

Always compare and contrast the performance with the tone of the comments.

Red Flag 7

If a Company Has Had a History of Over-Optimistic Forecasts

When companies issue their quarterly results, they often give indications about what they expect sales and profits will be like for the next period, whether a quarter or longer. If companies have a history of hyping their prospects and missing their own forecasts, be wary. Also, companies that say they really can't forecast what is going to happen in the next year or that offer a wide range for their projections may be more trustworthy than the guys who firmly predict a fixed percentage growth. The reason is that the latter are more likely to get up to tricks with their accounts to meet the target. An increasing number of companies, including Coca-Cola and McDonald's, are declining to produce earnings forecasts.

Red Flag 8

A Company Doesn't Include Accounting Policy Details in Its Press Release

Without information about accounting policies, it is again difficult for investors to tell whether the CFO is an honest figure or a creative genius. Waiting for the filing is not good enough—investors may already have been taken for a ride. The company should say how it has accounted for asset sales and purchases, pension income and deficits, and gains or losses from investments and what it considers revenue and when it is booked. For cable TV companies, financial disclosures should also include important information such as churn rates, which tell us the speed at which they lose customers, and how fees from long-term advertising contracts are booked.

Red Flag 9

Stock Options Accounting Policy and Its Impact Are Not Fully Explained

If the company has decided to expense stock options handed out to management and employees, as encouraged by corporate reformers, then it has to tell us, preferably in the press release and not just in a footnote to its financial statements, clearly how it reached the calculation because there are 101 different ways to do it. This isn't just a case of comparing apples and oranges, but more like pieces of an exotic fruit salad.

Red Flag 10

Too Much of the Wrong Kind of Disclosure Can Bury Vital Information

You want disclosure? Boy, we'll give you disclosure. Disclosure with a capital D!

That seems to sum up the response of some companies to various demands for more disclosure in recent years. Instead of distributing sharp, simply written documents, they are burying investors under releases full of legalistic mumbo jumbo that can sometimes stretch to 1,000 pages.

I began this chapter with a line from one of the footnotes in Enron's annual financial statement issued in April 2001—when the company was still riding high. The sentence, which can be found in "notes to the consolidated financial statements" under the heading "related party transactions," is one clue to some of the nefarious goings-on at the company. (There had been others in previous periods and in proxy statements.) It meant, in effect, that the company's chief financial officer, Andrew Fastow, was benefiting from partnerships he had set up to do business with Enron.

The Enron statements weren't extraordinary in length, but it still takes a lot of time and patience to read through all the footnotes—let alone understand them. So, imagine how easy it is to miss pertinent information in a document that is more like a telephone directory, like telecom company AT&T Corp.'s 2002 proxy statement (more than 846 pages long on my printer) or copier maker Xerox Corp.'s 2001 annual financial statement (889 pages).

Life is getting more, not less, complex for shareholders. More disclosure is going to mean more massive documents full of legalese. There will be more places for executives to hide relevant information than ever before, and then, if there is a controversy, they can turn around and say, "but it was fully disclosed in our 10K, 10Q, 14A, 8K," even if by full disclosure they mean a note to a footnote on page 656, sub-section 17 (ii).

Veteran publicist Howard Rubenstein says that often the lawyers and financial officials will tell their public relations teams to put press releases out that just use the language of a formal document, however obscure that might be. "They say, 'Let the media do the interpretation.'" Former SEC Chairman Arthur Levitt said that a profusion of footnotes is a possible danger sign for investors. If companies produce 1,000-page reports, they are carrying disclosure to "a ridiculous level that is just another form of obfuscation," he said. Former Federal Reserve chairman Paul Volcker is just plain gloomy in his assessment of who can understand the complexities of modern financing. "Ordinary investors can't follow it; the fact is, directors can't follow it, members of the auditing committee can't follow it."

Of course, some market experts believe that if you aren't prepared to put the time into reading annual and quarterly filings with the SEC along with the footnotes, then you shouldn't be invested in the stock in the first place. "Most investors and analysts are lazy—they don't read the footnotes," said short-seller James Chanos. "It's much easier to pick up the phone and call the CFO and ask for an explanation that may or may not be true than to dig through the footnotes and try to understand what is really going on."

Note

Annual and quarterly statements can be read on companies' own websites, the SEC's website (*www.sec.gov*), or from *freeedgar.com*. Also ask yourself whether the company has really shown that it wants to explain complicated financial disclosures to investors—perhaps through jargon-free writing, graphs, summaries of key information, and the like.

Red Flag 11
When a Company Says it Has Changed
Its Revenue Recognition Policies

A lot of the accounting frauds in recent years have been due to companies deciding to book revenue when a sale hasn't been completed or booking the revenue but delaying or fudging the way it accounted for the related costs under, say, a five-year service agreement. Therefore, any mention of a change in accounting for revenue should be closely monitored. It may be that the previous policy was dodgy and the company is being pressured by the SEC to change to a more conservative approach, or the change may be an attempt to goose up revenues.

> **Note**
>
> Look through a company filing online with a word search that includes such phrases as "revenue recognition" and "accounting policies."

Red Flag 12

Hidden Announcements of a Probe
by the Government or a Regulator

Companies will often slip these hidden announcements, which can reveal a probe by organizations such as the Justice Department, the Labor Department, the SEC, or the Food and Drug Administration, into their filings under such headings as "legal and environmental matters" or "additional factors."

Companies that hide time bombs deep in their SEC filings rather than disclosing them in a separate press release are treating their shareholders and the financial markets with derision, shareholder rights experts contend. The strategy often does not work because once the media and investors catch on, it can worsen the impact of the bad news.

One example of a company that only disclosed important information in the depths of a financial statement in 2002 was drugs producer Schering-Plough Corp. when it included a line about a "preliminary" criminal probe of its Puerto Rico business in paragraph 15 of a section titled "additional factors influencing operations," on page 16 (out of 22) of its quarterly statement filed with the SEC on May 15, 2002.

Investors didn't really care how preliminary all this was—it was still important news that shouldn't have been low down in a regular filing. Schering-Plough's shares dropped 12 percent that day.

"I think that their institutional investors should hold their feet to the fire on that kind of disclosure," said former SEC Chairman Levitt.

Note

Read filings thoroughly, especially any catch-all "additional factors."

Red Flag 13

Disclosure of Major Litigation Problems or Reserves for a Settlement

It is important to check what a company says under headlines such as "legal proceedings and contingencies," "litigation," and "commitments and contingencies" because this is often where a company will update investors on critical lawsuits it faces. For example, many major industrial companies are facing huge class-action lawsuits involving hundreds of thousands of claims because they manufactured or used asbestos products in the past.

With the rapid build-up of lawsuits against Wall Street investment banks in recent years, investors in this sector should certainly read any legal footnotes very carefully. With litigation over tainted analysts' coverage, unscrupulous IPO practices, and the involvement in creating some dubious transactions and partnerships at companies such as Enron, there are bound to be some major costs and charges taken.

Investors should also comb the quarterly and annual filings for the following (some of this will be found in footnotes and some will be flagged more prominently):

- Changes in pension policy

- Detailed information about takeovers and their accounting treatment over the year

- Any qualification of the annual results by the company's auditors or any unusual comments they make about the nature of accounting policies

- How the company accounts for long-term trading contracts— especially when there isn't an exchange on which they can be priced

- Signs that one part of a company is propping up another part through a cross subsidy

- The numbers of subsidiaries and limited partnerships in tax havens such as the Cayman Islands

Red Flag 14

When a Board or CEO Treats an Annual Meeting with Contempt

If Woody Allen's famous saying that "showing up is 80 percent of life" is true, the directors of Caterpillar Inc. didn't get much fulfillment in 2002.

None of the 14 board members of the world's largest construction and mining equipment maker, with the exception of Chairman and CEO Glen Barton, attended the company's annual meeting in Chicago in April 2002.

Their absence, despite the fact that four were up for re-election at the meeting, was seen as a gratuitous insult by shareholder activists. Some of those attending jeered their no show, according to the *Peoria Journal Star.* "It was one of the low points of the annual meeting season in 2002," said

The Corporate Library's Minow. "I think it is appalling, I believe that is one of those things that investors should look at as investment risk."

Barton had explained away the absence of the board members—who receive at least $60,000 each a year and only had to attend six full board meetings in 2001—by saying he didn't think it was worth their while to stay, according to *Business Week*.

"It tells me they don't believe that shareholders are important, and if they don't believe shareholders are important you shouldn't invest in the company," said Minow.

Some companies in the firing line hold their annual meetings as far away as possible from the majority of their shareholders and employees. And some, such as Tyco, which are domiciled in tax havens such as Bermuda, always hold their meetings at the island retreat—well away from most of their investors and employees. Tyco says it considers Bermuda the most appropriate place to hold the meeting because the company is incorporated there. In March 2003, Tyco said it would review the Bermuda incorporation.

Note

If you have time to attend annual meetings, take notice of the way management and the board treat shareholders. If they are contemptuous in public, imagine what they could be like in private.

Red Flag 15

When a Company Tries to Bury Bad News on or Just before a Holiday

One of the oldest tricks in the corporate book is the bombshell announcement just before a major holiday or late on a Friday night.

The idea seems to be to reduce media coverage and give investors a little time to think about news of a contract loss, expectations of lower profits, or a sudden CEO departure rather than immediately hitting the sell button. Invariably, it doesn't work and can actually make matters worse.

One of the most obvious examples of a holiday announcement was a warning about lower-than-expected profits from software maker Computer Associates close to midnight on July 3, 2000, when not only would markets be closed the following day for the Independence Day holiday, but also many Americans would be with their families and about as far away from the news as they ever get.

The result: Business columnists poured derision on the company and the stock dropped 42 percent when the markets opened on July 5. The company claimed that it released the information as soon as it was available, noting that the quarter had just ended.

> **Note**
>
> This is usually a very strong sell signal.

Red Flag 16

When a Company Doesn't Hold Conference Calls

This may indicate a lack of openness. Most companies hold conference calls at which analysts and investors have the chance to ask questions about quarterly results. One hold-out from this practice is drugs company Schering-Plough, which produces "listen-only" calls, meaning no questions are allowed. Wal-Mart also does the same sometimes. Usually, its conference call consists of little more than a reading of the press statement and a few more comments.

Red Flag 17

If a Call Is So Controlled That Probing Questions Are Not Addressed

If all the questions are coming from securities analysts who seek to ingratiate themselves with management rather than delve for more information, you may have a call that is so controlled that it is next to useless.

"We almost never get the chance to ask questions," said short seller James Chanos.

You can link to many conference calls through company web sites, but there are also services that specialize in them, including *www.streetevents.com* and *www.bestcalls.com,* and these provide archiving as well as live feeds.

Investors should also take note if a company ends a call abruptly, perhaps after an issue has been raised that it doesn't want to address.

Red Flag 18

When the Press Is Barred from an Annual Meeting

This is almost always a sign that a company is in trouble. The company may be doing it to prevent reporters from seeing how angry shareholders are over a particular issue or in an attempt to prevent executives from facing media scrutiny because of a scandal. One company to prevent the media from covering its annual meeting in 2002 was ImClone Systems Inc., which was embroiled in an insider trading controversy that led to the indictment of former CEO Sam Waksal. In explaining the decision, ImClone said that it wanted to be able to answer questions from shareholders without "distractions."

Red Flag 19

If a Company Delays Publishing Financial Results without Good Explanation

Companies delaying scheduled announcements, particularly if there is even a whiff of a possible accounting problem, get shown little mercy in the stock market these days.

Often this "take no prisoners" approach is correct. A delay in results, unless there is a reasonable explanation (the company may have lost its offices in the September 11 attacks, for example), can mean some accounting irregularities have been discovered and executives are worried about the accuracy of the numbers.

Now that CEOs and CFOs have to vouch for the material accuracy and completeness of the financial statements, there are likely to be more delays than in the past.

When the world's second biggest advertising agency firm, Interpublic Group of Cos., announced in August 2002 a one-week postponement of its second-quarter earnings statement at the request of its board audit committee, its shares plunged 25 percent. Over the next few months it announced a series of accounting problems, plunging profits and restatements of previous results, and that it faced an SEC probe. Its shares were about 75 percent below their 52-week high by March 2003.

Red Flag 20

If a Normally Talkative Company Official Suddenly Clams Up

When there is silence from a company that normally talks frequently with Wall Street, investors, and the media, it may be a signal that something major is on the horizon.

"Investors should watch out for a suddenly very open and communicative company becoming very quiet and not returning phone calls and not disclosing things it used to disclose," said Chanos.

Also, if a company is facing a growing crisis and isn't trying to get its story across to counter its critics, that probably tells you that it is in deep trouble.

An example in early 2002 was discount retailer Kmart Corp.'s rapid slide into bankruptcy.

On January 2, Prudential Securities analyst Wayne Hood slapped a "sell" rating on the company's stock and said he would not be surprised if the company filed for bankruptcy. That was enough to send the company's shares down about 25 percent in two days, and yet its management did virtually nothing to try to turn back the tide. A spokesman issued a short statement saying that the company had sufficient funds and available lines of credit to pursue its strategy. And that was about it.

If there had been nothing to what Hood had forecast, there would likely have been much more of an aggressive response, perhaps involving management doing conference calls, giving interviews to the media, and the like.

Sure enough, within three weeks, Kmart had filed for Chapter 11 bankruptcy protection.

Note

Always monitor closely how a company responds to criticism or key predictions.

Red Flag 21

When Drug Companies Spin and Obfuscate the Results of Drug Trials

One of the riskier areas for mainstream investors is the biotechnology industry, where U.S. regulators have done little to rein in companies making confusing or exaggerated claims about drug trial results. Clinical trials make or break a drug's chances of being approved by the U.S. Federal Drug Administration (FDA), so the results of a major trial can often send a share price for a ride and can make the difference between survival and closure for some smaller companies.

While companies must go to the FDA to get press releases about already approved drugs vetted before they go out, there is no such requirement for announcements about the progress of experimental drugs. The SEC tends to defer to the FDA on the legitimacy of medical claims in press releases.

One company that sparked controversy in 2001 was Alexion Pharmaceuticals Inc., which on January 23 of that year issued a press release about the strong efficacy of its drug, pexelizumab, in reducing death and heart attacks among patients undergoing heart surgery. Its shares soared 25 percent as a result. But, the following week, its share price almost halved after it issued another press release saying the drug failed its primary clinical objective, known as an endpoint, for reducing small heart attacks and other complications. The big difference? The first press release had only referred to a subgroup of patients tested. The second referred to the entire trial of 914 patients.

All was not lost for Alexion, even though investor confidence certainly took a battering because of the way it had issued the information. In November 2002, the company released results from an additional trial of 814 heart patients that showed promising results, giving its shares a 37 percent boost in one day.

The small investor should also know that news about trial results, whether for drugs being tested by biotechnology companies or the mainstream pharmaceutical groups, may have been available to a large number of medical specialists well before the press release reaches the media and the public.

Often, summaries of trial results, known as abstracts, are posted on web sites by professional medical groups, sometimes ahead of a full presentation at their conferences. These are only accessible by group members and are embargoed for release until the presentation, which will be covered by reporters and will probably be the subject of a separate press release. However, it doesn't take a genius to work out that potentially market-moving data can easily get from a heart or lung specialist to friends on Wall Street or investors elsewhere. There have been a number of cases in recent years of share prices moving on such information before it is widely available.

Note

Make sure you fully understand drug trial information.

7

Culture of Greed: Sports Stadiums, Shooting the Messenger, and Rank and Yank

"Did you ever expect a corporation to have a conscience, when it has no soul to be damned and no body to be kicked."

—Lord Edward Thurlow, English jurist and statesman, 1731–1806

When your favorite rock star is a punk, has punk attitudes, has produced nothing but punk music and one day you hear him or her singing country, talking country, and acting country, it is disconcerting. It may indicate that there is something terribly wrong.

Well, the same goes for a company that spends years building up a certain kind of image and then demolishes it overnight. That is what Tyco International, which had been an investors' darling until the Enron collapse focused the world on sharp accounting, signaled in January 2002. After years of gaining a reputation as a brash, acquisitive conglomerate with fingers in all sorts of pies and with a CEO who indicated he was going to create the next General Electric Co., Tyco suddenly announced that this wasn't how it was going to be any more.

The bigger-is-better philosophy had gone. Instead, the company, which sold everything from security gear to medical products to plastics and financial services, planned to break up into four pieces. Descriptions such as "u-turn," "about face," and "retreat" were bandied around by analysts, investors, and the media to describe the plan.

The change was a sign of a corporate culture that had little durability. Investors felt deceived and increasingly suspicious—rightly so, as it turned out. Companies can't expect to do a Grand Old Duke of York on their shareholders, marching them up the hill one minute and down the next.

We have already looked at how the attitudes of CEOs and boards make the difference between a company ripe for fraudulent accounting and one where honesty and integrity rule. Here, we look at problems in a company's culture and behavior that should be a big deterrent to investing.

Red Flag 1

When a Company Abruptly Transforms Its Corporate Strategy

According to short seller James Chanos of Kynikos Associates, Tyco's sudden announcement that it was no longer the great acquirer was a big, fat sell signal.

"Boards and management spend a lot of time thinking about what the company is all about, where it's going, and how it is positioned in the marketplace with investors. And very abrupt changes to that usually signal to us either some sort of accounting game that has come to the end of its rope, or something that management has uncovered and is about to drop on you in the form of bad news," he said.

Red Flag 2

If a Company Fires a Whistleblower or Faces a Suit from a Whistleblower

Knowing that an employee who suspects fraud, bribery, or some other horrendous practice can have a complaint treated seriously and confidentially and can have access to independent directors if necessary is a vital comfort for investors.

In at least four of the companies embroiled in accounting scandals in 2002, staff had tried to blow the whistle and had been either ignored or fired.

For example, a senior staff member at copier maker Xerox Corp. and another at telecommunications company Global Crossing, both of whom had complained about accounting policy, were fired well before the worst was publicly revealed at either company.

Enron whistleblower Sherron Watkins' expression of grave concern that the energy trader was about to implode because of fast and loose accounting policies was also given short shrift, with the contents of her letter not even released to the company's board in the fall of 2001.

And, while WorldCom's admission of a $9 billion accounting scandal after costs had been wrongly capitalized arose after internal auditor Cynthia Cooper went around CFO Scott Sullivan and talked directly to the chairman of the board's audit committee, attempts by others to report concerns about the company's accounting had been thwarted.

I should say here that I am using the term whistleblower loosely—some say that a true whistleblower has to go outside the organization rather than just informing higher-ups or the board of a problem. Prominent executive coach Marshall Goldsmith says the simplest litmus test for an investor deciding whether a company has good practices is the staff's freedom to express their opinion on ethical issues without fear of retribution. "The best companies don't give you an opportunity; they make it an obligation," he said. "The best companies don't need whistleblowers because every employee has the right to challenge right up to upper management without fear of getting punished."

Top public relations expert Howard Rubenstein says that there has to be an effective process set up for concerns to be expressed from any level in a company. "If someone discovers something they think is wrong, they should be able to go not to the person who managed that thing but go around or above them, and that would involve sexual harassment, hostile work environment, accounting procedures—almost anything that could be considered inappropriate."

One clue about a company's openness may be whether it has an anonymous telephone hot line for employees to express concerns about ethical practices and other issues. After the Enron scandal, there was an increase in calls to the hot lines, which are run by companies such as Pinkerton Consulting & Investigations. The Sarbanes-Oxley corporate reform act also introduces new whistleblower protection that prohibits retaliation against employees who provide any "truthful information" to law enforcement officers about a crime. It may help a little. Though rare are the times when companies say they are firing a worker for whistleblowing, they will usually find some other reason, such as a poor work record or job cuts.

Red Flag 3

A Company Cuts Research and Other Spending for the Future

Whenever there are signs of tough times ahead, if a company's first move is to slash its spending on research and development or other initiatives meant to improve its longer-term prospects, you may be dealing with a shortsighted management team. This is particularly the case if the cuts are the way the company gets to meet earnings growth targets.

Cuts in such discretionary spending are one of the biggest red flags for short seller David Tice. Companies feel they can cut research and development spending because it won't benefit them with a new product now, but Tice said investors have to ask what happens in subsequent periods when there aren't the new products there should have been. "Also you might have guys who handle current orders and you have other people who find new orders, and you can fire the guys who go out and find new orders to keep the earnings per share up, but then where is the next order going to come from?" he asks.

> ### Note
> Check growth in research and development against earnings and revenue growth; if it lags badly, there could be a problem brewing.

Red Flag 4

A Company Doesn't Handle a Crisis Directly or Quickly and Allows It to Fester

When a company is facing any kind of crisis, a fast and very public response from the CEO and other top officials is essential or else the silence is likely to be seen as arrogant or deceptive. If the crisis holds any suggestion of health risks concerning the company's products, hesitation in confronting the issue head-on can destroy years of work building a brand name and an image. Everyone in public relations at major companies should know that, and they should all have a plan to handle a crisis quickly and effectively. It doesn't always happen that way.

Take Coca-Cola Co.'s response to a health scare in Belgium, France, and some other European countries in June 1999 when scores of students and schoolchildren reported becoming ill after drinking the company's products. Public relations experts say that the company's initial response may have worsened and prolonged the crisis, threatening its entire European image. The crisis also hurt its earnings.

The company did not put out a statement from then Chairman and CEO Doug Ivester until June 16, more than a week after the crisis began, and it wasn't until June 18 that he flew into Belgium to handle the crisis personally. The company, which at the time denied it responded inadequately, had also stopped many of its outside public relations partners from talking to the media during this period.

"Don't allow yourselves to become a political issue and don't let the stories fester," said Richard Edelman, president and CEO of the public relations agency Edelman Worldwide.

Coca-Cola's response is often contrasted with the speed with which drugs maker Johnson & Johnson recalled all its Tylenol pain reliever drug from U.S. store shelves after tampering on two separate occasions in the 1980s led to some deaths. The huge sum of money that cost was seen as worth spending to defend the company's image.

Red Flag 5

A Company Hides Behind Anti-Takeover Devices and Ignores Votes to Change

Many boards and managements hide behind barriers meant to make it more difficult for a corporate raider to take over a company. These may have been suitable for the 1980s when junk bond-funded bids threatened many companies and were often not in the interests of many shareholders. But, in the view of many institutional investors nowadays, they are more likely to be used to protect weak managements and compromised boards.

The barriers include so-called "poison pills," which create mechanisms to prevent a hostile bidder from accumulating more than a certain percentage of its target's shares and to give a board effective veto power over any takeover proposal. They also include the use of staggered boards, which are sometimes referred to as classified boards. These allow for the election of only a percentage—often one third— of directors each year, preventing a shareholder group from taking control of the board at one meeting.

Critics argue that such devices are being used to ignore shareholder rights, particularly as a supermajority vote of shareholders is often required to overturn them. For six successive years, shareholders of drugs maker Bristol-Myers Squibb Co. passed a proposal to get rid of its staggered board and replace it with elections of all directors every year by a majority of votes cast at annual meetings. Yet, the company has kept the staggered board, arguing that the resolution still didn't get majority support of all shareholders (not just those voting) and that the board structure "provides continuity and stability in the management of the business and affairs of the company since a majority of the directors will always have prior experience as directors of the company." It also argued that if there were an unfriendly or unsolicited effort to acquire the company, the staggered system would give Bristol-Myers more power to negotiate with the bidder and to consider alternative proposals. However, at the time of writing in early 2003, that stance crumbled. It said in February 2003 it would agree to the shareholder demands for full annual board elections.

Companies that continue to stonewall when faced with such votes should face the wrath of investors, shareholder advocates say. "The shareholders need to step in there and change the board. If a company continues to ignore shareholders year after year, then shareholders should focus on the board," said Richard Koppes, a former general counsel for the giant California public employees pension fund group CalPERS who was elected to the board of ICN Pharmaceuticals in 2002 as part of a dissident shareholder group.

Red Flag 6

When Companies Are Legally Incorporated in Unusual Places

The majority of publicly traded American companies are legally incorporated in the State of Delaware, which has built its state finances partly on the corporate fees and taxes it can earn. While the Delaware courts have been far from the friends of shareholder activists over the years, they are at least a known quantity.

A shareholder activist such as Providence Capital President Herbert Denton is very suspicious of companies that incorporate in other states because they may be doing so to use esoteric local laws to thwart shareholder campaigns. For example, Ohio and Pennsylvania created additional obstacles to the purchase of large blocks of stock. This helped Ohio-incorporated defense systems and auto parts group TRW Inc. to mount a strong resistance to a takeover bid from Northrop Grumman Corp. in 2002. (TRW eventually agreed to a higher bid from Northrop.)

If, for example, Denton sees a company incorporated in the state of Nevada, he is immediately wary. "Being incorporated in a quirky place indicates that people who control the company don't want to be challenged," he said.

Red Flag 7
A Company That Buys a Stadium, a Sports Team, or Their Naming Rights

It seemed to come with the territory. Almost every company embroiled in a scandal in 2002 was also the owner of either a sports stadium or a sports team. The correlation was getting to be so frequent that some on Wall Street were wondering whether they should use the sports connection as a reason to sell a stock.

Short seller James Chanos said the sports link had "a wonderful predictive ability" as the weirdest sell signal throughout the Internet bubble and had in some ways supplanted an indicator that was most popular in the 1960s and 1970s, which was a company with a lavish corporate headquarters (see below). "There is an unbelievably high correlation," he said, between a corporate blowup and naming rights to a stadium. "The CEO is spending the money on something that probably benefits the senior executives more than the shareholders."

David Tice, who is also a short seller, says that he believes CEOs who become bigger names in their hometowns by investing in the local sports teams are probably not always doing it for sensible marketing reasons. He wonders whether people going to a stadium named after a company are any more likely to buy its products. "To me it is more of an arrogant move to have friends in a hometown or people look up to them, because it doesn't make economic sense."

Among the scandal-plagued companies that had such links are Enron, which had named the new Astros' baseball stadium in Houston Enron Field, and telecommunications company WorldCom, which had named the MCI Arena for the Washington Wizards basketball team. John Rigas, the former chairman of cable operator Adelphia Communications, was among the most active in the sports world. The Rigas family owned the Buffalo Sabres hockey team, got the company to pay for naming rights to the Tennessee Titans football stadium in Nashville, and allegedly used company money to build a golf course.

There are plenty more. It really is uncanny. But by early 2003 AOL Time Warner, News Corp., and Walt Disney Co. all indicated that they would be willing to sell their sports team holdings.

> **Note**
>
> Don't mix sports with investment decisions.

Red Flag 8

The Edifice Complex: Lavish HQs Can Signal Waste and Excess

Companies that build monuments in the form of lavish corporate headquarters buildings have raised investors' eyebrows for some time. Sometimes, such excesses can be partially excused as a marketing tool to appeal to customers or as a way to keep employees motivated, but often they are little more than a sign of a celebrity CEO wasting shareholders' money.

"Grizzled analyst wisdom says sell the stock of a company building a new headquarters that is owned, not leased," writes Kathryn Staley in her book *The Art of Short Selling*. "It is a top-of-the earnings cycle clue."

Emerging markets investment guru Mark Mobius said he became increasingly suspicious of Hong Kong businessman George Tan's Carrian group, which at one stage was the territory's sixth-largest company, after visiting its headquarters. "His whole office was done in a French boudoir style and I began to think this is rather a strange decor for an executive office. It gives you some insight into how these guys are thinking, where they are coming from." Carrian collapsed in the 1980s in Hong Kong's largest bankruptcy and corporate scandal involving corruption, false accounting, and illusory profits.

No such style for Wal-Mart Stores Inc., which sells more than $240 billion of merchandise a year—dwarfing the economies of many countries. Its offices are the antidote to any executive struck with the edifice complex. All displays of ostentation are out, while frugal— some would say miserly and cheap—is in. The spare brick and metal buildings that sprawl haphazardly over the muddy red clay of Bentonville, Arkansas, are symbolic of the discount giant's business philosophy: spare any expense.

Red Flag 9
Companies That Treat Staff Ruthlessly May Signal a Screwed-Up Culture

One of the key red flags for veteran public relations man Rubenstein is evidence that top management treats the staff badly. Unbearable behavior means they will not only lose talented people, but they will also likely face expensive lawsuits, he says.

"Let's assume they are brutal to their own staff. We have seen a lot of that—using inappropriate language, calling someone an idiot—and you see that in someone's management style. That doesn't work anymore," he said.

At Enron, employees suffered from a brutal appraisal system, called "rank and yank," that placed 15 percent of employees in the lowest of five categories, facing the prospect of being yanked, which meant fired or forced to quit. They were usually given six months to improve or leave.

"In practice, however, with new waves of 15-percent yanks coming every six months, it was difficult for those in the bottom category to escape for very long, so they usually chose to accept a severance package rather than stick it out," wrote Peter Fusaro and Ross Miller in their book *What Went Wrong at Enron*. "Furthermore, those in categories 2 and 3 were effectively put on notice that they, too, were liable to be yanked within the next year." Fusaro and Miller say that by threatening half the workforce, the company pitted employee against employee, which proved demoralizing and created a cutthroat culture.

Red Flag 10

Companies Confronting Rather Than Talking to Pressure Groups

Investors may want to take increasing notice of controversies about social policy issues at major companies. A failure by boards and managements to address them could lead to boycotts and other campaigns that could damage their share prices.

Arguments over human rights in Myanmar and other countries, gay rights policies, and renewable energy investing are all likely to become increasingly sore issues in the next few years in proxy fights at annual meetings.

Institutional Shareholder Services (ISS), which has huge influence through advising hundreds of major pension and mutual funds on shareholder voting, turned up the heat in 2002 by backing two resolutions, one on gay rights and the other on renewable energy, put forward by shareholders at oil giant ExxonMobil's annual meeting. Advocates of gay equality have called on ExxonMobil to add "sexual orientation" to its equal employment opportunity statement, but the company has resisted, saying it is not necessary because it doesn't discriminate against gay workers. Exxon has faced a boycott from gay activists for rescinding a policy banning anti-gay bias at Mobil, including providing insurance coverage for the partners of its gay employees, when it took over the oil company in 1999. A Catholic group also called on ExxonMobil to outline its plans for the promotion of renewable energy.

Explaining why ISS believes shareholders should really start to worry about such issues, its director of corporate programs, Patrick McGurn, says he fears that ExxonMobil's stance will "open the door for potential value diminution."

"They have chosen for whatever reason to make themselves the poster boy for all environmental activists, for example," he said. By seeking to declare itself right and its opponents wrong, Exxon has distracted attention away from the company's overall performance.

Expect this kind of issue to become much more of a battleground and a potential influence on share prices in the future.

Note

Don't ignore what may initially seem peripheral issues; they have a nasty way of taking center stage if they aren't addressed.

Red Flag 11

When Unexplained Events Cast Doubt on an Entire Investment Story

The Bre-X gold fraud has been described as the perfect international crime.

A Canadian company reports a massive gold find in the jungles of Borneo, one of the remotest corners of the planet, and follow-up tests show it is probably the biggest ever. Then, many major brokerage analysts and journalists in North America become true believers and help the company hype the discovery and its stock, pulling in some of the world's top mutual funds as well as thousands of individual investors. Meanwhile, the family of Suharto, Indonesia's then leader, plans to get its share of the riches that could flow from this El Dorado, as do some of the world's biggest mining companies, and in so doing, they add to the credibility of the discovery. And then, just as the fraud—based on the salting of thousands of test samples with gold brought in from elsewhere — is about to be discovered in 1997, the one company official who had all the knowledge of how it happened and could say who did what, chief geologist Michael de Guzman, plunges from a helicopter to his death in the jungle.

Six years later, the world is little the wiser about who did what. Nobody is even certain whether de Guzman jumped or was pushed. But top geologists don't drop out of helicopters without a reason, and those who didn't sell Bre-X stock on that news put hope ahead of reason and suffered big losses as a result. There had already been plenty of signs suggesting Bre-X was a dubious investment. For example, in January 1997, an unexplained fire destroyed the Busang camp's geological offices, including many of de Guzman's notes explaining the gold discovery's formation.

> **Note**
>
> When really inexplicable things happen, it is a very bad sign.

8

Earnings Tricks and Games: Manipulating the Numbers and "Creative" Fraud

"Now little beads of sweat appear. Soon he is creating charts with earnings on one side and Wall Street expectations on the other... As the quarters proceed he finds himself keeping bad accounts receivable, delaying the recognition of expenses, and altering inventory levels. At one point, dispensing with all formality, he finds himself directing his accounting staff to cross out real numbers and insert false ones."

—Michael Young in his book *Accounting Irregularities and Financial Fraud* on how the head of a company division can become drawn into a massive financial fraud

In one recollection in his autobiography *Straight from the Gut*, Jack Welch crystallizes the ease with which executives have been able to hide holes in their financial results. The former chairman and chief executive of General Electric recounts the nightmare he faced in April 1994 when told that Joseph Jett, a star government bond trader at the conglomerate's then investment banking unit Kidder, Peabody, was accused of making a series of fictitious trades that had left a $350 million hole in GE's accounts. Welch held a conference call with 14 of the leaders of GE's diverse businesses to deliver the bad news and to apologize for an event that was sure to hurt the company's stock price and for which he blamed himself.

The corporate chieftain, who has been deified by the media and management experts, recalled that "the response of our business leaders to the crisis was typical of the GE culture. Even though the books had closed on the quarter, many immediately offered to pitch in to cover the Kidder gap. Some said they could find an extra $10 million, $20 million, and even $30 million from their businesses to offset the surprise."

So, here we have the heads of some very large businesses within GE who are not only able to discover some extra money but who felt it was appropriate two weeks after the end of the first quarter to offer it up as a sacrifice to the head office. As it turned out, Welch—who declined to be interviewed for this book—said he turned down the offer because it was too late. The implication was that if it had been discovered a few weeks earlier, the Jett hole in the accounts could have been smoothed away.

Welch's praise of the pitching in as a hallmark of the strength of the GE culture—he contrasts it with the "disgusting" selfishness he encountered at Kidder, which was later sold—is also worrying to some analysts and investors. It begs the question of whether the heads of operations produce money out of thin air on other occasions to make up for shortfalls.

"It is called earnings management, and it is not kosher," said James Grant, who runs Grant's Interest Rate Observer, in reference to the offers from Welch's managers. "And yet he was most proud of these unbidden offers from the subordinates." Grant, who has been a frequent critic of GE's accounting policies, said that during his 20-year reign, which ended in 2001, Welch managed to condition people to believe in his ability to deliver the numbers rather than work out how the numbers were reached. "Despite all the analysts who followed GE, there was probably less analytical sweat expended than on almost any other company in the world," said Grant. "People were content with GE coming in predictably with one penny per share in earnings better than expectations every quarter."

In this chapter, we will look at the accounting sleight of hand that companies can use to disguise their earnings performance in a particular period. In the following two chapters, we examine manipulation of sales and costs and balance sheet tricks.

Answering critics in his book, Welch said that from the day he sought to become GE's CEO, he made "consistent earnings growth" a theme, but he claimed that he managed businesses, not earnings. He said that gains from sales of assets went to fixing problems elsewhere in the empire, using the analogy of fixing a leak in a house when you have the money. He said that one reporter suggested that if the company took a loss on the closure of one business in one quarter and a gain on the sale of another in the following quarter, then its earnings wouldn't have been consistent. Welch's reply to that: "Duh!!! Our job is to fix the leak, when we get the cash. If you didn't do that you would be managing nothing."

This doesn't seem to entirely answer the point—which is that any one period of results should reflect what happened in that period. GE managed to hit or just beat Wall Street earnings forecasts in every quarter, bar two, over a 10-year period (1992–2002), and some believe that just isn't possible for any company to do if it fully reflected what actually happened in each period.

Former SEC Chairman Richard Breeden says that he is highly suspicious of companies that almost always hit earnings targets. "Life doesn't produce nice straight lines," said Breeden, who was not specifically talking about GE. "That company is not necessarily engaging in fraud, but it is certainly managing earnings—the economy never looks like that, and the real world never looks like that. Orders don't all get shipped by the last day of the quarter. Some days they went out four days into the new quarter, and some people have the courage to admit that and other people find ways to fudge the rules."

When Jeff Immelt took over from Welch as GE's CEO and was faced with post-Enron skepticism about how GE made its numbers, there was some hope of a new era of openness at the company. Faced with a declining share price, Immelt said he was quite prepared to publish a report the size of a Manhattan phone book if that is what it took to dispel doubts about the way the firm reached its earnings numbers. GE did indeed release more information in its annual financial statements for 2001, breaking down the figures for a larger number of businesses and disclosing more about its accounting practices.

Yet, when it came to its third quarter earnings in 2002, the GE way seemed to have changed little. The company issued a statement on September 25 saying that its earnings for the quarter were "on track" to rise as previously forecast by 25 percent on an 8–10 percent increase in revenue. Then, at an analysts' meeting the following day, the maker of everything from light bulbs to jet engines and financial services, disclosed that the earnings would include a gain from the sale of its Internet commerce business. Analysts said that, without that one-time fillip, declining growth in some of its other businesses meant that it would miss the forecasts. A negative reaction from analysts helped drive the shares down after they had initially gained on the "on track" comment.

Some would say that many top executives are caught between a firing squad and the guillotine in the current environment. If they miss Wall Street expectations by reporting entirely straightforwardly, they are taken out and shot, and if they massage the numbers, they can be beheaded.

There are clear signs that chief financial officers often find themselves being asked by CEOs to manipulate results to meet targets. In 2002, the results of a CFO magazine survey of 141 CFOs at publicly traded companies with more than $1 billion in revenue showed that 17 percent admitted that their CEOs had pressured them to misrepresent results at least once in the past five years, and 5 percent said that they had violated accounting rules at least once in that period. In an advertising supplement in July 1998, BusinessWeek released even more worrying results from a poll of CFOs who had attended a forum the magazine had run in April of that year. The 160 delegates were asked to respond to the following statement: "As CFO, I have fought off other executives' requests that I misrepresent corporate results." Using electronic keypads to respond, 55 percent answered, "yes, I have fought them off," and 12 percent answered, "I yielded to requests," with 33 percent answering that they had not received such requests.

"That is an amazing, amazing survey result that shows there really is a situation in the corporate reporting right now where there is a very good likelihood that the numbers are not reflecting reality," said short seller Jim Chanos.

I began this chapter with a quote that shows what often happens to the manager who wilts under such pressure. It starts with small things—delaying a few costs, bringing forward some revenue, changing some accounting assumptions to make the outcome rosier, or perhaps reducing some reserves held for a rainy day. This helps to cover up a problem—perhaps a fundamental problem such as lower-than-expected orders or a cancelled contract. Of course, rarely is such a problem only going to hit home in one quarter, so the CFO or the divisional head has to pull another rabbit out of the hat the next quarter. When he or she has gone through all the rabbits, he or she may have to simply start making up numbers, and then the fine line between accounting manipulation and fraud has been well and truly crossed.

One of the biggest difficulties for investors is that there is always a lot of room for judgments and assumptions in any accounting system—particularly, it seems, under the U.S. Generally Accepted Accounting Principles, or GAAP. That net profit of $200 million that your favorite company has reported might be built on very aggressive estimates and assumptions. On a more conservative basis, it could be $190 million. And we are talking here not about the Enrons and WorldComs of this world but about highly respected, well-run companies.

One of the problems at Enron, for example, was that it was making assumptions about the value of energy contracts that went many years into the future—with no exchange or market prepared to independently value them. Sometimes, all the assumptions behind such estimates aren't disclosed, leaving investors completely in the dark.

Such vagueness creates huge room for the artful, the manipulative, and the truly crooked to conjure up whatever final numbers they want. As Breeden puts it, "Financial reporting moves from photography to impressionist painting." Some even say that quarterly reporting—and the incessant focus on one critical earnings number and the forecasts ahead of its announcement—should be done away with.

"The whole environment has put too much pressure on the short term numbers. I think that is a lot of the problem," says James Gerson, chairman of the accounting industry's Auditing Standards Board, which helps to set U.S. auditing standards. "I think the world would be a lot better if net income was stated as a range instead of one number—which is probably closer to reality when you figure in the kinds of estimates that go into these numbers," he said.

During the bull market at the end of the last millennium, there was incredible demand from the whole Wall Street circus—in which I include investors, traders, analysts, and the media—for companies to at least meet and usually beat the consensus forecasts of Wall Street securities houses. In fact, at the height of the mania, just matching the consensus estimate from analysts was also reason enough for punishment in the form of a stock price dive. A company had to be able to beat the forecast by at least a penny and sometimes more. The argument in the market was that if you couldn't beat the analysts' number given the rampant use of all kinds of manipulation, it was a very bad sign. Clearly, Old Mother Hubbard's cupboard was bare without a dog's bone in sight. There was even a cottage industry formed around so-called whisper estimates, which were almost always higher than the formal estimates from analysts. Several web sites specialized in collating such estimates from public investors.

Of course, in this whole equation, we shouldn't forget the role that compensation policy played in creating an incentive for managements to beat earnings forecasts so that the value of their options would soar. Stock options, which give the recipient the right to purchase shares at some specified point in the future at a price set at the time of the award, had been heralded as a way of aligning executives' interests more closely with those of the shareholders. There had been popular revulsion at the piles of cash some chief executives were being paid in the early 1990s even if their companies' performance was awful and their share prices were getting trodden into the ground. So, the idea that CEOs would only get a modest cash salary (though modest in this context probably means about $800,000 plus) and that a lot of the rest of their compensation would come from a bonus based on meeting certain targets and from stock options was seen as a move in the right direction. The argument was simple: If the shares rose, the CEO made more money from his or her options and the shareholders were also happy.

But this didn't take on board the notion that executives could pump up short-term performance, driving the shares up, and then pocket huge windfall gains as they cashed out the shares they bought with their options. Even more than that, it didn't take account of the chances that the pumping might involve stealing growth from the future, lying to investors, and fraud—all of which of course can bring the shares back down to earth with a bump. Oh, and stock options could be handed out like confetti without the need for the company to expense them under U.S. accounting rules, as must be done with other compensation. And, when they were exercised by the recipients, there were even some tax benefits for the company.

So, there we have it—a dangerous combination of fear and greed: fear of missing the numbers and losing your job as a result, and greed from beating your numbers and collecting the pot of gold at the end of the options rainbow.

In the rest of this chapter, we are going to view some of the red flags to watch out for when analyzing a company's financial reports. However, here is a word of caution: When executives have reached the stage where they are crossing out numbers and inserting false ones, the clues may be found not so much in the financials but in a wider pattern of behavior and in comparisons with rivals.

Red Flag 1

Companies That Always Meet or Beat Earnings Expectations

Diversified electronics and engineering group Emerson, whose products include fans, garbage disposals, and power and climate control systems for buildings, suffered its first earnings setback in 44 years in 2001 due to a sharp decline in profits from its electronics and telecommunications business, and restructuring costs. The first decline in earnings for such a long period was worth noting in itself, but the way that Emerson announced that the downturn was going to hit home was even more interesting and sheds a lot of light on the leeway companies think they have to tinker with the final numbers delivered to the public. "After careful consideration, our management team made a proactive decision to not continue Emerson's record 43 consecutive years of increased earnings per share," Emerson's CEO David Farr said in a statement. "We could have pared back restructuring and other investments, or taken other operating actions as we have done in the past, to continue the record."

So, the failure to record a forty-fourth year of earnings growth wasn't a decision taken by the marketplace and wasn't due to a lower order book and recession-hit economy—it was a decision taken by management. In the event, Emerson recorded a 27.5 percent drop in net profit to $1.03 billion in the year to September 30, 2001. Investors should probably be appreciative of Emerson's decision not to indulge in the manipulative behavior so prevalent in the rest of corporate

America. However, the honesty shows how investors can be easily duped into thinking that earnings are growing when a company's business is less than cheery.

So, the message is clear—don't take earnings numbers at face value; there may have been a lot of masking and maneuvering involved to get there. We will see as we go through this chapter that companies can use 101 different ways to reach earnings targets, including gains on sales of assets, pension fund adjustments, the raiding of so-called "cookie-jar reserves," and beneficial changes in accounting assumptions.

Breeden says that the perfect track record "shows a willingness to manage earnings that then can lead to other problems, and I as an investor can't police that. I can't know. All I know is that they are not telling me the full truth."

Note

Don't be frightened of companies, other things being equal, that show some volatility in their earnings.

Red Flag 2

The Use of One-Time Gains from Asset Sales to Reach Earnings Targets

International Business Machines Corp. (IBM) said that it had cut selling, general and administrative expenses, the main expenses line in its accounts, in the fourth quarter of 2001. The reduction by 3.8 percent to $4.18 billion made it look as if the company really had a handle on costs despite sagging revenues, and it helped it to beat Wall Street's earnings expectations by a penny. It seemed that the company had managed to squeeze out costs from an area that includes everything from headquarters staff salaries to office supplies to travel expenses. However, what IBM didn't tell investors in the press release announcing the results in January 2002 was that the expense reduction was helped by a $280 million gain on the sale of an optical transceiver business to JDS Uniphase that was included in the expenses calculation but not separately disclosed in the press release. The company only acknowledged the way the gain was booked when *The New York Times* ran a story about it and the company's shares dropped.

Indeed, IBM has been putting such one-time gains and charges into the expenses line rather than announcing them as separate items for many years. It argues that sales of what it deems intellectual property are part of its normal business and shouldn't be seen as one-off or in any way extraordinary. The only problem is that the investor was often left in the dark or otherwise searching through the footnotes of its full financial statements, which are issued some weeks after the press release.

IBM, which has been criticized for its use of other such maneuvers—including pension gains and stock buybacks—to meet or beat earnings forecasts, has, like GE, agreed to disclose more financial information given the changed climate. "Given increased accounting scrutiny, IBM's proclivity to stretch to make earnings on disappointing revenue was becoming a liability," Merrill Lynch analyst Steven Milunovich told Reuters in April 2002. Still, the world's largest maker of computers is defiant about such accounting practices. "Let me just say once and again that we are proud of our accounting and disclosure practices," IBM's Chief Financial Officer John Joyce said on a conference call (also in April 2002). He said it would be "absurd" to characterize intellectual property sales as non-recurring items. However, the company has recently been disclosing such gains in a separate line in its earnings press releases.

Still, this is a lesson for us all. When a company as prestigious as IBM can behave like this and still keep on the right side of securities and accounting regulations, then many others will be doing the same, and a significant number will be stepping over the line. Be very wary of even the sniff of the use of one-time gains to bolster earnings. Remember, once a business is sold, the earnings stream is lost and any gains really are one-time—you can't sell an asset again.

> **Note**
>
> Always try to strip out one-time items from earnings before deciding whether they are a true reflection of recurring performance.

Red Flag 3

When a One-Time Charge Becomes a Permanent Part of Results

Imagine every year telling your bank manager that spending much more than you are earning is not a problem because you have decided to take a one-time charge to restructure a part of your life, your job, or your relationship with someone. Well, that is exactly what companies do to investors when they constantly take one-time charges for this restructuring or for those lay-offs or for this or that liability arising from a lawsuit—and any number of other reasons. The idea they try to get across is that as these are so-called one-time items, this isn't real money. They try to get investors to focus on earnings before these items.

This might be okay if this one-time problem really happens only once in a blue moon, but the serial one-time chargers are to be regarded with great suspicion. The fear is that real costs of the business are being chucked into a one-time charge bucket. One company that has had a preponderance of one-time charges is mobile phone and chip maker Motorola Inc., which reported a $203 million pre-tax charge in the fourth quarter of 2002 for the costs of restructuring and asset impairment, including employee severance and debt redemption costs, making it the sixteenth successive quarter it had reported a one-time charge.

If you have to spend a large amount of money to close down a project that failed, it should be regarded with as much concern as any management mistake and not cast off into some separate hinterland in the accounts.

Shareholder activist Herbert Denton said that when a top official from health group Aetna gave "a dismissive wave of his hand at one annual meeting, saying, 'well that $3 billion is a non-cash charge,' I felt like saying, 'Well it used to be cash, it used to be cash.'"

> **Note**
>
> Think of one-time charges as real money that is slipping out of the company's grasp and not just as some kind of irrelevant bookkeeping entry.

Red Flag 4
Companies Dipping In and Out of Cookie Jar Reserves

One of the tried and tested ways of disguising bad performance in a particular period is the use and abuse of reserves. Most companies set some money aside for a rainy day to allow for bad debts, or to cover the costs of integrating an acquired business. Various assumptions go into deciding how much there should be in these reserves, such as how many customers go bankrupt in a typical year, an estimated cost for closing a factory following a takeover, and so on. The size of the reserves should be based on conservative assumptions, so there is more than is likely to be needed.

However, just like children finding a cookie jar open on the kitchen table, executives, too, often find these reserves too big a temptation to resist. After all, here are funds that can be used to cover up holes in the accounts, which means that perhaps a CEO doesn't have to front up to the market and admit that he or she missed earnings forecasts and made some mistakes with that expensive marketing campaign. Not only could "borrowing" some money from these reserves save the CEO's and CFO's hides, but it could also prevent a plunge in the company's stock price and their stock options with it. Indeed, some companies even set up special reserves just for this purpose.

Raiding the reserves is, however, a dangerous game. Take, for example, a wine distributor selling to hundreds of restaurants. He knows that some of the restaurants are likely to go out of business, and he also has his eye on some that are slow in paying their bills. He has therefore created a reserve for doubtful accounts that would cover 15 such bad debtors, even though in a normal year he would expect only 10.

Suddenly, his costs have gone through the roof and he is in danger of reporting lower earnings than he had forecast. So, instead of taking the hit and risking the market's wrath, he reduces the reserves so that they can only cover 12 customers who don't pay.

The result: He meets the forecasts, his share price is untouched because investors are oblivious to what is going on, but he has increased the risks within the business. The next quarter, he reduces the figure to 10, this time to cover another drop-off in revenue.

Eventually, though, he gets caught out. The economy suddenly heads into a recession and 15 of his customers close their businesses in a year. With the doubtful accounts reserve depleted, he has to take a hit to earnings and also expose himself to accusations of reckless risk taking.

The SEC said in June 2002 that Microsoft kept seven reserve accounts between 1994–1998 that allowed it to artificially change its income in various quarters. The software behemoth was ordered by the SEC to cease and desist from committing violations, though the company didn't admit or deny the commission's findings. The total balance of these accounts, which was affected by a whole range of items including some sales, depreciation charges, and interest income, varied from $200 million to $900 million. In a good quarter, Microsoft would set aside some money to add to these reserves, but in other quarters, it would raid the cookie jars to bolster its profits. "By including these adjustments in its financial statements, Microsoft failed to accurately report its financial results, causing overstatements of income in some quarters and understatements of income during other quarters," said the SEC in a statement at the time of the order.

Red Flag 5

Serial Acquirers Who Disguise Performance with the Next Big Deal

Companies can use acquisitions to artificially boost earnings in a number of ways. One of the easiest is the manipulation of a target company's results around the time an acquisition is completed. By raising its costs just before that key date (through, for example, getting management to pay staff bonuses and other expenses before they were due), the company can reduce the costs of the business in the year after acquisition. It can play a similar trick with revenue by delaying the booking of sales until after the completion, boosting sales performance later.

Of course, at some stage, the music stops and the acquisitions dry up. This is especially the case with companies that were using their stock as an acquisition currency and then found it had lost a lot of value.

An investigation conducted for Tyco by law firm Boies, Schiller & Flexner LLP concluded that during the reign of indicted former CEO Dennis Kozlowski, management was aggressive in its accounting for acquisitions with the aim of increasing reported financial results, according to a report by Tyco issued at the end of 2002. The former management had sought out techniques that would boost profits while shying away from those that would reduce them, the investigators' report said. Tyco appeared to boost post-acquisition earnings in some of the companies it was acquiring by influencing management of the takeover targets to artificially reduce revenue or increase expenses in the quarter immediately before the deal was completed, in a process known as springloading.

Fortune magazine reported in April 2002 that five former employees and a former consultant at electronics manufacturer Raychem, which was bought by Tyco in 1999 for $2.9 billion, said they were asked by Tyco officials to accelerate costs and hold back payments with the implied purpose of boosting the acquirer's cash-flow. This went on between the time the deal was announced in May 1999 and its completion in August of the same year, the magazine said.

Red Flag 6

Using Aggressive Pension Fund Assumptions to Reach Earnings Targets

In the second half of 2002, many companies were waking up to a massive hangover as they realized that the days when they could drive up their earnings with gains from their employee pension funds were fast coming to a close. Indeed, negative returns on pension fund assets because of the plummeting stock market mean that many face a deficit in funding their company pension plans, and instead of recording windfall gains, they are having to stump up cash and take a hit to earnings. A study by Credit Suisse First Boston, published in the autumn of 2002, estimated that of the 360 companies in the Standard & Poor's 500 index that have pension plans, 325 were set to have shortfalls by the end of that year. According to the study's author, David Zion, in dollar terms, the shortfall was estimated to reach a staggering $240 billion. "It is a huge issue because pensions have been almost a profit center for some companies, and we think that the rate of return assumptions are too high and there will be significant shortfalls because the market is in decline," said short seller David Tice.

Hardest hit tend to be manufacturing companies with union workers because they often have defined benefit plans that provide guaranteed pensions to retirees. This group includes General Motors Corp. and Ford Motor Co. and conglomerates such as 3M, United Technologies Corp., and GE. Many companies have been sticking their heads in the sand and keeping to assumptions of 9–11 percent returns on pension fund assets when they have been suffering losses. Investor Warren Buffett, who has criticized such high assumptions, pegged the rate for his Berkshire Hathaway Inc. at 6.5 percent in recent years. Anything higher than that might be fine if stock prices were going to rally back to levels of two years ago, but at the time of writing, that seems unlikely anytime soon. General Motors, for example, made a negative 7 percent return on its pension assets in 2002, though it retained a 10-percent-a-year returns assumption.

Under current accounting rules, companies are allowed to smooth pension fund returns over a number of years so that the impact of a year or two of market declines will be balanced by returns in previous years without a hit being taken by profits. However, a third year of the bear market means that for many companies, the gains made in the tech-boom years are being more than wiped out. Even more of a concern for investors is that many large companies have been quite legally propping up earnings by billions of dollars because of the higher return assumptions—even as the pension funds were losing money. These assumptions can also be tweaked upward even when there is little justification, helping to boost earnings and perhaps cover a shortfall elsewhere. For example, phone company Verizon Communications pushed its assumptions up in 2000, helping earnings.

Concern that future stock market returns won't match those of the past 10–15 years began to force many companies to reduce their pension fund return assumptions to around 8–9 percent from 9–10 percent in the second half of 2002. But the new levels may still be too high. "I don't think companies have come clean yet," said analyst Robert Friedman of Standard & Poor's in February 2003.

Others are also worried that the ability to smooth returns over a long period of time means that investors get a misleading impression of the performance of a pension plan. "I think the danger of smoothing is that it creates a controversy over whether a company should be using 8.5 percent or 9.5 percent when the plan is actually earning 20 percent or losing 30 percent. It focuses everybody on a silly question rather than what is happening," said Patricia McConnell, an accounting analyst and senior managing director at brokerage house Bear Stearns.

Investors should always be suspicious of any upward adjustments in the assumptions about pension plan returns. There should also be concern if there are any signs that a company is painting a rosier picture than really exists because eventually any shortfall will have to be funded.

> **Note**
>
> Always read pension entries and footnotes in financial statements and look for changes in returns or assumptions as well as shortfalls or overfunding.

Red Flag 7

Companies That Talk of New Paradigm Measurements of Performance

We all should have learned our lesson from the Internet stocks boom and bust, but you never know. Remember, in those crazy days in 1997–2000, money was being pumped into companies that had little chance of selling much, let alone turning a real net profit. We were told that it didn't matter and that sales were less important in the early stages of Internet growth than clicks, eyeballs, or unique visitors on or to web sites. In her book *Now or Never: How Companies Must Change Today to Win the Battle for Internet Consumers* (published in 2000), Mary Modahl of Forrester Research Inc. captured much of the wrongheaded thinking of that age when she told us that the Internet newcomers "change the components of revenue and cost in such a way that traditional companies find it difficult to counterattack." She further writes that "superliquid venture funds and individual investors can bankroll years of gigantic losses in a bid to win market share from traditional companies." Modahl cites Internet retailer Buy.com as an example of a company for which "advertising from corporate sponsors creates a revenue stream that supports lower prices."

Well, the problem was that in many cases, the web retailers could not transform the components of cost and revenue, and the money ran out quickly. They could only sell products that cost them $1 for 50 cents—while still burning through the initial financing from venture capitalists and initial public offerings. And, while Buy.com has survived, it only held on by its fingertips. In 2001, the company, which once had a market value of $5.5 billion, was taken private by its founder Scott Blum, who paid just $25 million.

If future "new paradigm" measurements of a company's health are thrust down investors' throats by executives, their image people and their bankers, the riposte clearly has to be "show us the money." And, the money should be real revenue and net profit without anything being excluded.

Red Flag 8

Beware of Companies That Use Risky Stock Hedging Strategies

When times are good and a stock price is riding high, it is difficult for a company to consider the risks it may face if there is a reversal. However, it is vital for investors that companies think the unthinkable because failure to do so can lead to a far uglier setback than could be caused by the economy or competition. This was the case with computer services giant Electronic Data Systems Corp. (EDS), which sold "put options" to investors when it was in a go-go period as a way to offset costs associated with employee stock option programs.

A put option gives its owner the right to sell shares back to the company that issued it at a set price at some point in the future. EDS issued such options with an exercise price of about $62, making them worthless if the price of the company's stock went above that level (it headed above $70 late in 2001) and allowing the company to pocket the money it received for the actual price of the options. But, as when the tech boom fizzled and the stock price plummeted in 2002, EDS was suddenly faced with having to buy back shares at $62 that were only trading in the market at about $17. The total cost of settling these options and related forward contracts was $225 million, which led to fears of a cash crunch and prompted investors to drive its share price down even further, to just above $10 in September 2002. "It was free money as long as the stock kept going up," Abe Mastbaum, managing director at New York money management firm American Securities told Reuters. "But once it turns round it becomes significantly less pleasant."

Note

Keep a close eye on hedging strategies that may lead to major liabilities if a share price drops or some other event occurs. Of course, this is easier said than done because it often means combing through pages of complex footnotes to find such information—if a company discloses it fully in the first place.

Red Flag 9

When Net Profit Is Rising but Cash Flow Is Declining or Negative

When Lucent Technologies reported its financial results on October 26, 1999, the telecom equipment maker's then CEO Richard McGinn boasted of achieving the strongest quarter and the strongest year in the company's history. "Lucent enters the new millennium with momentum," he declared. The figures the company issued in its press release seemed to bear out his confidence. The company's net profit (including one-time items) had more than quadrupled to $4.77 billion from $1.04 billion the year before, and even after taking non-recurring gains and losses out of the picture, profit was still up 46 percent.

Crucially, though, the release didn't include either a balance sheet or a cash-flow statement. When those were finally given a public airing almost two months later, the picture was very different. Cash flow from operations, which can be a very useful measurement of a company's ability to produce cold, hard cash from its everyday business and can also be a key indicator of its ability to pay back debt, was a negative $276 million against a positive $1.86 billion in the previous year. Major reasons for this setback for cash flow were a surge in receivables (money owed to the company by customers for goods and services) and a surge in inventories (the supplies in hand in the form of finished and unfinished goods and raw materials or goods on consignment to customers). To some analysts, this indicated that Lucent was suffering from reduced demand, had an increasing number of customers who were finding it difficult to pay for the company's goods, or was boosting its sales and net profit by supplying customers with merchandise on consignment that they didn't want.

McGinn's confident statement was soon proven wrong. The company headed into a period of 11 successive quarterly losses (and still running) at the time of writing. McGinn was forced out in the fall of 2000 because of the financial setbacks, its stocks dropped to less than $1 in 2002 from more than $80 at their peak in November 1999, and Lucent faced a probe by the SEC into whether it recorded revenue improperly. In February 2003, Lucent said it had settled the SEC probe by consenting to a prohibition against future violations of various securities laws, while not admitting or denying wrongdoing. Still, some analysts were even talking about bankruptcy as a possibility in the longer run for Lucent if it continues to burn through its remaining cash and the market for telecom equipment doesn't pick up.

A statement of cash flows is in some ways like a bank statement that takes information from both the profit and loss account and from the balance sheet while adding some additional data. It can usually be found just after the profit and loss statement in a company's financial statements. There are three parts. First and most important is cash flow from operating activities, which is supposed to give you a picture of how much cash is being produced by a company's normal operations—taking the net profit figure and then stripping out all the non-cash elements such as changes in inventories and accounts payable. Then, there is cash flow from investing activities (which includes payments for property, plant, and equipment), proceeds or costs from investments, and changes in cash from making and collecting loans. Finally, there is cash flow from financing activities, which includes changes in cash balances due to debt or equity raisings or repayments, stock repurchases, and dividend payouts.

Former SEC chairman Breeden says that investors should be suspicious if net earnings aren't being at least matched by cash flows. "I believe a profit has happened when a profit is in the bank and everything else is a model," he said.

Note

Always check the cash flow statement and particularly cash flow from operating activities. Contrast the percentage change in cash flow from operations with the rate of earnings growth.

Red Flag 10

Now, a Contradictory Warning— Cash Flow Can Also Be Manipulated

I've just given you a tool with which to detect possible shenanigans, and a moment later, I am casting doubt on its credibility. I have suggested that investors tired of being deceived by management manipulation of earnings before interest depreciation and amortization (Ebitda), pro-forma earnings, core profits, and even good old net profit could try going with the flow—cash flow from operations.

However, in the accounting scams of the past few years, cash flow suffered as much as any other benchmark in the hands of a chief financial officer who wanted to monkey with the numbers. By engaging in some accounting tricks, companies can "improve on their apparent operating performance and potentially gain some of the rewards of the financial numbers game ... by taking steps to boost operating cash flow even in the absence of changes in total cash flow," write Charles Mulford and Eugene Comiskey in *The Financial Numbers Game.*

For example, those who turn regular business expenses into costs that are capitalized over a number of years, who use complex securities or commodities trading arrangements that are designed to artificially inflate or be opaque, or who securitize receivables can radically change the cash flow picture. Tax benefits, particularly those from stock option plans for employees, can also have a big impact.

Take energy trading and pipeline company Dynegy Inc., which set up a multi-year natural-gas transaction called Project Alpha that enabled it to use a $300 million loan from Citigroup Inc. to raise its reported cash flow from operations by $300 million and cut its tax bill at the same time. After the SEC began to investigate in April 2002, Dynegy decided to put the questionable $300 million into a separate financing part of the statement. Three months later, it issued a warning that its cash flow would slump by as much as 40 percent from previous forecasts, sending its stock price down 60 percent in a day and casting doubts over its viability as a standalone enterprise. In September 2002, without admitting any wrongdoing, Dynegy agreed to make a $3 million payment to the SEC for alleged accounting improprieties and potentially misleading energy trades. It also restated earnings for three years in November 2002.

I realize that understanding this may take a little effort. Many analysts will play around with the basic cash flow figures and add or subtract various items to come up with what they believe to be a purer representation of recurring performance. You may, for example, hear the phrase "free cash flow," which is cash after the subtraction of replacement capital spending and dividends. Creditors sometimes look at "net cash after operations," which is cash after the addition of interest payments, to get an idea of the cash available to service debts. Indeed, some analysts say that these kinds of measurements are too complicated for the average mainstream investor. "Every text an investor looks at is going to define cash earnings differently," said McConnell at Bear Stearns, who believes it is probably too confusing for most individual investors to look at various cash flow measurements when they have limited time and knowledge.

Red Flag 11

A Company Grows Much Faster Than Its Rivals with No Clear Explanation

This one goes in the "too good to be true" category of warnings. You have to be able to understand how a company can report sterling results while rivals in the same industry have been struggling. For example, WorldCom's, Global Crossing's, and Qwest Communications' relatively high growth rates around the start of the millennium infuriated some competitors in the telecommunications industry because they couldn't work out why they were lagging. Of course, WorldCom's declaration of a massive accounting deception over the summer of 2002 and Qwest's announcement in the autumn that it was restating at least $950 million of revenue and costs from swaps of network capacity with other carriers answered many of their rivals' questions. Global Crossing, which operated a fiber optic network in 27 countries and filed for bankruptcy protection amid crippling debts, has also been investigated by a congressional committee looking at whether it used sham transactions to boost revenue and mislead investors.

Accounting analysts say that companies recording extraordinary growth in revenue should be treated skeptically. "For crying out loud, all this growth people were seeing in revenue and nobody questioned it," said Jack Ciesielski, the publisher of the *Analysts' Accounting Observer*. "Where are the people asking the questions about how the growth was being achieved and about the specific transactions? I mean, those are kind of embarrassing questions that should have been asked at analysts' meetings," he said in reference to the lack of skepticism that he perceived existed among Wall Street analysts.

Manipulation of results can have an impact on an entire industry. *The New York Times* suggested in the summer of 2002 that telecommunications group AT&T Corp. may not have been broken up if it weren't for the skewed comparisons with WorldCom. The newspaper quoted AT&T vice chairman Charles Noski as saying the company's executives would dissect all of WorldCom's public information but couldn't understand how it came up with its results. "We were certainly frustrated because we couldn't figure it out," he was quoted as saying.

So sometimes the better a company's results, the more suspicious you should be. At least make sure you know that the company reached the Holy Grail through legitimate means—perhaps by cutting a bloated bureaucracy or launching a successful new product—and not just through accounting sleight of hand.

Note

Always compare and contrast performance across an industry.

Red Flag 12
When Earnings Growth Is a Lot Faster Than Sales Growth

When a company's earnings are increasing at a much faster pace than its sales, especially over a long period, it can be a sign that a company is either using various accounting tricks or that it is recklessly slashing spending. It is fine if costs are being cut through increasing productivity and a leaner and meaner approach to suppliers. But, too often, companies may be cutting spending that is necessary for longer-term growth. "We like to see earnings grow at roughly the same pace as sales," said short seller David Tice. "If earnings are growing a lot faster than sales, then it could be that the company is cutting back on discretionary expenditure, like selling expenses, research and development expenses, and advertising expenses. It will help earnings per share now but it will hurt it later." In the next chapter, we look more closely at how revenue and costs can be manipulated and ways to spot companies that do it.

9

Goosing, Stuffing, and Faking: Tricks of the Trade to Drive Revenue Up and Costs Down

"In the corporate world, some things aren't exactly black and white when it comes to accounting procedures."

—President George W. Bush at a news conference on July 8, 2002, a day before announcing a crackdown on corporate criminals and as he defended his own past business dealings

Now let's look at the truly creative. Playing around with a few asset sales, some pension gains, or "cookie jar" reserves to prop up earnings is one thing. But this is small time crookery to the real manipulators and deceivers. They prefer to simply scratch a few billion dollars from one column and put the money in another, to stop the computer clocks so that a late order can have a timestamp before the end of a quarter and be counted in that period's revenue, or to send trucks of goods to their own warehouses and declare them sold. Some prefer faking invoices, forging colleagues' signatures, or adding figures ahead of or after the original numbers in an email so that a contract appears to have the value of millions rather than thousands of dollars. All this has happened at publicly traded companies in recent years as the desperate and greedy not only cook the books but dice and stir fry them, too. Sadly, such behavior has been far from limited to penny stock companies.

The aim is usually to either artificially raise revenues or depress costs—and, in doing so, to boost reported earnings or cash flow. Under U.S. accounting rules, to record revenue, there should be evidence of a sale, delivery has to have occurred, or the service has to have been rendered, the price is fixed or easy to determine and payment must be reasonably assured. Unfortunately, executives under pressure to reach Wall Street expectations will too often ignore one or more of those requirements. Also, they will use flexibility within the rules to get their auditors to give the nod to barely legal maneuvers. "Revenue recognition, sales growth, depends on very judgmental factors—when is the sale complete has always been a tough one," said Jack Ciesielski, the publisher of the *Analyst's Accounting Observer*.

Sometimes, the fraud can be stunningly simple, requiring little more guile than needed by the guy who holds up a gas station. Other times, the trickery will include complex financial structures that would take a team of lawyers and accountants months to tear apart and understand. Often, though, there will be telltale signs that can let investors know that something just doesn't add up—sometimes literally.

In this chapter, I am going to describe some of the main deceptions related to revenue and costs and outline some of the ways you may be able to detect them before it is too late.

Red Flag 1

Any Signs That Companies Are Reducing Costs by Capitalizing Them

Corporate spending can be divided into two categories. There are the purchases of raw materials and payment of wages, rent, and advertising costs that are clearly operating expenses. These have to be offset against revenue on a quarterly basis. Then there is the purchase of some big-ticket items that are used over a number of years, such as a fleet of new vehicles for a trucking firm. The latter costs are capitalized, which means that an asset is created on the company's balance sheet and is then written off (through an annual depreciation charge) over its productive life. This asset is going to be used to produce revenue over a longer period than a quarter or a year, and therefore the costs should be taken over a longer period to reflect that. At the same time, the annual depreciation charge is an acknowledgment that the asset will eventually be spent and will have to be replaced.

Now, the big temptation for a company under severe financial strain is to capitalize costs that should be part of its regular expenses. Let's say a company capitalizes a $100 million purchase of raw materials over five years on the fallacious basis that this is the period over which the benefits from their use would accrue. That means in the year in which the raw materials are used to produce finished products, the company will only take one fifth of the cost and yet get all the benefit from the resulting sales of goods. Result: an immediate lift to earnings. In essence, this is what WorldCom did when it capitalized the costs of leasing line capacity from other telecommunications companies, which was a major part of its $9 billion deception. Such costs were clearly regular costs that should have been reported in the period in which they occurred rather than written off over a number of years. Until it was discovered, though, the deception did the trick—while some of its rivals were being routed amid a vicious price war in 2001, WorldCom continued to report profits.

"I was instructed on a quarterly basis by senior management to ensure that entries were made to falsify WorldCom's books to reduce WorldCom's reported actual costs, and, therefore increasing WorldCom's reported earnings," the company's former controller David Myers said in September 2002 when pleading guilty to securities fraud charges.

Among other major companies alleged by regulators to have capitalized costs was America Online Inc. before its takeover of Time Warner. In May 2000, AOL agreed to pay the SEC $3.5 million as part of a civil case brought by the regulator against the Internet company for reporting the marketing costs from gaining new subscribers in the mid-1990s—which was mainly sending computer disks to potential customers—as an asset to be depreciated rather than an ordinary business expense. It made the difference between AOL's reporting profits in six out of eight quarters and reporting losses. AOL paid the penalty and agreed to stop doing such things in the future, but it did not admit to or deny the charges.

One of the cheekiest moves of all was by accounting company PricewaterhouseCoopers (PwC), which according to the SEC helped two of its audit clients, wireless tower operator Pinnacle Holdings Inc. and cosmetics group Avon Products Inc., to improperly account for costs, including consulting fees for PwC in 1999–2000. In July 2002, PwC agreed to pay a $5 million penalty, and to settle charges that its auditors approved improper accounting and that it violated independence standards. It was the second-largest such payment ever made by an accounting firm, though it also didn't admit to or deny the charges.

Other maneuvers to look out for include the capitalizing of costs for the hiring and training of staff for a new operation, such as a store or restaurant. And, some companies even try to reverse the usual attempts to postpone costs by instead burying them in quarters that have already passed. Investors should be particularly on the lookout for any change in accounting policy regarding the way costs are accounted for, though often a lack of disclosure is also part of the problem.

Note

Getting to know what the normal policy is in an industry can help a lot. If a company has a policy that is more aggressive than its rivals and that is making it look better by comparison, then it may be best avoided as an investment. This is where common sense comes in. If a company is doing better than its rivals, there has to be a logical explanation.

Red Flag 2

When Companies Depreciate Assets over an Unrealistically Long Time

You may think the electrical appliances in your kitchen will last for 5 to 10 years before they either start to break down or look tacky, and you may budget for replacements within that timeframe. Now, say you were suddenly strapped for cash—and it is already year 9: You might well extend the life of the appliances until your finances were back in better health after year 12. Well, companies will sometimes do the same—but they won't say that they are doing it because they are short of cash. Instead, they will often hide the change in the footnotes to their financial statements. By extending the life of assets—say a fleet of vehicles or seats in a movie theater—to 15 years from 10 years, a company will be able to prop up its earnings because the cost of depreciation will now be spread over the longer period. If the company has discovered a way of keeping that piece of machinery running longer in an efficient manner, there is no problem. Yet, too often, the extension is just an accounting trick to cover up a shortfall somewhere else. One way to see which is the case is to do a comparison with a company's rivals. If an oil company decides it can depreciate a pipeline over 40 years when everyone else is using 25, it suggests aggressive accounting.

So, even when costs are capitalized properly, there is still plenty of room for trickery. Waste disposal and haulage company Waste Management Inc. is alleged to have claimed that its garbage trucks had much longer lives than they really did and then to have inflated the salvage values. This was part of an alleged massive fraud lasting more than five years. The SEC filed suit against the founder and former CEO Dean Buntrock and five other former officers in March 2002, alleging they inflated profits by $1.7 billion to meet earnings targets and reap almost $29 million in ill-gotten gains and describing it as "one of the most egregious" cases it had ever seen. Buntrock and at least three of the others have said that they will fight the charges.

> **Note**
>
> Two signs that there may be a problem include indications of past writedowns of assets because depreciation policy was too favorable (meaning the assets didn't retain their value as long as was allowed for in the accounts), and an average depreciation period for a company's assets that is much longer than for similar companies in the same industry.

Red Flag 3

Fabrication Is Possible When a Company's Top Customers Don't Check Out

Sometimes, fraud goes beyond switching numbers between columns or using a misleading accounting policy—sometimes it consists of pure fabrication. Take, for example, the case of German technology company Comroad AG, which said it developed traffic information systems for operators of public transport. Well, it rode the technology stocks boom to reach a market value of more than $1 billion and received a positive reception from analysts and the media in 2000. Even after the boom turned to a bust in 2001, Comroad defied the gloom, reporting sharply stronger earnings and sales and talking up its own prospects. Then, suddenly, in February 2002, its auditor KPMG resigned after expressing some doubts about some of Comroad's business relationships; KPMG refused to approve Comroad's 2001 accounts. A special auditor was called in and found that a company through which the vast majority of Comroad's sales were processed in 1998–2000, a Hong Kong company called VT Electronics, didn't exist, and there was no evidence that it ever had. It turned out that 98.5 percent of Comroad's 2001 reported sales of about $90 million could not be verified. Comroad's then CEO Bodo Schnabel was convicted of fraud and faking accounts in November 2002—accusations that he had said were "objectively and subjectively" correct, according to the Associated Press.

So, if someone wants to create fictitious companies, sales, and earnings—and auditors and banks don't find out for years—how is the mainstream investor supposed to find out? First, you should get some idea about who a company's major customers are. If the auditors can't be relied on to find out, perhaps it's up to you—especially if the company is not well known. Clearly, if there is even a hint that the customers aren't legitimate, it's time to hit the road. There had already been some warning signs in the media concerning Comroad. The German investor magazine *Platow-Boerse* expressed concern about the company's sales targets in April 2001, though Schnabel at the time denied there were any problems. This shows that clearly if investors are going to take their chances on international markets they have to get wired into relevant local media as well as international publications and news services.

Red Flag 4

If a Company Pumps Out Too Many Goods in a Particular Period

Shipping more products than customers want is a favorite way of boosting revenue and income toward the end of a quarter. The company books all the revenue from the shipments in the period they were dispatched, even though the goods may be gathering dust on the shelves of a warehouse. It may also have offered customers incentives to take the goods, such as discounts or favorable terms for returning the goods if they can't be sold. The result of this practice, sometimes known as channel stuffing, is either a rapid growth in accounts receivable or lower orders in future quarters—or both. The business is essentially stealing sales from a future period, usually to cover up a shortfall somewhere else.

Drug maker Bristol-Myers Squibb, the company behind such drugs as the breast-cancer treatment Taxol, is accused by industry analysts and class action lawyers of indulging in some channel stuffing in 2001 by encouraging wholesalers to buy more drugs than they could sell. Indeed, it sold the equivalent of around 56 weeks of drugs in 2001, which left a bulge of inventories at the wholesalers that meant they didn't need so much of the company's products in 2002. As a result, sales dropped in 2002 and the company had to restate its results amid probes from the SEC and the Department of Justice. Of course, companies hope they can counter the impact of any excess shipments by selling new products at greater speed in future periods. In Bristol-Myers Squibb's case, this wasn't achievable. In a statement in April 2002, the company said that it had "begun to reduce shipments in an attempt to lower inventories to levels more consistent with market demand." However, in July of that year, when acknowledging the SEC inquiry, Bristol-Myers said it believed "that its accounting treatment of the domestic wholesaler inventory buildup has been completely appropriate." In March 2003, the company said it had overstated sales by $2.3 billion between 1999 and 2001, and cut $900 million from previously reported earnings.

One famous alleged channel stuffer was Al Dunlap, the former CEO at kitchen appliance maker Sunbeam. He got retailers to buy the company's products such as gas grills well before they were needed through the use of discounts and other inducements, according to the SEC. In some cases, the customers didn't receive the grills immediately—they were shipped to a warehouse leased by Sunbeam—and received discounts for the early orders. They didn't have to pay for them straight away either, though Dunlap didn't delay booking the sales, making Sunbeam, which eventually filed for bankruptcy protection, look as if it was doing much better than it was. Dunlap agreed to make a payment of $500,000 to the SEC and consented to being barred from serving as an officer or director of a public company, without admitting or denying this and other allegations of accounting shenanigans included in the settlement.

When receivables and inventories are soaring, it can be a sign that a company is bringing forward sales through channel stuffing or other means. At Sunbeam in 1997, for example, sales rose about 19 percent but receivables surged 38.5 percent and inventories 57.9 percent. As a result, the company reported a negative cash from operations figure even as its net profit climbed. Clearly, a lot of goods weren't being sold or were not paid for quickly. Climbing inventories can also mean that a company is having difficulty selling its products for another reason—perhaps because a competitor has slashed prices.

Note

Always check inventories and receivables growth against sales growth.

Red Flag 5

When a Company Is Taking Longer to Convert Sales into Cash

It is all very well to have strong sales growth, but when a company is taking longer than usual to convert those sales into cash, it can be a sign of trouble ahead. For example, in 1999, telecom equipment maker Lucent Technologies needed about 40 percent longer to convert an average sale into cash than in 1997—93 days versus 68 days. Both inventories and receivables were climbing faster than sales at the time. Lucent struggled from the end of 1999 as cutbacks in telephone company spending forced it to slash jobs and money-losing production, post billions of dollars in losses, and watch as its market value collapsed.

You can work out a cash conversion cycle for any company by calculating the amount of revenue a company makes per day in a period and then use this to figure out how many days it would take to drain or turn its inventories (days inventories outstanding) and how many days of sales it is owed by customers through the receivables (days sales outstanding). You add these two together and then take away the number of days a company waits before paying its bills, which is the days of accounts payable outstanding (calculated based on costs of goods sold). The result is the length of the firm's cash conversion cycle. On this basis, Wal-Mart had a cash conversion cycle of just 8 days at the end of its financial year in January 2002, little changed from 7 days a year earlier, which shows just how much of a generator and conserver of cash the retailing behemoth is.

Red Flag 6

Companies Bringing Forward Revenue from Longer-Term Contracts

Companies will often push the envelope by booking a large proportion of revenue from a longer-term contract on signing, which has the potential to pump up earnings in the short term and risk a future setback. The reason that such a practice is dangerous is that the revenue is being taken early but some of the costs of servicing that contract will occur in subsequent years. Take, for example, a company that is leasing construction equipment and providing follow-up service as part of a five-year deal. If it pushes the entire revenue through its accounts in the first year, it could get an earnings boost because the offsetting costs will be only partial. However, in years two-through-five, it will face nothing but costs through its accounts while it pays staff to service the equipment, and its earnings could be hit as a result.

Copier maker Xerox Corp. paid a record $10 million penalty to the SEC in April 2002 after charges that it used highly questionable accounting policies to inflate its earnings between 1997–2000. In the complaint that led to the settlement, the SEC charged that Xerox "created the illusion that its operating results were substantially better than they really were." Xerox had recorded revenue it expected to receive from servicing the equipment and financing the leases as if the revenue was from equipment "sales" that could be recognized immediately rather than over the period of the contract. Under accounting rules, only a portion of the contract—related directly to the leasing of the equipment—can be accounted for straight away. Xerox had also retroactively increased the "residual value" of the equipment it was leasing, something that is banned under accounting rules. Residual value is the estimated fair market value of the equipment at the end of the lease. These, and related indiscretions, were far from minor.

The company had accelerated the recognition of $3 billion of revenue and increased its pre-tax earnings by about $1.5 billion, according to the SEC. In the fourth quarters of 1998 and 1999, such accounting techniques had generated 37 percent of the company's pre-tax profit, and without them, it would have fallen well short of Wall Street earnings expectations in almost every quarter between 1997–1999. (Of course, as we are seeing happens often in SEC actions, Xerox settled with the SEC without admitting or denying the charges.) The SEC's director of enforcement, Stephen Cutler, said in a statement at the time of the settlement that Xerox had used its accounting to "burnish and distort" its results. "For Xerox, the accounting function was just another revenue source and profit opportunity. As a result, investors were misled and betrayed," he said.

> **Note**
>
> Always check a company's revenue policies in its financial statements and compare and contrast them with accepted practice in the industry concerned. For example, if you are analyzing the number three company in an industry, compare its revenue policy with number one and number two.

Red Flag 7

Companies That Record Bogus Revenue Achieved through Swaps

At one stage in 2002, it seemed that just about every major telecom company and energy trader in the United States had been using some kind of swap agreement that had no real economic purpose; the tactic merely made it seem as if revenue was growing rapidly. These agreements had all kinds of weird names—wash trades, round-trippers, boomerangs, lazy Susans—but they all added up to one thing: a distorted picture of how well a business is doing.

When demand started to sag in 2000–2001, a number of telecom companies, including Qwest Communications International and Global Crossing Ltd., exchanged approximately equal values of fiber-optic line capacity and recognized the deals as revenue. Amid investigations by the SEC and the Department of Justice and following the appointment of new management, Qwest announced in September and October 2002 that it was reversing or deferring $1.48 billion in revenue from such swaps and sales of network capacity for 2000 and 2001. Global Crossing also restated some earnings and revenue in October 2002 and cut both its assets and liabilities by $1.2 billion on its balance sheet as a result.

Both blamed advice from auditors Andersen for the way the transactions were improperly recorded. "Confronted with shrinking markets and declining business volume, executives at Global Crossing and Qwest used capacity swaps to conceal slowing growth by booking fictitious revenues," said the chairman of the U.S. House Energy and Commerce subcommittee on investigations, James Greenwood, at a hearing in September 2002.

Meanwhile, in the energy industry, a whole series of companies have either admitted engaging in "wash" trades to boost revenue or are under investigation for it by the SEC. Energy trader Dynegy agreed to pay a $3 million penalty as settlement of SEC charges that it overstated its trading activity and concerning improper accounting of another transaction in September 2002 (again without admitting or denying the allegations). "Dynegy misled investors about the level of its energy trading activity by failing to disclose that the company's publicly released numbers included results inflated by such sham trades," said Harold Degenhardt, administrator of the SEC's Fort Worth, Texas, office. Regulators fear that such artificial boosting of activity recorded in the electricity and natural gas markets may have helped to raise power prices during the California power crisis of 2000–2001. In October 2002, Enron trader Timothy Belden admitted in a San Francisco court that he was part of a conspiracy to raise electricity prices in the state, a conspiracy that boosted Enron's profits at the time.

It is very difficult for an outside investor to know whether a company is engaging in such sham trading. A comparison with rivals' revenue growth would be helpful, though only if they weren't engaged in exactly the same practices. Certainly, investors should steer clear of companies they hear indulge in artificial transactions. For one thing, it suggests that such companies would be capable of other deceptions.

Red Flag 8

Beware of Companies That Record the Entire Value of Trades As Their Revenue

Some companies are extremely generous in the way they decide what really constitutes revenue, and it is important that investors know whether this makes their financial statements directly comparable with those of competitors. Enron's booking of the value of all its energy trading contracts as revenue, rather than just its trading revenue, helped to propel the company to the number five spot in the *Fortune* 500, even as it was heading into bankruptcy. Enron recorded $138.7 billion in revenues in the year of its collapse, putting it ahead of General Electric Co. and Citigroup. Clearly, this is nonsense—even at its height, Enron was nowhere near as important to the U.S. economy as companies like those. A decision by accounting rulemakers in 2002 to require energy traders to subtract the cost of sales from gross revenue figures to produce a "net revenue" number is reducing this practice, though the gross revenue technique is still used by some companies in other industries.

Red Flag 9

Companies That Indulge in Barter Deals Should Raise Suspicions

Companies that sell their wares and don't receive cold hard cash in return but instead get payment in goods and services or through other arrangements should be watched carefully. Too often, such barter arrangements blow up or lead to accounting scandals. During the Internet stocks boom, such arrangements were normal. The problem was that when the companies at the other end of the transactions went out of business or provided services of dubious value in return, the barter often collapsed. "If you go back to the beginning of the Internet boom, I think that is where a lot of the emphasis on revenue got started because there weren't any profits, so let's do what we can to show things gross rather than net, let's do barter with my web site or yours," said Ciesielski.

AOL Time Warner was involved in some barter-type deals and in some round-trip arrangements with the likes of WorldCom and Qwest, and they have come back to bite the media mammoth. In October 2002, AOL Time Warner said it would restate two years of results—cutting $190 million in revenues partly due to allegedly improper accounting for advertising deals. The restatements cut both operating earnings and net earnings in the periods concerned. Both the SEC and the Department of Justice were holding their own probes into AOL's accounting, with no sign of a formal announcement of progress at the time of writing.

Red Flag 10

When Companies Provide Vendor Financing, It Can Backfire

When companies provide their customers with financing to buy their products, it can be a very risky business. If the customers get into trouble, they can default on their payments and suddenly the contract can turn into a nightmare. Even worse, the financing is sometimes not fully disclosed, leaving investors flat-footed when it becomes a problem. Take the example of wireless phone makers Motorola and Nokia, which lent the family that owns Turkey's number two wireless operator, Telsim, more than $2.5 billion and at the time of writing were suing for their money back and alleging fraud under U.S. anti-racketeering laws. Motorola had to write off almost all its share of the loans less than a year after it had triumphantly announced a third-generation mobile phone network deal with Telsim. Motorola has received repayments of only $170 million of $2 billion in loans to Telsim. In

December 2002, a British judge sentenced a member of Telsim's controlling family, Turkish media baron Cem Uzan, to 15 months in prison in absentia for contempt of court after he failed to show up at hearings in which Motorola and Nokia had asked for a freeze on his assets. The Uzans deny the allegations from the telecom companies that they never intended to repay the loans and have been seeking arbitration of the matter in Switzerland.

Note

Look for disclosure of large vendor financing deals and ask yourself what will happen if they go bad.

Red Flag 11

If Companies Use Their Own Assumptions to Assess the Value of Contracts

We have already seen that there is plenty of room for tweaking revenue and profit figures depending on accounting methods used, but in the energy trading sector, use of the word "tweaking" would be an understatement. One of the issues that arose over the disintegration of Enron was the wildly optimistic assumptions that went into the energy merchant's assessment of profits and revenues from long-term energy contracts. The contracts, often stretching many years into the future, were not traded on an exchange, so companies made their own assumptions about their worth. This practice, of course, left plenty of room for manipulation and deception. It is very difficult for an investor to decide whether the delivery of electricity or natural gas in 2007 is being priced fairly within a company's accounts. In October 2002, accounting rulemakers appeared to close the door on some of these practices by declaring that on some types of contracts, energy traders will only be able to record the revenue and income from the contracts at the time of delivery and billing. However, many derivative contracts can still be valued based on a model that might have little to do with their eventual value.

Red Flag 12
When Plane Makers Use Wrong Assumptions to Spread Project Costs

Investors in aircraft makers can sometimes get a rude awakening when they realize the companies have been using over-optimistic assumptions in their accounting for spending on aircraft production. Under a controversial accounting method known as "program accounting," the plane makers can use an assumed average cost of production in any one period rather than declaring the cost actually incurred in that period. The argument is that initial costs of a project are greater than costs incurred once production has been cranked up. That reasoning is all very well as long as the average cost is at least matched by revenue from sales, but if it isn't, the company could suddenly be forced into a big write-down of these deferred costs that investors weren't expecting. This was the case with defense contractor Lockheed in the 1970s and also contributed to a $2.6 billion charge announced by Boeing Co. in October 1997 because of a surge in production costs that started some time before.

Red Flag 13

When Construction Companies Include Disputed Cost Overruns in Revenue

If you ever wanted proof that accounts don't actually reflect money that came in and out of a company in a particular period, have a look at the way that some construction companies record revenues that have not only not been received but are actually in dispute. This occurs when the cost of a project exceeds original estimates and the builder seeks to reclaim the additional money from the customer.

Under U.S. accounting policies, companies such as oilfield services and construction group Halliburton Co.—which had U.S. Vice President Dick Cheney as its CEO between 1995–2000—say that including claims for cost overruns on contracts in revenue is a perfectly legitimate practice. "Claims and change orders which are in the process of being negotiated with customers for extra work or changes in the scope of the work are included in revenue when collection is deemed probable," Halliburton said in its notes to accounting policies in its annual financial statements beginning in March 2000.

This is a case study in how such footnotes are used to quietly disclose important changes. In 1998, the company had said the opposite, declaring that "claims for additional compensation are recognized during the period such claims are resolved." That year, with Cheney at the helm, Halliburton began to claim such revenue, although it did not disclose the change until the 2000 filing with the SEC. Lawsuits filed against Halliburton by investors in 2002 as a result of the accounting policy change allege that it overstated revenues by as much as $445 million. In December 2002, the company said that the SEC had intensified a probe into disclosure and accounting practices at the company, though both Halliburton and securities analysts say that the policies were appropriate. Cheney has refrained from commenting concerning the probe.

Of course, from an investor's perspective, whether appropriate or not, the biggest concern when a company can book revenue it hasn't received is that it opens the floodgates to over-optimistic assumptions and therefore possible manipulation.

Note

Always read and contrast notes to accounting policies with those disclosed in previous years.

10

Beyond Their Means: Balance Sheet Clues That May Stop You from Losing Your Shirt

"Profits are an opinion; cash is a fact."

—unknown

Early in 2001, one of the security guards in my apartment building was fired for borrowing money from many tenants without returning it. I was among the lenders, getting hit for $10. The guard was very convincing. Others in the building got hit for much more. We were all suffering from a lack of market information—this person was a bad credit risk and as individuals we only had a small part of the picture. Of course, if we had pooled our knowledge and realized how much we were all owed, we could have turned off the credit tap, but this is New York City, and many people don't chat with their neighbors.

Many stock market investors are too often snookered in a similar way, but they have less excuse, and instead of risking $10, they often risk $10,000 or more. They invest in companies without finding out about debt levels, interest costs, credit risk, and the prices at which that debt is trading. Stock prices, especially when there is a bull market, often don't reflect any of this until it is too late. As we shall see in this chapter, a little understanding of how the debt markets work and what to look out for can prevent a lot of heartache.

Debt is important because, quite simply, we are talking survival. Too much debt can destroy a company—and your investment with it. Think of any of the major corporate meltdowns in 2001–2002, and the debt burden became the critical element. In a bear market, when there is little positive news about sales growth or profit margins, the credit markets side of the picture becomes even more crucial. Sometimes, as in Enron's case, the collapses were caused by obligations that suddenly emerged after being cleverly disguised and hidden off the balance sheet. Even if it isn't enough to kill off a business, the financing costs that come with a big debt burden can eat into profits and reduce funds for expansion.

Therefore, your first stop before investing in a company should be the balance sheet and the line in the profit and loss account that details interest and financing costs. "To me the critical thing about any company is what the balance sheet looks like," said former SEC chairman Richard Breeden. "That is where the real wealth is, and that is where the real exposure is, that is how deep your pockets are, and how much adversity you can absorb is shown by the balance sheet."

Just as important as the level of debt on a balance sheet is when it is due to be repaid. For that information, you may need to wade through footnotes to the financial statements. One of the reasons that Tyco International's stock and bonds got hammered in 2002 was investors' concern that it wouldn't be able to refinance a mountain of debt maturing in the next few years. As a result, the company sought to offload some assets, which led to the resale at a big loss of the finance company CIT Group, which Tyco had bought only the previous year.

One of the first things any prospective investor in a company's stock or bonds should do is check out how the bonds are trading. This information, and an idea of the company's credit ratings (see section later in chapter), will give you an immediate idea of whether the company is in danger of defaulting on its debt and heading into bankruptcy. In bankruptcy, remember, stockholders often lose everything and bondholders are the first in line to claim the company's assets. Bond prices also give you an idea about how bond investors, who often have a more conservative bent than typical stock investors, view the company. Also, a company's troubles aren't fully reflected in the stock market sometimes, but they are in the bond market.

Brokers dealing directly with the public won't often talk about the company's debt prices, but investors mustn't let them get away with it. Unfortunately, bond markets are much less transparent than equity markets. There is no freely available real-time pricing, but any of the big Wall Street brokerages have trading desks that can give their broker an indicative price in a flash. If the broker won't do this for you, change brokers. You are already at a disadvantage compared with the Wall Street professionals, and any sign that you are to be thwarted in efforts to narrow this handicap is unacceptable.

You can also get an indication of bond prices from the web site of the National Association of Securities Dealers (*www.nasdbondinfo.com*). Click on bond search and then insert the name of a company and you can find prices for its bonds. For example, I can type "Ford Motor Co." and get a list of prices for many of its bonds. In March 2003, I could see that the automaker's 30-year bonds (the simple plain vanilla variety without any sprinkles) were priced around 71–80, well below "par" of 100. This pricing means that a $1,000 Ford bond was being sold for $710–$800, a level not much above junk bonds and well below where a blue chip company's debt should be priced. The yield on the bonds, which rises as bond prices fall and vice versa, ranged from 8.84 to 9.71 percent. Similar bonds issued by the financing arm of Ford's main rival General Motors Corp. were trading at around 95, or about $950 for a $1,000 bond, and had a yield of 8.48 percent.

So, what does all this tell us? It suggests that bond investors aren't as confident of Ford's future as they are of GM's. Purchasers of the Ford bonds have to be offered lower prices to guard against the higher risk they perceive. It also tells us that when raising money, Ford may be at a disadvantage compared with its main competitor, which can probably borrow at cheaper rates. A quick perusal of news reports and research shows us there is growing concern that Ford, which lost $5.45 billion in 2001 and $980 million in 2002, is trying to preserve its market share by offering costly incentives to buyers of its vehicles. This, plus fierce competition from foreign automakers in the U.S. market and a costly pension burden, is adding to investors' fears that it won't be able to return to sustained profitability anytime soon.

To see a really distressed situation, I looked at the bonds of insurance and finance company Conseco in October 2002. This was two months before it filed for bankruptcy, and the bonds told us that was likely to happen. Conseco's unsecured bonds maturing in 2004 were trading at just 4, meaning that $1,000 of face value of the bonds could be bought for $40, and the yield was 1,200 percent. (The NASD system does have some quirks. If it quotes a bond at 99.99 percent, as it did in this case, it invariably means the yield is above 100 percent.) This price and yield said that investors thought the company was likely to collapse and that in a bankruptcy they didn't expect unsecured creditors, like holders of these bonds, to be left with much once secured creditors had been paid out.

The Balance Sheet and Those Beloved Footnotes

So, we know we should look at the balance sheet and see whether the company we may want to invest in is "leveraged" with large amounts of debt. There are, however, two possible problems. First, perhaps we can't find a balance sheet in the company's latest quarterly earnings press release. Second, looking at the balance sheet isn't going to be enough.

Yes, in an era when investors have begun to demand more than just a dreamed-up earnings figure to trade from, many companies are still not issuing full balance sheets and cash-flow statements when they announce quarterly earnings. In October 2002, 24 of the 30 blue-chip companies that make up the Dow Jones industrial average did not break out a separate cash-flow statement in their latest release and a number of the most prominent—including General Electric and Walt Disney Co.—did not include balance sheets either, while others only included selected data such as assets and accounts receivable. Investors are told to wait a few weeks until the company files the full documents with the SEC—by which time the share price may have gone to the moon and back based on the earnings release.

The balance sheet is supposed to be a snapshot of the company's health at the end of a particular period. One of the problems is that it is far from a complete picture without the footnotes, and even after looking at those, we may have more questions than answers. For example, the balance sheet itself will only give us some combined figures for "current" or short-term debt obligations of less than a year or for long-term debt that falls due after that. It is in the footnotes that we will discover whether the company has a big debt payment in any particular year, which could mean the company is facing a cash crunch and may have to negotiate some kind of extension with its lenders.

Also in the footnotes, we may discover evidence that the company has hidden various debt obligations off its balance sheet, perhaps in so-called special purpose entities (SPE), or that there are "triggers" within agreements with some of its lenders—such as a slump in its share price, a reduction in its asset base, or a cut in its credit rating—that could allow the lenders to demand repayment of some debt immediately. There may also be references to "related parties" being involved in some of these financings. This term is usually code for a member of management or a member of the board, which is a warning sign for investors.

I must say here that off-balance sheet financing was far from restricted to the corporate miscreants of recent years, so we shouldn't blast any company that has ever used an SPE or packaged assets and sold them to reduce balance sheet debt. It is a genie that has been let out of the bottle by many highly respected corporate chieftains. A lot of companies are now selling their receivables—things like the credit card and store card payments we owe banks and retailers—to other investors by creating asset-backed bonds. This allows the companies to use their available capital more effectively, to borrow more cheaply, perhaps to lend to some other customers, or to develop a new store concept. However, if a company retains ties to these assets, anything that goes wrong can hurt it. Which brings us to the first red flag in this chapter.

Red Flag 1

If There Is Any Sign a Company Retains Risks from Off-Balance Sheet Items

Either a company has completely severed its ties to an asset and any related liability, such as debt, or it should remain on the balance sheet. Otherwise, the balance sheet doesn't present a true picture of a company's risk profile.

The use of financial engineering to change the way financial statements look is so pervasive that entire industries, such as the airline industry, rely on it, and even a company like Krispy Kreme Doughnuts used a so-called "synthetic lease" to finance a mixing factory, allowing it to remove the project from its balance sheet. *Forbes* magazine in February 2002 described the structure of the Krispy Kreme deal as "an off-balance sheet trick in which a corporation has all the practical effects of a heavily mortgaged piece of real estate but tells its shareholders it neither owns the property nor has debt on it." Following the criticism, Krispy Kreme reverted to more conventional financing. Irish-American drugs company Elan faced a continuing SEC probe at the time of writing into allegations that it shifted research and development costs off its books and into a highly complex web of joint ventures. Elan has denied doing anything fraudulent. Still, investors' loss of confidence in the company's accounting led to a drop of more than 90 percent in its share price in 2002.

Note

Be skeptical when assets are transferred off a company's balance sheet into another entity, and ask whether the risk has gone too.

Red Flag 2

Avoid Anyone Boasting About Using Financial Engineering to Reduce Debt

Back in June 1999, Enron's Fastow boasted to *CFO* magazine of his ability to raise lots of capital without its showing up on the company's balance sheet. In those days, it was the kind of maneuver that won financial engineers like Fastow awards. There was little thought in the mainstream investment, accounting, or media communities that this wasn't quite kosher. "We accessed $1.5 billion in capital but expanded the Enron balance sheet by only $65 million," he said, noting that this was "a very significant amount of leverage" that was not on the balance sheet. Fastow, who was talking about the debt associated with Enron's $1.5 billion purchase of three New Jersey power plants, also told the magazine that "we have much more complex transactions as well." Fastow did, though, say that the assets were completely segregated and couldn't hurt Enron if anything went wrong. The bankers advising Enron seemed to fully understand what their master wanted. According to *USA Today*, one email discovered by congressional investigators had one Chase executive George Serice writing that "Enron loves these deals," as they "are able to hide funded debt from their equity analysts because they (at the very least) book it as deferred rev [revenue] or (better yet) bury it in their trading liabilities." Suffice it to say that when a new generation of Andrew Fastows comes along (and it will) and starts claiming to have played God with balance sheets, this should send shivers up any investor's spine.

Shot by Both Sides: The Credit Rating Agencies

The three main international credit rating agencies, Standard & Poor's (S&P), Moody's Investors Service, and Fitch Ratings, were castigated for their failure to detect Enron's deteriorating financial position or to reduce the ratings they gave it until only days before it sank into bankruptcy. Their top officials were hauled before Congressional committees to explain themselves amid suggestions that they were either asleep at the wheel or too cozy with their corporate clients who foot the bill for the ratings. As a result of the criticism, the SEC was expected to propose measures to regulate the three agencies in 2003.

The agencies fired back that Enron had kept them in the dark and they were victims of fraud as much as anyone. You might think their failure to spot the Enron problem sooner means that the agencies have become less relevant. But, nothing can be further from the truth. Indeed, they have been criticized by some investors for becoming trigger-happy with downgrades in the wake of the pummeling they received over Enron.

Fitch and S&P rate companies on a 22-notch scale (from the best rating of "AAA" to the lowest at "D") and Moody's uses a similar system with 21 notches (from "Aaa" to "C"). Anything below "BBB-" for S&P and Fitch and "Baa3" for Moody's is viewed as a junk rating—which means that the bonds are regarded as speculative in nature and not "investment grade." In essence, a credit rating tells investors and bankers how likely a company is to default on its obligations to lenders. Often, a change in the rating for one major player in an industry may be followed by similar action for others unless the reasons for the change were entirely company-specific. Companies need credit ratings to obtain any significant financing, and many investors will not put their money into junk issues because they see too high a risk of default. As a result, companies that suffer a downgrade to junk usually have to pay significantly higher borrowing costs.

A downgrade can be a critical decision, and it can make the difference between life and death for a company. A company's banks and investors will likely be concerned, its suppliers may begin to demand payment sooner, and its customers may start to look for alternatives among its rivals. Last but not least, a credit rating cut can also speed up the timetable for debt repayments, leading to a worsening spiral downward.

Moody's is now letting investors know much more precisely what its next move may be, so that if it is considering a downgrade or thinks one is possible, it will say so. "We have heard from investors that they want us to be a lot clearer about how we are thinking," said Moody's credit policy head Chris Mahoney.

With that in mind, here are the main warning signs you need to look out for from the credit rating agencies.

Red Flag 3

Rating Agencies Cut a Company's Long-Term Debt to Junk Status

This is just about the biggest flag of them all. Likely results of junk status include sharply higher borrowing costs, loss of some investors, a probable drop in the share price to go with a decline in the company's bond prices, and (particularly if it is the latest in a series of downgrades) concerns expressed in the media and elsewhere that the company faces a troubled future, and could even be heading for bankruptcy.

Red Flag 4
A Rating Downgrade Triggers Obligations, Such As Debt Repayments

A survey by Moody's of 771 U.S. companies with a rating of Ba1 or higher showed that 88 percent of them have triggers based on their ratings incorporated into their borrowing agreements, yet less than a quarter of these triggers are publicly disclosed in financial statements. Altogether, these companies had 2,819 triggers, with 41 companies reporting 10 or more, and Moody's said the figures were almost certainly understated. Results of the survey, which were released in July 2002, show how investors are kept in the dark over such triggers, which usually stipulate mandatory changes in contract terms once a rating drops below a certain level. While many of the triggers are benign, Moody's said that a significant number have potentially severe consequences, including the acceleration of payments on a company's debt, a technical default on its debt, or permission for the lender to demand the company repurchase the debt. "Such triggers exacerbate liquidity strains at the precise moment when an issuer is least able to deal with such problems," Moody's said in the report. The rating agency said it will seek, where it can, to highlight the existence of such triggers in the future.

Notes

Among other ratings agency actions, look out for:

• Standard & Poor's placing a company on "CreditWatch" with a view to cutting the rating or Moody's doing the same with its "Watchlist" review

• A negative rating "outlook" from the agencies

You can check a company's current ratings by going to *www.moodys.com, www.standardandpoors.com,* or *www.fitchratings.com.* Also worth having a glance at are Morningstar's financial health ratings from "A+" to "F," which are based on a company's debt levels and cash-flow and can be found on its web site (*www.morningstar.com*), while RiskMetric's web site (*www.creditgrades.com*) provides a measurement of how the markets are pricing credit risk.

Red Flag 5

When a Company's Debt Levels Are Much Higher than Those of Rivals

You can measure debt levels in a number of different ways, and it is always best to use more than one method. Among the possibilities are:

- Consider the ratio of debt to shareholders' equity, which is the investment in a business by shareholders and reinvested profits. Anything over 50 percent is a cause for major concern and suggests that a business may be over-extended, which basically means living beyond its means.

- Compare long-term debt (from the balance sheet) and annual revenue (from the income statement). If the relationship is anything close to one-to-one it is a signal that the debt is too high.

- Look at the ratio of operating cash flow to interest charge. This should be at least two-to-one for the company to be able to finance its debt adequately and have money with which to run the business.

In all these cases, the most important issues are both the trend (Is there a sign of a marked deterioration or improvement over several quarters or years?) and the way the figures compare with those of competitors.

Red Flag 6

When a Company Has Large "Contingent" Liabilities

Companies often guarantee the debts of subsidiaries, affiliates, and even sometimes their suppliers, customers, or executives, and this guarantee has often been hidden in the footnotes to the financial statements or is sometimes not disclosed at all. Investors should make sure to check the footnote usually termed "commitments and contingencies" and should look at any guarantees as liabilities. Steer clear of companies that are less than forthcoming about the size of such potential obligations, and always assume the worst. Adelphia Communications' collapse into bankruptcy in 2002 owed a lot to the $2.3 billion in mostly undisclosed loans the company made to subsidiaries and firms owned by the founding Rigas family. Under the agreements, the family entities were responsible for repaying the money, but Adelphia was liable if they couldn't do so.

Red Flag 7
When Insurance Against Defaults on Bonds Goes through the Roof

Investors in corporate bonds can buy a form of insurance against default by a borrower—called a credit default swap—that is proving to be an early warning signal of financial trouble. As a leading indicator ahead of the bankruptcies of Enron and WorldCom, it was more reflective of the risks than bond or stock prices. The price of buying such insurance for both companies climbed in the months ahead of their downward spirals into bankruptcy as investors sought to protect themselves against the worst possible outcome. The swaps aren't exchange-traded, so retail investors will have to ask their brokers for information about how the cost is changing.

Red Flag 8
A Company Whose Return on Capital Is Below Its Costs of Funding

Enron was wiping out its shareholders and heading for liquidation well before it collapsed. That's the contention of short seller James Chanos, who detected Enron's troubles about a year before the company hit the wall. Chanos says that Enron's low return on capital was the cornerstone of the negative view taken by his firm Kynikos Associates when it began selling Enron's shares short in late 2000. The energy trader was only returning 6–7 percent of capital employed before tax and interest, whether the money was provided by shareholders, by owners of its debt, or through financing from firms it was trading with. However, the cost of that capital was at least 9 percent and could easily have been above 10 percent, Chanos estimates.

Enron wasn't really earning any money at all. "It was liquidating its shareholders—they just didn't know," said Chanos. "Return on capital is a very hard number to fudge because it shows that often companies that are growing rapidly, that appear to be great companies, are actually relatively poor companies that have just been given a lot of capital by Wall Street."

In some ways, we are dealing with an easy concept—anyone who has ever thought of setting up a business, however small, has considered the cost of capital and the likely return on that capital. But Chanos said that, amazingly, a lot of Wall Street analysts and investors don't understand a concept that can really separate a good business from a bad one. He said that Enron's return on capital was abysmally low given the signs of aggressive accounting and its hedge fund style of operating. To put it into context, Chanos says that U.S. manufacturing companies would normally be expected to have a 12–18 percent return on capital and retailers something like 10–14 percent. "The ratio has probably tipped us off to more bad businesses than any other thing," Chanos said.

> **Note**
>
> Even a back-of-the-envelope calculation can be useful in comparing the cost of borrowing a company faces against the money it is making on investments.

Red Flag 9

When the Interest Coverage Ratio Drops Below One-to-One

The interest coverage ratio is an indicator that Sean Egan pays a lot of attention to when his team at credit analysis firm Egan-Jones Ratings Co. goes through a company's financial statements. When the ratio of income before interest and taxes divided by interest drops below one-to-one, it means a company is going to struggle to keep up with interest repayments on its debt. A drop below this level can be an early warning sign of major financial difficulties ahead. In early 2002, Egan-Jones cut Ford Motor Co.'s credit rating to junk status because its interest coverage had fallen to around one-to-one. "It has interest coverage that gives it no room to spare," said Egan. "If a company goes below one-to-one, it means it is going to have to look for other sources of capital." Throughout 2002, Ford consistently denied that it had faced any difficulties financing its huge debt load.

Red Flag 10

When a Company Is Rapidly Burning through Its Cash

When a company is consistently recording losses and there is little sign of a turnaround, the amount of cash it has becomes critical. During the Internet bust, the media, led by *Barron's*, kept a death watch on companies that showed little evidence of ever recording a profit, with the rate at which they were burning through their cash the key indicator. It is remarkable how quickly a troubled company can burn through a pile of cash. In a report in September 2002, Merrill Lynch estimated that telecommunications equipment maker Lucent Technologies would have only $600 million cash left by the end of 2003 and $300 million by September 2004—compared with $5.4 billion at the end of June 2002. That drop leaves it little room to maneuver. Lucent, which has been plagued by losses in recent years, would burn through the cash because of further losses, restructuring costs, short-term borrowing repayments, interest and dividend costs, and capital spending.

chapter

11

Snakes and Ladders: Spinning, Flipping, and Walking through Wall Street's Walls

"What used to be a conflict is now a synergy."
"Objective? The other word for it is uninformed."

—comments by Salomon Smith Barney's controversial former telecommunications
analyst Jack Grubman, quoted in *Business Week* on May 15, 2000

L ittle illustrated the dilemma facing Wall Street more than the response of Goldman Sachs Chairman and Chief Executive Henry (Hank) Paulson to the public's loss of confidence in corporate America in the summer of 2002. In a rare speech, this publicity-shy powerbroker told an audience at the National Press Club in Washington, D.C., that he couldn't think of a time when U.S. business had been held in less repute. He also laid out an agenda for change in the boardrooms and the accounting profession more than a month before President Bush went to Wall Street to deliver his own plan to get tough with corporate fraudsters. "In my lifetime, American business has never been under such scrutiny," said the one-time adviser to President Nixon's White House. "To be blunt, much of it is deserved," he acknowledged. "The Enron debacle and subsequent revelations have revealed major shortcomings in the way some U.S. companies and those charged with their oversight have gone about their business. And it has, without doubt, eroded public trust," he said.

With many other corporate leaders seemingly cowering in silence as every day brought an avalanche of reports about freshly discovered corporate skullduggery, Paulson's speech earned him mostly positive front page and opinion page treatment, the reaction making it appear in the words of *International Herald Tribune* columnist Jim Peterson as if "Moses had reappeared carrying another tablet of commandments."

This nature-loving Christian Scientist had become "a violet that shrinks no more, spanking business in a well-received speech over bad accounting and soiled laundry," wrote *Wall Street Journal* columnist Holman W. Jenkins Jr. The contrast with Goldman's normal discretion made his intervention "compelling and unusual," according to *The New York Times.* "He ought to be heeded," it declared.

Yet Paulson said little about what investment banks could do to improve Wall Street's image and restore investors' confidence. The measures outlined in his speech included changes to the structure of Goldman's research department to strengthen Chinese walls with the firm's investment banking arm. Arguably there was not much to suggest that there would be widespread and far-reaching Wall Street reform to clean up the mess left behind by the wild stock market party of the late 1990s.

A lot has been written about the troubles at Merrill Lynch and Citigroup's Salomon Smith Barney, particularly concerning the allegations of tainted research, but Goldman had mainly steered clear of the public spotlight—as it has tried to do throughout its history.

And yet, at the time of Paulson's speech, Goldman was also facing, or about to face, a series of potential problems such as probes by the Securities and Exchange Commission, state attorney generals, and Congressional investigators. The firm agreed at the end of 2002 to pay $110 million as part of a $1.5 billion Wall Street settlement of charges that investment banks and brokers put their interests ahead of investors by issuing tainted research and doling out hot stocks to favored clients in the expectation of winning investment banking business. The Goldman penalty includes $50 million in fines and restitution and $60 million to pay for independent research and investors' education in the future. Goldman's was only the fifth-biggest penalty in the settlement, behind Salomon (top with $400 million), Credit

Suisse First Boston, Merrill Lynch, and Morgan Stanley. However, given that Goldman has little dealing with mainstream investors, preferring to make its money through deal-making and out of institutional investors and the rich, that was no cause for celebration.

Certainly, Goldman's role in the stock market bubble should not be underestimated. Goldman was the biggest underwriter of initial public offers (IPOs) during the Internet mania. In the year to November 26, 1999, Goldman's net profit doubled to $2.6 billion and then climbed above $3 billion the following year, in large part driven by its investment banking fees from IPOs and advisory work on acquisitions.

The embarrassment level for Goldman increased as summer turned to fall in 2002, with the House Financial Services Committee releasing a list resembling a who's who of American CEOs who received allocations of shares in hot IPOs from Goldman during the technology stocks boom years. Among those listed were eBay CEO Meg Whitman, Yahoo! Inc. co-founder Jerry Yang, and Ford Motor Co. CEO William Clay Ford Jr., the great-grandson of company founder Henry Ford.

Also, among the beneficiaries were several of those in the prosecutors' sights, including Enron's former CEO Kenneth Lay and Tyco's former CEO Dennis Kozlowski. Goldman spokesman Lucas van Praag described the congressional committee statement as "an egregious distortion of the facts," and denied that banking clients received favored treatment. In a statement issued by House Financial Services Committee Chairman Michael Oxley, Whitman, who only joined the Goldman board in 2001, was named as among executives who "flipped shares for quick and easy profit." Whitman resigned from the Goldman board in December 2002. EBay spokesman Henry Gomez said at the time that "she didn't want there to be any perception whatsoever of any conflict," adding that Whitman wanted eBay to have the opportunity to use Goldman as an adviser in the future.

The venerable 134-year-old Goldman was also among the main targets in an avalanche of class-action lawsuits by investors seeking damages for allegedly being defrauded by those who launched and underwrote IPOs. Class-action lawyers and regulators were looking at allegations that IPO prices had been manipulated through the use of laddering—a term for a series of orders put in at higher prices when an IPO stock begins trading, in a deliberate attempt to push it higher. Clients were allocated shares by underwriting investment banks during the tech IPO boom on the condition that they put in such orders, investors' lawsuits alleged. At the time of writing, the SEC was still investigating that matter.

Even one of those issuing companies, one-time online toy retailer eToys Inc., sued Goldman, alleging that the investment bank underpriced the 1999 IPO and then received kickbacks from investors who profited when the shares initially soared.

And, as if that weren't enough, Goldman was fined $1.65 million, the same as four other investment banks, for failing to preserve email. (Much of the incriminating evidence against Salomon and Merrill had come from emails uncovered by investigators.)

Paulson and Goldman have also become vulnerable to criticism because one of their analysts was one of the main cheerleaders for Enron in the year before its collapse, despite his own admission that he didn't understand the company.

While it would be understandable if investors held most of Wall Street's energy company analysts by their ankles from the Brooklyn Bridge for keeping buy recommendations on Enron even as the media and some investors were raising red flags, it was Goldman's David Fleischer who heaped some of the biggest helpings of praise on the Houston company. Goldman's van Praag said in reply to questions from the author that the firm doesn't believe it has engaged in laddering and that it considered the eToys lawsuit "entirely without merit." It decided to join the Wall Street settlement with regulators as it was "in the best interests of shareholders" to draw a line under the issue. Van Praag also said that any problems with its stock research during the technology bubble were due to "honest mistakes rather than mendacious behavior." He said it was Paulson's view that Wall Street collectively didn't do as good a job as it could have done in its role as gatekeeper of the capital markets.

Fleischer, who is a Goldman managing director, had Enron on the investment bank's coveted recommended list of stocks until November 21, 2001, just nine days before it filed for bankruptcy. Only five months earlier, he had gushed on a conference call with Goldman Sachs clients, some of whom were skeptical, about how he thought Enron was "one of the best companies in the economy" and how its then CEO Jeff Skilling was "brilliant," a man who has "grown dramatically," according to transcript extracts published by the U.K.-based *The Financial News*. Goldman, like many other investment banks that gave Enron positive ratings until the last gasp, had an investment banking relationship with Enron. It was a dealer for Enron's commercial paper program and had arranged a number of preferred stock sales.

Paulson, whose cash compensation alone in 2001 was $12.2 million, did say in his June 2002 speech that "the next time something looks too good to be true, we hope to have the wisdom to see it and the courage of our conviction to act accordingly." And, when asked about Fleischer during an appearance on CNBC a few weeks later, Paulson said this was "an analyst who was very, very wrong," though "he did his best." In that interview, there was a familiar refrain that we are capturing throughout this story: It's not fair to blame us—everyone else was wrong, too. Paulson built on the blame others theme when he told an investor group in October 2002 that it is the investment banking clients who should shoulder a lot of the responsibility for tainted research because they put "relentless and sometimes intense pressure" on analysts. Van Praag said Fleischer remained an analyst with the firm, though in a different, unspecified role.

It remains to be seen whether Goldman will live up to its reputation, as seen by former Saloman Brothers head John Gutfreund, as a company that always seemed to wear a suit that "was impervious to slings and arrows."

Taming the Beast

Eliot Spitzer said that he was "putting a tourniquet on the bleeding" when he got Merrill Lynch, the world's biggest brokerage, to pay $100 million in May 2002 over allegations that it published tainted research to gain lucrative investment banking business. That eventually became part of the overall $1.5 billion Wall Street settlement. The New York Attorney General, whose campaign to clean up Wall Street made America's then top securities cop, SEC chairman Harvey Pitt, seem comatose by comparison, said investor confidence had been shattered so badly by some of the practices at major U.S. brokerages that aggressive intervention was essential. "We needed to say, wait a minute, something is broken, get this information out there, get the process of controlling this beast underway," Spitzer said in an interview for this book.

His most potent weapon was the publication on April 8, 2002, of a large number of embarrassing emails that showed Merrill's then star Internet analyst Henry Blodget and his staff promoting Internet investment opportunities in public while privately ridiculing the same companies, sometimes describing them as "a piece of junk" or "a piece of shit."

It was a public relations coup for Spitzer and a watershed in the public's understanding of what had really been going on during the technology stocks bubble. It made Spitzer look like the good knight battling Wall Street's dark forces, while creating a perception that Pitt and the politicians in Washington might be either bumbling fiddlers or compromised by previous business ties and campaign donations.

Within three weeks, Merrill's Chairman and Chief Executive David Komansky had publicly apologized to the clients, shareholders, and staff of the firm, which is known as the thundering herd.

It was the second $100 million payment by a Wall Street firm in 2002. In January, Credit Suisse First Boston had paid that amount to settle a case leveled by the SEC and the National Association of Securities Dealers (NASD). The suit charged Credit Suisse with participating in a "pervasive" scheme to get a large slice of customers' profits from hot IPOs through kickbacks in the form of extraordinarily high commissions. CSFB, a unit of Swiss financial services giant Credit Suisse Group Inc., also agreed to adopt new procedures in the way it handled IPOs. It settled without admitting or denying the charges.

The regulators were pushed into instituting reforms in the way research departments operated. In the settlement with Wall Street, analysts will be prevented from going on investment roadshows and participating in deal pitches. Each firm will also contract with at least three independent research firms so that customers will get access to their views.

The firms themselves, under pressure from Spitzer and other regulators, also instituted some changes. The biggest at the time of writing was Citigroup's decision to split off its stockbroking and research business from the rest of its investment banking empire into a new unit under the name Smith Barney.

The NASD, the brokers' organization that also acts as a markets' regulator, also announced new rules aimed at preventing abusive practices, such as "spinning," by underwriters of IPOs in allocating the shares.

So, adding all this together, on the surface it looks like Wall Street is on the mend, and confidence can soon return, right? That's not guaranteed.

First, further embarrassing and damaging revelations may still dribble out over a long period of time. Government and regulators' probes into the accounting scandals at companies such as Enron, WorldCom, and Global Crossing are unlikely to be concluded for some considerable time, and many of them implicate banks and securities houses. Prosecutions in some of these cases are likely to stretch well into 2004, providing a drip-feed of news about corporate wrongdoing and Wall Street's role in it.

Increasingly large and complex class-action lawsuits are also likely to keep the courts occupied for a long time, as investors seek to recoup some of their losses from the companies at the center of the scandals as well as their executives, auditors, and investment bankers. Class action lawyers who tasted victory in diet drug and breast implant cases have been eyeing Wall Street as their next big honey pot. In some cases, they are chasing money managers who invested pension money and mutual funds in companies right up until they sank into oblivion. Also, in early 2003 there was a mass filing with the NASD seeking arbitration of complaints against Salomon and telecommunications analyst Jack Grubman by a large group of small investors concerning their investments in WorldCom.

During 2002, I asked some of the financial statesmen who were around during the insider trading scandals of the 1980s for some clarity on how low Wall Street had sunk and what the chances were of rebuilding trust anytime soon.

One of them, Richard Breeden, summed up the views of many. Breeden, who was chairman of the SEC from 1989 to 1993 (as regulators were cleansing Wall Street of the insider trading scandals of the 1980s), said that some of the practices used in initial public offerings in the technology stocks boom were little different from those used by boiler rooms set up by criminal gangs. The investment banks "were not only getting kickbacks in the form of cash kickbacks in various forms for the allocation of stocks, but through a process known as laddering they were actually organizing subsequent buying down the road, which looks remarkably like penny stock fraud. I mean this is market manipulation writ large," he said.

Helping to build the expectations for a big run-up in new technology stocks were the analysts, said Breeden, who was appointed by a court to monitor management behavior at WorldCom following the discovery of fraud. "People would only agree to ladder if they thought they were going to get a big run-up. Why were they thinking that?

Well, because of course you have this massive hype machine that meant Wall Street went from providing research on stocks to becoming stock touts in a classic 1920s sense."

Some question whether the model on which Wall Street firms now operate can be viable without analysts helping the dealmakers to pull in the dollars. The problem is that after fixed stock trading commissions were abolished in 1975, investment banks became a lot more reliant on deal-making rather than trading for their income. Slowly, the purpose of research changed from helping to generate trading interest to helping promote deals for the investment bankers' corporate clients. This culminated in some investment bankers promising that their research departments would provide positive coverage of a stock issue as part of the whole advisory package.

Of course, it would be wrong to say that there haven't been some signs of improvement. According to Thomson First Call, the percentage of negative calls on stocks had risen by September 2002 to 7.3 percent of all stocks covered—from less than 1 percent at the height of the bull market in 1999. By early 2003, the figure had crept over the 10 percent mark. The analysts, though, often try to avoid the dreaded word "sell," preferring to use such euphemisms as "underweight" or "underperform." Mind you, the switch to tougher calls was spotty with Goldman and Merrill, for example, at around 6 percent negative calls, while Lehman Brothers was at 28 percent in September 2002.

Also clearly, increasing restrictions on the involvement of investment bankers with analysts mean that the next generation of Jack Grubmans are unlikely to be encouraged to get so close to the companies they cover that they attend board meetings and expense a trip to a CEO's wedding, as Grubman did when WorldCom's CEO Bernie Ebbers got married.

And yet, the Chinese walls still have holes. Whatever the structure, there is still likely to be a nod and a wink about the need for positive research coverage for clients, though it will be much more subtle than in the past to avoid falling foul of new prohibitions. Analysts' compensation may not be linked to individual deals anymore, and they may be working for a different subsidiary than the investment bankers, but there will still be some links with the firm's overall performance, including the lucrative investment banking. Also, there will still be little to stop companies from trying to freeze out analysts who write unflattering reports about them, though some investors believe that the absence of a cozy relationship with the CFO might actually be a plus. Again, the way companies punish analysts who issue negative reports may be more subtle than in the past.

And, there has been little sign of the IPO system becoming democratic, by means of an auction system through which anyone in good standing can bid. The investment banks and brokerages still jealously guard their right to dole out hot IPOs to favored clients—as long as there isn't a direct investment banking link. West Coast investment bank W.R. Hambrecht has been pioneering an IPO Dutch auction system that opens up bidding to the public, but there is open hostility to such an idea from Wall Street.

With all that in mind, there are clearly still going to be some major red flags for investors when handling Wall Street analysts and brokers. Here are some of the main ones.

Red Flag 1

When an Analyst Doesn't Kick the Tires or Even Read a Company's Filings

If you read a brokerage research report and everything seems to be based on company presentations and comments by a CFO rather than independent inquiry, you may be dealing with an analyst who mightn't be able to tell you what a tire is, let alone kick one. In the past 10 years, the pressures on many analysts to help win deals for their firms' investment banking division and the lack of incentive for hard-nosed research meant that much of what was produced was spoon-fed to the analysts by companies. Sometimes, the companies even helped write the reports by suggesting changes to drafts they were sent ahead of release. Of course, this is bad, lazy, tainted research—no ifs, ands, or buts.

Investors should increasingly keep an eye out for the analysts who don't just rely on the official sources for their information but get to know suppliers, customers, those who provide services to the company concerned, and staff at lower levels. This applies to all analysts, whether they work for investment banks or independent research houses. You want the airline analyst who knows who to talk to at the unions about labor dispute flashpoints, you want the media analyst who knows the advertising agencies well enough to get early indications of demand in the forthcoming TV season, and you want the analyst covering home appliance makers who knows what's in fashion with home builders. You should be able to get a sense of who's a live wire and who's dozing or who's an apologist for the company they are covering, from their research reports and sometimes from their behavior on conference calls. As James Grant of *Grant's Interest Rate Observer* says, "The level of sycophancy was beyond nauseating" on conference calls during the stock market boom. Often analysts would start a question to a company's management with a comment (such as "great quarter guys") that immediately gave away their lack of objectivity.

Of course, none of this is ever a guarantee, but at least it shows you that they are thinking and that they are doing their homework rather than acting as a doormat for the company's management. Former CSFB Internet analyst Lise Buyer complained to *Fortune* magazine in June 2000 that the level of research was so low at times during the stock market boom that she can't remember the last time she read a 10Q thoroughly because "nobody cared." (A 10Q is a company's regular quarterly financial statement that is released publicly usually a few weeks after the quarterly earnings press release, and it should be essential reading for anyone studying a company.) Buyer, who was speaking around the time that she was leaving CSFB to go to a venture capital firm, said that the job of an analyst in that era changed from being about solving puzzles to being about "who can make the most noise." Analysts were being rewarded for being cheerleaders for stocks and setting outrageous price targets, she said.

Contrast that dismal picture with the way Todd Slater does his job. When he wants to know what's going on with the retailers he examines for brokerage firm Lazard Freres, Slater doesn't just read their financial statements and industry publications or talk to the companies; he religiously heads for a suburban shopping mall. In October 2001, I was part of a group of Reuters journalists who joined Slater and an analyst from one of his clients on a shopping trip to Roosevelt Mall in Garden City, New York—only we were looking for bargains not in the shops but in the stock market.

Slater, a former senior executive at Macy's, hunts for the next $200 pair of jeans that will sell like hotcakes for a report to Wall Street clients that he calls "Scenes from the Mall." We watched him stop to examine a pair of jeans that "had everything" at Limited Inc.'s Express store. With a strip of rhinestones down the side, frayed edges, a whisker wash, and, of course, no waistband, they were what Slater calls "kitchen sink" jeans—they had all the hot trends for denim at that time. Slater handed us all a list of criteria by which to measure the stores we visited, including the level of markdowns, number of customers, appearance, and service. Slater also chats up store managers, asking about their best and worst sellers without immediately disclosing that he is an analyst. At times, our presence is unwelcome, especially when Slater gets a camera out to snap photographs for his report. Often, he is shooed away. Still, Slater reckons that he gets a big advantage over the analysts who prefer to sit at their desks and only crunch numbers, getting most of their information from company managements.

So, it is not a guarantee, but it might make you more comfortable to find out whether analysts you follow have scuffed shoes. It seems to be a case of the grubbier the shoes, the better. If they are too polished, the wearer is probably spending too long in boardrooms on investment banking deals and not enough out on the road.

Note

When reading research reports, look for an indication of the sources of the information. A good analyst should indicate that he or she talks to more than just company officials.

Red Flag 2
If an Analyst Hypes a Stock or Uses Superlatives to Describe Management

We have already seen the hyping of Enron by Goldman's David Fleischer. In the same vein was the language often used by Salomon's Grubman when he promoted WorldCom and its prospects, including aggressive calls on investors to buy lots of the stock. A study by attorney Stuart Goldberg (see *www.publicinvestorsattorney.com*), who is representing some WorldCom employees in legal action against Salomon, includes some of the most striking comments from Grubman in the 20 research reports he issued on WorldCom between 1998–2000. Here are a few.

— "WorldCom's President and CEO, Bernie Ebbers, is a true visionary." (April 9, 1998)

— WorldCom is a "must-own, large-cap, growth stock in anyone's portfolio." (November 16, 1998)

— "WCOM is likely to double earnings every two or three years for the next decade. We think that any investor who does not take advantage of current prices to buy every share of WCOM they can should seriously think about another vocation." (August 20, 1999)

— At one point, Grubman exhorts readers to "load up the truck" with WorldCom stock. (August 20, 1999)

— WorldCom is as "cool a cat" as any company out there. (February 15, 2000)

— "We think this is the bottom and would be massively aggressive buyers of the stock." (November 2, 2000)

At one point, Grubman writes as if he is Ebbers' spokesman after the CEO announces his own sale of company stock, suggesting it is of no concern. "We would like to point out that the sale is due to a margin call," Grubman writes.

If you come across this kind of language and tone in a research report, it is probably best to put it down and move on. You are looking for objective analysis, not soap powder sales techniques.

In the parallel universe of Wall Street securities analysts, nothing means what it says. As we have seen from the Blodget emails, from Grubman and the telecommunications industry, and from Fleischer on Enron, analysts have felt able to keep a "buy" recommendation on a stock even when it is plummeting to earth and burning up investors in its wake. Whether such analysts did this because they were the bag carriers for the investment bankers or because they just got it very, very wrong I'll leave to you, the regulators, and the courts to decide. But one thing's for sure: Investors should never take such recommendations at face value again unless they really know the track records of the analysts concerned and feel that they can be trusted to tell it like it is. A "hold" could still mean a "sell," and a "buy" could still mean a "hold."

Investors should also take note of analysts' risk ratings and, in some cases, volatility indicators. For example, Goldman Sachs' new system, introduced in November 2002, rates individual stocks as either outperformers, in-line performers, or underperformers, but it also has a rating for the relevant sector: attractive, neutral, or cautious. Wall Street firms criticized for putting buy recommendations on collapsing Internet stocks have often pointed to a high risk rating that was also put on the stock as a "we told you so" defense.

Red Flag 3

When an Analyst's Estimates and Recommendations Often Don't Pan Out

If you are going to follow the advice of analysts, you have to get to know whether their earnings estimates and recommendations pan out or not and what potential conflicts of interest they may face within their investment bank or brokerage. This is a lot to ask of any retail investor, but without doing your own research, you could easily end up chasing the picks of the next Jack Grubman into bankruptcy hell. One way of getting an indication of who is hot and who is definitely not among brokerage analysts is to read *www.starmine.com*, a web service that provides independent ratings of Wall Street securities analysts by measuring them on their stock-picking performance and the accuracy of their earnings forecasts.

While StarMine charges a lot for its main service—fees start at $1,300 a month at the time of writing—it provides some information for free. You can find out who the top performing analysts are on a particular stock and the latest "SmartEstimate," which is the firm's own earnings forecast taken by getting a consensus of forecasts from only the most successful analysts. In the summer of 2002, StarMine had one set of ratings—from one star to five stars based on how accurate an analyst's earnings forecasts were—with a particular emphasis on the times when an analyst had a different view from the consensus and got it right. It is the people who "stick their necks out" and do so at the right times who are rewarded under the system, said StarMine vice president for marketing David Lichtblau.

At the time of writing, StarMine was planning to produce a second set of one-to-five star ratings based on how well an analyst's portfolio of stock picks performs. Often, a five-star analyst in one category won't be as good in the other, said Lichtblau. It is rare to have somebody who is top ranked on both, and, when someone is, that is a real star. To get five stars in either category, an analyst's performance has to be in the top 10 percent. Four stars go to the next 22.5 percent, three stars go to the next 35 percent, and so on down to just one star for the worst performers.

A number of major brokerages such as Merrill Lynch have signed up for StarMine, and according to Lichtblau, they are looking at using the ratings system when doing their own appraisals of analysts' performance and how they are going to be compensated. Unfortunately, StarMine's free service is only a "happy service" and doesn't list the one-star folks you want to avoid.

Investors should remain skeptical of research quality even if it is dubbed independent and handed out by Wall Street brokers as part of the global settlement. Such research should be judged using the same criteria—it's all very well to rely on independent research, but it must be quality independent research.

Red Flag 4

When a Highly Reputable Analyst Cuts a Rating, It Is Often a Sell Signal

While it is tempting to dismiss Wall Street analysts and their absurd system of coded warnings, like it or not they still move stock prices. The most important thing to remember as an investor is that the changes in the ratings, the trend, is more important than what those ratings are. A top-ranked semiconductor analyst can cut the rating on Intel Corp. from "a strong buy" to "a buy" and drive the company's share price down sharply. "What you are really looking for as an investor is a change of opinion," said Lichtblau.

When a brokerage stops covering a stock altogether, unless it is pulling back its coverage from a sector because of its own cutbacks, it may be a sign that the company has collapsed or is worth very little. Analysts were criticized during the Internet bust for quietly stopping coverage without issuing a final report announcing the decision. They will now be expected to put out such a concluding announcement that will at least draw investors' attention to the issue. Sometimes, the changes, especially when a company gets into trouble, can be remarkably abrupt. For example, Goldman Sachs went from recommending Tyco to not rating it at all in July 2002, citing concern about its accounting practices.

Red Flag 5

When an Analyst Stops Covering a Company without Notice

If an analyst suddenly stops issuing reports and recommendations on a company it is often bad news, unless, that is, they have moved to another job. When the Internet boom turned to bust, some analysts quietly stopped covering once-high-flying companies as they slipped into bankruptcy and liquidation or fire sale—without formally telling investors. The reports and the recommendations would just stop coming out. That practice is supposed to stop under new rules that require brokerages to notify clients when an analyst has stopped covering a company.

Red Flag 6

You Are Probably Behind Wall Street's Top Clients on Research News

It is clear that major brokerages still provide their top clients with an early heads-up on major ratings changes before releasing the information to their small investor clients and the media. This isn't a democracy. If you have more money, you get faster advice: Those are the rules of the game. Traders within a brokerage also have plenty of opportunity to find out about analysts' calls ahead of time. So, when you see a ratings change headline pop into your email from your brokerage (and often small investors don't even get access to research reports) or when you see a headline on the television or Internet, understand that you may be hours behind those with more money and influence. You will often find, for example, that the stock price has already started to move on electronic trading platforms such as Instinet in trading occurring before normal U.S. market hours. That head start doesn't mean you never trade off such announcements, but it does mean that your disadvantage will be stark.

Red Flag 7
Buying Hot IPOs After Trading Begins Is an Easy Way to Lose Your Shirt

Unless the system for initial public offerings is completely overhauled and there is an opportunity for all to bid through an open auction, investors should remain very wary of being sucked into buying a new issue in the days immediately after it starts trading. One of the biggest transfers of wealth during the recent technology stocks boom and bust was from smaller investors ignorant of the risks to Wall Street's most prized clients, such as WorldCom's Ebbers, and insiders at the companies going public. The top clients knew full well that the stocks they had been given in the IPO allocations were getting ridiculously overvalued and got out within minutes, hours, or days (at a big profit), while the uninitiated were left holding the baby, the bath, and the bathwater.

If you do buy shares in an IPO either at the launch price or in the market afterward, be sure to find out whether there is a "lock-up agreement" that prohibits company insiders from selling shares over a specific period of time, usually 180 days, without the underwriters' permission. When the locks come off, a wave of selling from insiders can drive the shares down, and you should at least consider whether to sell before that date. Also, be aware that the underwriter can end a lock-up period early. To find out whether a company has a lock-up agreement, check the "underwriting" or "plan of distribution" headings in the IPO prospectus.

Please see Appendix A for ways to decide on and judge a broker or financial adviser.

12

At the Scene of the Crime: Funds Became Part of the Happy Conspiracy

"Let the buyer beware; that covers the whole business. You cannot wet nurse people from the time they are born until the day they die. They have to wade in and get stuck and that is the way men are educated and cultivated."

—H.O. Havemeyer, leader of the powerful sugar trust, in Congressional testimony in 1899, arguing that investors should be left to fend for themselves

Somewhere out there—scattered across cities, towns, and villages in the United States and Germany—are thousands of individuals whose shares were at the center of high stakes allegations of vote-buying involving one of the world's most powerful banks and the $19 billion merger of two of the biggest makers of computers. And, most of them probably haven't got a clue they had anything to do with it.

There is little that illustrates the lack of knowledge, let alone influence, that investors in mutual, trust, and pension funds have over the voting of shares that were bought with their money than the battle over the Hewlett-Packard Co. (HP) takeover of Compaq Computer

Corp. in the winter and spring of 2002. It offers us a bleak starting point from which to look at ways investors can be kept out of the picture by funds in which they are invested.

Often, the institutions that run these funds and have a fiduciary duty to act in the best interests of their clients haven't even told them how they voted at a particular shareholders' meeting. As for the why, how, and by whom the decision was made—forget about it. Even new SEC rules requiring more disclosure will only partially open up the process.

Thanks, though, to former dissident Hewlett-Packard director Walter Hewlett and to the leaking of a voice mail from HP CEO Carly Fiorina to the *San Jose Mercury News*, we now know a little more about a decision-making process that is often wholly secretive.

Deutsche Bank Asset Management (DBAM) ran funds that owned at least 17 million shares in Hewlett-Packard, which was facing strong opposition from Walter Hewlett to its proposed takeover of Compaq.

DBAM initially decided in separate decisions taken in the United States and Europe to vote the 17 million shares against the takeover, and that looked like it might be enough to sink the plan, given that the vote was expected to be close.

On hearing of this, HP management demanded an eleventh-hour meeting to try to get the decision reversed, and it achieved just that on the morning of the vote on March 19, 2002. In the event, the takeover proposal narrowly won by a margin slightly larger than would have been swayed by the 17 million votes.

However, in a lawsuit challenging the result of the March 19 vote, Mr. Hewlett alleged that HP management improperly coerced and enticed Deutsche Bank, which denied the allegations, into voting the 17 million shares for the takeover. The claim was based partly on the disclosure after the vote that HP had paid Deutsche Bank a $1 million fee for helping it with advice and analysis during the takeover battle— with an extra $1 million when the deal went through. Mr. Hewlett suggested that the Deutsche Bank group, which had other business ties with the computer maker, was therefore persuaded to vote with HP management through some combination of carrots and sticks.

He lost the suit, but the Delaware judge in the case expressed concern about the lack of Chinese walls between Deutsche Bank's asset managers and investment bankers.

The leaking of the voice mail from Fiorina, who has been described as America's most powerful businesswoman by *Fortune* magazine, also put HP on the spot.

"We may have to do something extraordinary for those two to bring 'em over the line here," Fiorina said in the message to HP CFO Robert Wayman. The "two" refers to DBAM and another smaller investor.

However, Fiorina contended in court that "something extraordinary" meant nothing more than needing to do something at the last minute to talk to the Deutsche Bank unit, including possibly flying to New York for a personal presentation. Wayman, in a memo to HP employees hours after the *Mercury News* story ran, said that he and Fiorina "never, ever crossed any ethical or legal lines" in presenting the case for the takeover to shareholders, according to George Anders in his 2003 book on Fiorina called *Perfect Enough*.

Without going into whether Walter Hewlett's case had merit, the most important issue from an investor's perspective is that the people who were the beneficial owners of the shares knew nothing and heard nothing. That meant it was easy to make allegations that there were backroom deals.

Shareholders' rights activist Nell Minow said that the episode showed how important it is to focus on seeking reform of the institutional investors as much as companies themselves. She said that "there is something horrendously wrong" about the last-minute switching of the vote, the payment of fees to Deutsche Bank for advisory work on the merger, and the lack of Chinese walls. Minow described it as "the most upsetting corporate governance event in a very upsetting year. Let's assume you have invested your money with Deutsche Bank, you are curious to know how it is voting your stock in the HP-Compaq merger. You don't know, there is no way for you to know, but there is one person who knows other than Deutsche Bank and that's Carly Fiorina. She knows because the votes are coming in and she can count them before the meeting date."

Minow said that Fiorina should not have been allowed to know the way the votes were going and who to pressure to change when the real owners of the shares know nothing.

DBAM said in a statement to the author that Hewlett's allegations were false. It said that following the court case it has reviewed the Chinese walls between the investment banking and asset management sides of the bank and made revisions to its policies and procedures that it believes have created some of the strongest such barriers in the industry. "Discussion of pending proxy votes is never allowed under any circumstances," it said. DBAM also said that it discloses its voting policies to the boards of its mutual funds and specific votes to "affected clients" who ask, though it hadn't at the time of writing clarified what was meant by "affected."

Yet, this is just one area in which the people who run our pension and mutual funds (and now charge us about $100 billion a year for the privilege) have been seen to cozy up to corporations and Wall Street while denying investors the chance to influence their decisions. Many fund managers were, after all, far from innocent spectators during the market bubble—some certainly played the role of sirens luring investors onto the rocks. Here are some of the ways that they became part of the problem.

— Often, fund managers complained bitterly when analysts slapped a "sell" or "hold" rating on a stock they owned—even to the point that they suggested that their business with the analysts' brokerage was at risk.

— Major fund investors are still reliant on Wall Street for much of their research, despite some beefing up of their in-house teams. The reason is simple: They can get it without paying directly—provided that they give the brokerages commissions for stock trades. If they went outside to a research boutique, they would have to pay twice—once for the research and a second time to trade through a brokerage.

"They (the institutional investors) do all this bitching about research not being as objective or as thorough as it ought to be. Look in the mirror ... it's the old story. You get what you pay for," said Chuck Hill, research director at earnings tracking service Thomson First Call. "If they could soft dollar the janitorial service, they would, and some of them probably do," he said in reference to so-called "soft dollar" payments (the term for "free" brokerage research and other services provided to institutional investors in return for commissions from their trading).

— In some cases, it was the mutual funds that were getting allocations of stock from the brokerages in hot IPOs and then "flipping" (selling) them within minutes of the stock starting to trade, adding to the mania at the height of the bull market. While a lot of the IPOs went to hedge funds and rich individual investor clients of the investment banks, some of the mutual funds were also favored in allocations because of the huge commissions they paid for trading. The allocations may have come at a price, as in return for the IPO shares, Wall Street firms in some cases demanded kickbacks in the form of high commissions or the promise of orders for the stock at higher prices. The uninformed small investor, of course, was often left with losses on the stock bought at the top of the market after the "flip" had taken the air out of it. "It became a question of not what you knew but who you knew as to whether or not you got good returns," said Don Phillips, the managing director of funds research company Morningstar.

— Institutional investors have been leaning on the credit rating agencies to try to persuade them against making more regular changes in credit ratings. This is despite the criticism of the agencies for keeping Enron's investment grade rating (as opposed to a junk rating for high-risk companies) until just before it filed for bankruptcy. "The criticism is that we are too volatile and that we are trigger-happy. They don't want us to change ratings," said Chris Mahoney, chairman of the credit policy committee at Moody's Investors Service. "There is a conflict of interest ... people who own securities don't want them to depreciate in value. They want rating agencies to upgrade them and not downgrade them."

— Mutual funds that call for more disclosure from companies they invest in often don't practice what they preach. Many decline to release quarterly statements to shareholders that detail their holdings—they are currently only required to do so twice a year, though the SEC seemed poised in 2003 to demand quarterly filing. And, as we have seen, many mutual funds—including the largest, Fidelity—have in the past declined to tell anyone how they are voting at shareholder meetings. Some major fund groups have been refusing to tell their shareholders who the money manager in charge of a fund is and when he or she departs or is replaced. "They regard it as their money, which they manage for you," said Bill Patterson, the head of the investment office run by the AFL-CIO, the umbrella organization for U.S. labor unions. "There is a mystification of asset management—an attempt to make it far more complicated than it needs to be and to under inform."

In January 2003, the SEC voted to require mutual funds to disclose how they voted in shareholder meetings. The new rules will also make them reveal their voting policies and how they deal with conflicts of interest. However, the disclosure of the voting record would only be required once a year, by August 31 for votes taking place in the 12 months to June 30. This would still give a Hewlett- Packard and a Carly Fiorina key voting information well ahead of DBAM investors—who might only learn of the direction of a vote months after it had taken place. It will still be far from easy for investors to compare how funds voted on various issues in any timely manner.

— Institutional investors have played a key role in pressuring managements into meeting or beating earnings targets, many being unmerciful in selling shares in companies that miss Wall Street forecasts. This has, in the view of many senior financial figures, helped to cause accounting fraud, as managers desperately try to make their numbers. One of the reasons for this is that the institutions' time horizon for ownership of a stock has shortened dramatically. In 2001, for example, one out of every ten equity funds turned its portfolio over at an annual rate of more than 200 percent, four out of ten at a rate of more than 100 percent, and only just over one out of ten at a rate of less than 25 percent, according to John Bogle, the founder of the Vanguard Group of funds and a vocal critic of some practices in the fund industry. "By focusing on short-term stock prices rather than long-term corporate values, the fund industry has helped to create the over-heated financial environment of the recent era," he said. "We have become not an own-a-stock industry, but a rent-a-stock industry."

— Fund managers have, with a few exceptions, spent little time on shareholders' rights and corporate governance issues in recent years. During the boom times, few complained about excessive executive compensation, poor disclosure, dubious accounting, and questionable deal-making. Many didn't even vote at shareholder meetings, or when they did, they supported management and the board without question. It was all aboard the merry-go-round, with little thought of how dizzy they might feel when it stopped.

A number of fund managers, such as Legg Mason's Bill Miller, are taking a more aggressive stance on such issues, but there are still many who prefer to sell a stock when the smell gets too bad rather than force the company into improving its plumbing. "I think that the balance of power has shifted so dramatically to the companies and the boards becoming the creatures of the CEOs that the institutional shareholders are obligated to get a lot more active to protect their clients' interests," said Miller.

Still, many would agree with the head of Third Avenue Funds, Marty Whitman, who says that the cost of an effective campaign to change a management and board can be just too expensive for a medium-sized fund. "Probably you have to bring a suit, hire an attorney, and maybe get an investment banker," he said.

— Many funds are rife with conflicts of interest, and it is far from clear that Chinese walls are being honored, as seen from the judge's view of the Hewlett-Packard case. For example, funds that manage a company's pension money, or want to manage it, are unlikely to create a noise about management or board issues, said Sarah Teslik, executive director of the Council of Institutional Investors, which mainly represents pension funds. If a fund "wants General Motors pension business, is it going to vote against General Motors board—you bet it is not," she said. Funds that are part of major banking groups can also be influenced by the interests of the bankers in retaining or snaring business from the company concerned, she said.

— Some of the biggest U.S. funds were caught as flat-footed as any Wall Street analyst by Enron, WorldCom, and some of the other recent corporate disasters. Alliance Capital Management, for example, added to its Enron stake up until almost the very end. Alliance Premier Growth Fund Manager Alfred Harrison said that he missed key warning signs. "We had been buying from $80 on down," he said in December 2001. "All the way down the stock looked cheap."

Alliance is the subject of a lawsuit from the agency that oversees Florida's pension fund, which says it lost more than $300 million on the Enron stock purchases by Alliance. The presence of Frank Savage, an Alliance director and former top executive of the fund company on the Enron board, further muddied the waters, though Alliance said that he had no role in investment decisions. Alliance also had a significant stake in WorldCom around the time of its bankruptcy. "Where was the skepticism?" asked Vanguard's Bogle. "Where are the accountants in the mutual fund firms?"

— The fund management industry has become a huge promotional machine focused much more on marketing than on how to improve performance for shareholders, according to Bogle. He said that he went back to look at *Money* magazine at the peak of the bull market in March 2000 and counted 44 mutual funds advertising their returns, which averaged 85.6 percent, for the previous year. "They weren't advertising a year later, or if they were advertising, they were advertising their bond funds or were advertising their stars and not their percentages," Bogle said in reference to the Morningstar relative performance star rating system for funds. "The problem with this industry is a very simple one in that we have too much salesmanship and not enough stewardship," he said.

So, with all that in mind, here are some of the red flags you should note when they are indicated by the fund industry. And, always remember that it is your money they are handling.

Red Flag 1

Your Mutual or Pension Fund Has Clear Conflicts of Interest

If a fund shows signs of being conflicted because it is part of some larger financial services organization that includes an investment bank and brokerage, then consider giving your money to an independent boutique instead. The conflicts can take all kinds of forms, but at the end of the day, they mean only one thing: Your interests as an investor are not primary.

Examples of possible conflicts follow:

- pressure on fund managers to support investment banking clients or potential clients in shareholder votes

- pressure on fund managers to promote the research produced by the group's brokerage division

- a fear of losing pension fund business means that a fund manager is unquestioning of a weak or venal management and board at a company

- independent fund directors who agree to hikes in management fees without a thorough examination of the justification. Often these directors are compensated well and may not want to upset the applecart

- pressure to invest in certain securities as a favor to other parts of the group that may be doing a public offering

Red Flag 2

Funds That Won't Tell You How They Are Voting Your Shares at the Time of the Decision

In days when everyone from President Bush on down is demanding more disclosure from American companies, it may seem extraordinary that mutual funds still felt in 2002 that they didn't have to disclose information about the way they vote at company meetings.

Let's consider the biggest mutual fund company of them all, Fidelity. When labor unions tried to get shareholders of defense contractor Lockheed Martin Corp. to vote against the re-election of director Frank Savage in 2002 because he had been on the Enron board during the executive mischief that led to its collapse, they turned to Fidelity, which was the largest outside shareholder with about 9 percent. But, Fidelity wouldn't tell anyone how it was going to vote, and even months after the union move was defeated, it won't disclose which way it went or whether it voted at all. Remember, the shares it is voting are mainly held on behalf of many individual investors in pension, mutual, and other funds.

Fidelity officials claim that disclosing such information would damage its attempts at quiet diplomacy on behalf of shareholders and that its public airing of any differences with a management or board could hurt a company's stock price.

"We are encouraging shareholders to demand this kind of disclosure," said Patterson of the AFL-CIO. "I don't know how you can go to your investor base and tell it you voted for an Enron director at Lockheed Martin and how that was a step to protecting shareholder value." (Patterson said that he was convinced Fidelity voted for Savage.)

The SEC's new rules still mean that Fidelity wouldn't have had to tell investors about how it voted on Savage for four months after the April meeting.

Phillips says that some kind of web democracy where mutual fund investors could let the fund's managers know how they wanted them to vote on specific issues would be "terrific in theory," though in practice getting enough people to vote to make it meaningful might be difficult. There are already web-based shareholder activist groups such as *www.eraider.com*, which was set up by two university professors, and Pax World Funds' web site (*www.paxfund.com*), and these might be an early sign of things to come.

Red Flag 3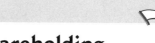
Funds That Don't Issue Shareholding Information Every Month

Many investors have only got to hear what stocks their funds have been buying and selling every six months—a lifetime when you think that Enron disintegrated from a top-rated company into bankruptcy in less than 60 days. This may soon change to required disclosure every three months, as we have seen, but that is still too infrequent.

The funds argue that premature disclosure of a shareholding before all the planned buying has been done could raise the cost of the targeted shares as other investors piggyback on the move. However, given that even monthly disclosures would still have some delay built in and that even the best disguised efforts at building a major position tend to get known by Wall Street insiders, this doesn't carry much weight.

The funds industry also argues that mailing out lists of stocks owned—especially for some funds that have hundreds and even thousands of individual holdings—every quarter instead of every six months will just raise costs. This could be overcome by using the Internet for more regular disclosures while keeping to the six monthly mailings.

Phillips says that more frequent disclosure is even more important given that the average U.S. stock fund now has a turnover rate of 113 percent a year—which means that the average holding period is only ten months. "These funds are being turned over at a massive, massive rate," he said.

It all means that if you are only told what is happening every six months, you may never get to know whether your fund owned Enron or WorldCom shares for a few crucial and painful weeks.

However, the industry's main lobbying arm, the Investment Company Institute, has been arguing for less disclosure, saying that funds should only have to disclose details about their top 50 positions or a holding worth more than 1 percent of a fund.

Red Flag 4

Funds That Play Cloak and Dagger Games with Fund Managers' Identities

One of the keys for any investors putting their money in a fund is finding out about the background and past record of the manager who is going to be making the key investment decisions. So, how about funds declining to tell you who that manager is, let alone announcing when they quit or are replaced?

Well, that's exactly what the world's fourth-largest funds group, Putnam Investments, decided to do for a brief period in 2002, designating its funds as merely "team managed." However, it reversed the decision a few months later amid a wave of criticism in the media.

By playing down who is at the helm, fund firms like Putnam had hoped to avoid scrutiny when managers quit or were fired. Instead, the policy can backfire by inviting more criticism, especially if funds are performing poorly, which has been the case with some of Putnam's.

Red Flag 5

When a Fund Manager Quits Suddenly, Especially if No Clear Reason Is Given

Like the overnight departure of a CEO, this can be cause for major concern, especially if it is explained with something meaningless such as "personal reasons." Does this mean that there has been an internal feud? Is there some bad news about the fund that hasn't been disclosed? Is there an experienced and well-regarded replacement?

You should be looking to the firm's management to answer these kinds of questions because you have been paying for the manager's expertise. You should also monitor the fund's subsequent performance very closely to see whether the departure has had any noticeable impact.

If the departing fund manager has been a star performer and is going to set up shop elsewhere, you shouldn't necessarily panic and follow close behind. A lot depends on whether the manager was thrust into the limelight as part of a marketing campaign while his or her team was really doing the hard slog, or whether there really was a star at the helm.

Red Flag 6

When a Fund Management Firm Is Dropped by a Big Pension Fund

If a fund management firm gets dropped by a big company pension fund, it is worth finding out why. If it was for poor performance, perhaps you should consider following the lead. Also remember that the loss of such business could also be followed by some turmoil within the money manager.

Maybe the loss is because a money manager has stood up for improved shareholder rights and upset the management of a company. In this case, the money manager should probably be congratulated for sticking to its guns even when threatened with losing business.

Red Flag 7

Lowered Ratings from Morningstar or Lipper

Investors should get to understand the fund ratings systems run by companies like Morningstar and Reuters Group Plc's Lipper Inc. as they can be a good starting point in winnowing down the massive fund universe when choosing where to put your money, and also a check against the comparative performance of what you already own.

It may seem fine to have an annual return of 25 percent on a precious metals fund at a time when the gold price is surging—until you realize that similar rival funds have been gaining at least 35 percent. If this pattern of underperformance had been repeated over at least three years, the gold fund you have invested in would likely be getting one of Morningstar's lowest ratings of one or two stars.

Under the Morningstar system, the top 10 percent performers in a particular category of funds get five stars, the next 22.5 percent receive four stars, the next 35 percent have the average three-star rating, the first 22.5 percent slab of under-performers getting two stars, and the worst 10 percent of the funds getting just one star.

The system is risk weighted so that a fund that has very volatile returns gets a penalty. It also takes fees into account when measuring returns.

If you hear that a fund you are invested in has dropped from five stars to four stars on the Morningstar system, it is almost certainly no reason to panic. However, if it has gone from three stars to one star, you should really be analyzing what has gone wrong and consider moving on. The system, which is based on monthly measurements, can only be a guide—it doesn't replace your own research into cost, risk, the background of the manager, and so on. Also, it is always worth remembering that yesterday's success stories can often turn into tomorrow's horror stories—past performance is never a guarantee.

Indeed, Morningstar was criticized after the stock market bubble burst because it gave a lot of the high-octane technology funds five stars, ratings that were used in advertising to help draw in investors at the top of the market. In mid-2002, the research firm changed its system so that funds are measured within a much wider range of categories, so that a technology fund would have to be performing better than 90 percent of other technology funds, rather than 90 percent of all equity funds, to get five stars.

Lipper through its *www.Lipperleaders.com* web site doesn't just go for the single rating, preferring to provide investors with a more complex set of measurements that not only show historical returns but

how consistent they have been, whether the fund is a safe place to preserve capital or is more of a casino play, and how tax efficient it is and
how the fees compare with similar funds. "We say that all investors
should review those five areas at a minimum," said Lipper's Global
Director of Research Robin Thurston.

Red Flag 8

When a Fund Has a History of Moving Away from Its Advertised Intentions

If you put your money in a fund set up to invest in lower-risk consumer products and food and beverage companies, you shouldn't
wake up one morning and find a big chunk gone because it invested
in here-today-gone-tomorrow telecommunications companies, such as
WorldCom or Global Crossing. And, diversified means what it says,
not a fund that is half energy traders like Enron and Dynegy.

Nobody minds money managers putting a big slab of money into
cash for a short period when they expect a slide, but otherwise, they
should be sticking to your original instructions. If there is any room
for so-called "style drift" (moving away from the original plan), you
should be told about it clearly in the fund's prospectus. During the
technology stocks' boom and bust, some investors discovered that
their supposedly average risk equity funds were stacked with big bets
on high-risk technology issues.

In this context, it is very important to know from the start what
flexibility the manager has at a fund you are investing in. It is no good
sleeping soundly because you think that he or she will have switched
a lot of money you put into a cable and media fund into cash before
the likes of Adelphia, AOL Time Warner, and Vivendi Universal
plunged, when the maximum cash the fund can hold at any one time
is 10 percent.

"What is a disaster is when you get a mismatch where the investor
is expecting X and the fund manager is saying my walking orders are
Y," said Phillips.

Red Flag 9
When the Shareholder Letter Is Merely Used As a Sales Tool

Investors should scrutinize the quarterly or half-yearly letter to shareholders from the fund manager closely for its depth and candor. If it is merely used as a sales tool, you should take a dim view.

"The worst one is where it is an attempt to sell you more of the fund—when they tell you no matter what the market conditions are, now would be a good time to add to your fund," said Phillips. "What you really want is a fund manager who is trying to help you understand how to use this fund intelligently—what might be right in a situation and what might be wrong."

He said that, ideally, the letter would indicate that the fund manager really sees the investor "at the top of the food chain."

Phillips said that investors should ask if fund managers are admitting mistakes and evaluating themselves fairly or merely taking credit for an overall gain in the market.

Red Flag 10
Managers Who Divert Hot Stocks into One Fund at the Expense of Another

Investors must feel confident that money managers are being fair in their allocation of hot issues and losers between different funds. In the mid-1990s, Dreyfus Corp. money manager Michael Schonberg diverted nearly all the hot IPOs he was allocated into one of three funds he managed, the Dreyfus Aggressive Growth Fund. The effect was to drive the new fund's return to a spectacular 119 percent in just eight months.

Dreyfus then marketed this performance to investors through advertisements, though there was little chance of repeating the feat as the fund grew in size.

Dreyfus Corp. settled charges filed by the SEC and New York state's Attorney General alleging that it and Schonberg made inadequate or false disclosures. It paid nearly $3 million in the settlement. The prospectus for the fund had disclosed that investment opportunities would be allocated equitably among all Dreyfus funds. Schonberg, who had to put up $50,000 of the payment, was suspended for nine months from the investment advisory business. Neither Dreyfus nor Schonberg admitted to or denied the charges in the settlement.

Investors should also be wary not only of the possibility of mischief between mutual funds but also between mutual funds and hedge funds run out of the same firm. There is plenty of leeway for such practices as front running, which occurs when a money manager buys a stock for a hedge fund he runs—and from which he would almost certainly earn higher fees—ahead of buying the same stock for his mutual fund. The investor in the mutual fund would then end up possibly paying a higher price because the first order may have forced it up.

Red Flag 11
High Fees That Suck Up Returns, Especially in a Bear Market

Losing two to three percentage points in fees to mutual funds may not have hurt much in the heady days of the bull market when some technology funds were more than doubling in value. But, try taking that off if, as some investors fear, returns settle down to a 5–7 percent average annual level for a prolonged period. Add in transaction costs for funds that have rapid turnover and taxes on distributions, and you would almost be better sticking the money under your mattress. (At the time of writing, bank deposit rates are extraordinarily low.)

Investors are likely to become a lot more cost conscious about funds, said John Biggs, who was the head of the giant TIAA-CREF pension fund system until he retired in November 2002. "We are skeptical of the whole damned industry because of the high costs and the need to maintain profit margins, which I think are always excessive," he said.

Once you have added up advisory fees and other costs and expenses, including hidden transaction fees, you are already 2–3 percentage points down on the annual return you will get from many equity funds. And, that is without taking into account some of the upfront "loads," or costs, that you may have to pay to sign up in the first place or the taxes you may be hit with on any capital gains.

The increasing importance of fund sales through major brokerages such as Merrill Lynch or Schwab, sometimes known as financial supermarkets, rather than through direct selling, is raising charges for investors, said Lipper's Thurston. "They now pay more load charges and in some cases higher fees because it costs money for the fund to distribute through the supermarket," he said.

Given the likelihood of lower returns over the current decade than in the last decade, Thurston says he expects charges to become a big issue. "Looking at relative expense ratios is very important because it has a huge impact on performance over time," he said. Investors should approach the issue of fees like they would buying products in a supermarket—which means they should go for the cheapest unless there is some overriding reason why one fund is better than another, he argued.

Information on fees and comparisons across a sector can be found on both the *www.morningstar.com* and *www.lipperleaders.com* web sites.

Of course, this is all an argument for buying an index fund that charges between 0.15–0.20 of a percentage point in fees, excluding transaction costs (which are much lower because there isn't the frenzied trading). That way you get returns pretty much in line with what an index, such as the S&P 500, achieved, and there are no risks of a stock picker lumbering you with some really bad bets and then charging you a lot for the privilege. The tax efficiency of index funds tends to be higher, too, because of the lower turnover.

Red Flag 12

Advertising That Boasts of Stellar Returns over a Short Period

We should all be careful about being sucked in by mutual fund advertising that promises the earth based on great returns in previous periods. At the height of the bull market, technology funds were particularly prone to do this, and in the eyes of some senior figures in the investing world, such funds played a dishonest role in pulling investors into a dangerous market.

When a fund is riding high, it may be precisely the worst time to buy. For example, during the 12 months ending March 2000, the month the technology bubble burst, investors poured $240 billion into technology funds and tech-oriented growth funds—while pulling money out of other funds that were poised to do better.

Investors should also realize that if a firm has killed off some badly performing funds, it can make the average performance of the remaining funds look artificially better.

13

Where Were the Auditors? Counting Fictitious Beans

"...We wonder if these fellows can be trusted with the grocery money, much less with restoring public confidence in shareholder capitalism."

—from a *Wall Street Journal* editorial about the big four accounting firms, April 23, 2002

Paul Volcker leans his huge frame back in the chair and chortles as he describes some of the absurdities he sees in modern-day accounting.

To the 75-year-old former Federal Reserve chairman, whose reputation for taming inflation in the 1980s matches his basketball player six-foot, eight-inch frame, very few people in business really know what is going on with many aspects of today's complex sets of accounts.

Volcker says that the leadership of the big accounting firms let investors down just when it was needed most to protect against manipulation of increasingly complex financial statements.

"Ordinary investors can't follow it. The fact is, directors can't follow it, members of the audit committees can't follow it, so you have

215

got to trust the professional guardians, of which the auditors are the designated last line of defense," said Volcker. "But unfortunately they haven't been doing as good a job as they should."

Through the debacles at Enron, WorldCom, Global Crossing, Adelphia, Tyco, and many others, a constant refrain has been "Where were the auditors?" Here I will attempt to answer that question in part and suggest how investors can monitor auditors of companies in which they are invested and identify danger signals.

Volcker says one of the main reasons auditors were found wanting is that accounting rules and standards are arcane and need a thorough overhaul. He harks back to the 1950s, when the business world and its accounting was much simpler. "You go out there and you count the inventory and you see if the oil is in the tanks and you can see the factory and you can count the receivables and so forth," he said.

Unfortunately, Volcker says, accounting standards haven't adapted to the information age and a complicated world of derivatives and the valuation of intangible assets, such as brand names or patents.

He delivers a withering criticism of the nonsense he sees in the worlds of accounting and financial engineering. Take these comments from an interview with this book's author:

- "The equity on the liability side is matched with something called goodwill on the other side, whatever goodwill is."

- "The Financial Accounting Standards Board [the accounting standards setter in the United States] has got some very complicated rules, which I am told nobody understands, on what conditions you mark to market and what conditions you don't."

- "My grandson said, 'I want to be a financial engineer.' My heart sank. Here is a whole profession that grows up and 85 percent of what they do is how to get around the rules."

If you don't fully understand what exactly goodwill is or marking to market is, or what a financial engineer does, don't worry—Volcker makes it clear that even many of those who must come to grips with such concepts can struggle with the industry's gobbledygook.

While Volcker is known for his straight talking, it is still refreshing to hear such no-nonsense comments from a man who served almost 30 years as an economic policy setter under five U.S. presidents and who is now chairman of the trustees for the group set up to establish international accounting standards.

Volcker, who was parachuted in by Andersen to lead a rescue effort after it became deeply implicated in the Enron collapse, blames the industry's unwillingness to reform itself for the failure of his attempts to save the accounting firm.

He said he didn't believe the leaders of the other Big Four accounting firms, PricewaterhouseCoopers, KPMG, Ernst & Young, and Deloitte & Touche, wanted Andersen to survive along the lines he was suggesting, which required it to focus solely on auditing and get out of the consulting business altogether.

"I think they said we don't want these Andersen reforms, so they are no longer part of our club," said Volcker, whose offices are high above Manhattan's Fifth Avenue in the Rockefeller Center complex.

That, and the economic self-interest of Andersen partners, destroyed the firm as much as its conviction in a trial over the destruction of Enron documents, he said.

Clearly, Volcker isn't the only financial statesman to have questions about the leadership of the accounting profession.

In 2000, then SEC Chairman Arthur Levitt tried to bar accountants from providing consulting services as well as auditing a client's books. He felt that the big money the major accounting firms were making out of consulting meant they were more likely to turn a blind eye to fraudulent or deceptive accounting.

At many companies, accounting firms were receiving more for consulting than they were for auditing. At Tyco International, the annual audit and quarterly reviews cost $13.2 million in 2001, while its accountants PricewaterhouseCoopers received $37.9 million for all other services, including tax consulting, work on acquisitions, and a new financial information system. At defense contractor Raytheon, the ratio was an amazing 20 to 1 in favor of non-audit work in 2001.

Levitt's move was met by a fierce lobbying campaign by the accountants' main professional body, the American Institute of Certified Public Accountants (AICPA), and three of the then Big Five accounting firms (Andersen, KPMG, and Deloitte & Touche). Levitt describes their approach as "intensive and venal."

Levitt received letters from 46 members of Congress, many of whom had gotten campaign contributions from the accounting industry, questioning his plan. According to The Center For Responsive Politics, which tracks campaign contributions, the Big Five accounting firms and the AICPA made nearly $39 million in political contributions between 1989 and 2001, according to the center's web site (*www.opensecrets.org*).

Wilting under the assault, which included threats from some senators that they would be able to get Congress to curb SEC funding if the plan went ahead, the SEC abandoned the Levitt plan—apart from forcing companies to disclose how much they pay their auditor for other consulting work.

After Enron and WorldCom, though, many of the politicians have had to eat humble pie and support the Sarbanes-Oxley corporate reforms, which include the ban on an accounting firm doing auditing and most kinds of consulting work for the same company.

In an interview, Levitt said that he believed the accounting profession is "probably the weakest led, least public-oriented industry" in the United States. "The AICPA does a vast disservice to the public by its fortress mentality and Neanderthal tactics," he said.

Another example of the accounting industry's resistance to any kind of outside regulation was its thwarting of the efforts of the now-defunct Public Oversight Board to investigate how widespread was the problem of auditors having financial links with their clients.

The board, which was set up in 1977, was supposed to help police the accounting industry. The only problems were that it was funded by the AICPA and had few powers.

The SEC asked it to carry out a sweeping probe of the Big Five's compliance with independence requirements for auditors after the securities regulator discovered in 2000 more than 8,000 violations of conflict of interest rules at PricewaterhouseCoopers. The violations included direct investments by partners in firms for which Pricewaterhouse was the auditor.

At first, the AICPA cut off money for the probe. When funding was reinstated after pressure from the SEC, the accounting firms raised other obstacles about issues such as confidentiality. The AICPA, the accounting firms, and their lobbyists "threw up obstacle after obstacle so that after a year and a half we hadn't done anything," said John Biggs, who was then a member of the board.

"It [the oversight board] was really a very distressing experience," said Biggs, who retired as head of the giant TIAA-CREF pension fund system in November 2002. "It was a thankless, horrible job."

He said the board faced "total hostility" from the AICPA. "If we were doing something they didn't like, they would say, 'if you continue doing that, we are going to de-fund you.'"

This frustrating battle with the accounting firms and a perception that the SEC wasn't giving it enough support were among the reasons for the Public Oversight Board's decision in January 2002 to dissolve itself.

To some, the 340,000-member AICPA got its just deserts when the Sarbanes-Oxley bill received the nod from President Bush in July 2002. The sweeping law takes away the AICPA's power, which it had held since the 1930s, to have the final say on auditing, independence, and quality control standards and hands it to a new Public Company Accounting Oversight Board.

It looked, briefly, as though attitudes might be changing.

In a speech delivered in September 2002, the AICPA's CEO Barry Melancon admitted that the profession had been "part of the problem" that had led to the wave of business scandals and that its reputation had been badly dented. He called for a reassertion of the traditional values of accounting, including putting the public interest first and showing no tolerance of companies that want to bend the rules or be deceptive.

The tone and the content of the speech, which was given to the Yale Club in New York City, were a far cry from the image of a bullying, politically powerful organization that the AICPA had presented to regulators in the previous few years.

Yet, few believe that a couple of soothing comments from Melancon and others mean that the trust and integrity of accounting can be restored quickly. The industry proved that it remains a formidable Washington power player when in October 2002 it helped to defeat an attempt to get Biggs to chair the new oversight board, industry analysts said. A divided SEC voted 3–2 to appoint former FBI and CIA head William Webster chairman of the new body. Biggs, who was favored by the SEC commissioners who lost the vote, was regarded by the accounting industry as too independent and radical in approach. "We got the Sarbanes-Oxley Act as the result of the uproar by typical American citizens," Joseph Carcello, a professor of accounting at the University of Tennessee, told Reuters after the decision. "But when things quieted down, the accountants found that what you can't accomplish through the legislative process, you accomplish through the regulatory process."

For some time, there had been warning signs about the accounting firms' determination to build their businesses at all costs—even if ethics and standards became secondary. For example, they were criticized by the United Nations and the World Bank during and after the Asian economic crisis of 1997–98 for their willingness to allow the lowest common denominator to rule by signing off on accounts drawn up to very low national standards.

"No one in the manufacturing or consumer industry would in this day and age even dream of saying, 'We have no standards; our standards go as low as a national regulator wants them to go,'" then World Bank vice president Jules Muis, who was a former managing partner at Ernst & Young in the Netherlands, said in 1999. In a speech to accountants at an international conference in Scotland in 2000, corporate governance guru Ira Millstein said that the major accounting firms were prepared to put their names and reputations to financial statements that they knew "do not meet the expectations or the needs of the critical users—the investors."

At companies like Enron, there existed the absurd situation of Andersen the auditor looking over the accounting treatment of partnerships that had been structured with the help of Andersen the consultant, and Andersen even monitoring an internal audit department dominated by Andersen the internal audit provider. What chance was there for an untainted audit on behalf of investors in those circumstances?

It was also quite clear that some of the accounting firms and major financial consulting groups were completely sucked in by the hype of the Internet boom. We shall see examples of that below, but first let's look at the most dramatic alarms that auditors can raise for investors.

Red Flag 1
The Auditor Suddenly Resigns or Is Fired without a Good Explanation

The sudden departure of an auditor without a really good explanation is just about one of the biggest sell signals going.

It usually means that either the auditor has discovered a possible fraud, in which case it is likely to report this to the SEC, or the auditor has upset the company by refusing to endorse attempts to manipulate the financial statements or create financial structures that may be illegal.

Given the current concerns about fraud, most auditors going to a board's audit committee with concerns about accounting mischief are likely to see an immediate investigation by the company as a result. In the few cases where they don't see a quick response, the threat of going to the SEC is likely to do the trick.

"If the auditor says, 'It is a shame you are not doing the right thing because now we are going to have to go to the SEC,' that strikes fear into the heart of the audit committee and suddenly they get religion," said Michael Young, a litigation partner at Willkie Farr & Gallagher and outside counsel for the American Institute of Certified Public Accountants.

An example of an auditor's departure that is worrying for more than one reason is the firing by the small, publicly traded company U.S. Technologies, an investor in young Internet companies, of BDO Seidman in August 2001. Initially, Washington, D.C., based U.S. Technologies said that it dismissed the auditors because BDO Seidman had raised substantial doubt about whether the company could continue as a going concern in its explanatory report for the company's 2000 financial statements. However, a few weeks later, it was forced to acknowledge, after BDO Seidman had written a letter to the SEC, that BDO had been fired after also telling U.S. Technologies' management and its audit committee in the summer of 2001 that the company lacked the internal controls necessary to produce reliable financial statements. Among BDO Seidman's concerns were the lack of an experienced chief financial officer, deficiencies in the timely recording of transactions, and problems with the organization and retention of financial documents and accounting records.

So what? I hear you say. This was a tiny company that few had ever heard of—and that would be right if it weren't for the presence of William Webster (who was named head of the new oversight board by the SEC) as the chairman of U.S. Technologies' audit committee during that period. Indeed, the criticism resulting from Webster's role at the company became so intense that he had to resign from the new body, and the controversy played a central role in the departure of SEC Chairman Harvey Pitt. Just over a month later, U.S. Technologies CEO C. Gregory Earls was charged in a criminal complaint with cheating investors out of $13.8 million. Webster had resigned from the board of the company, which is also facing investors' lawsuits, in 2002.

"Talk about taking away the credibility of the board even before it has started," Mark Cheffers, who runs the web site *Accounting-Malpractice.com*, told Reuters in reference to the oversight board.

Despite the accounting industry's continued attempts to prevent reform, auditors are expected to take a much harder line with clients who aren't giving them straight answers. In a signed statement that was part of an advertising campaign in December 2002, PricewaterhouseCoopers U.S. Chairman Dennis Nally said that "in any case where we cannot resolve concerns about the quality of the information we are receiving or about the integrity of the management teams with whom we are working, we will resign the client."

Red Flag 2

The Auditor Questions Whether a Company Can Survive

When an auditor believes that a company may fail within 12 months, it is required under U.S. accounting industry guidelines to issue a so-called "going concern" opinion—which means it qualifies the accounts by pointing out that the company could be heading for bankruptcy court.

Clearly, when an investor sees such a comment from the auditor, it is almost certainly time to bail out. Given the criticism auditors have faced after giving companies a clean audit only to see them topple over a few months later, the use of such "going concern" tags is likely to increase. It is also more likely to speed a company's collapse as investors, suppliers, customers, and bankers lose confidence in its future.

Red Flag 3
A Company Restates Its Results

The increasing focus of journalists, analysts, academics, and short sellers on possible accounting malpractice is likely to increase the pressure on companies to restate their financial results if anything even slightly dubious is discovered.

"I think there are forces in place which are going to lead to a continuing upsurge in financial statement restatements," said Young. "People now see that accounting can be interesting and one of the consequences of that is that there is a whole new industry of muckrakers out there, foremost among whom are journalists," he added.

He said that *Fortune* magazine's Bethany McLean, who was arguably the first journalist to raise red flags about Enron, seems almost to be regarded as financial journalism's answer to Watergate's Woodward and Bernstein. "Everybody wants to be the next to break the big accounting story," Young said.

Young, who says he doesn't consider this a bad thing, sees such pressure from outside fueling the rise in restatements, combined with demands on auditors for extra zeal and an increasing sensitivity to any problems from audit committees.

The number of restatements surged to 330 in 2002 from 270 in 2001 and just 116 in 1997, according to a report from the Chicago-based Huron Consulting Group in January 2003. The biggest single reason for restatements was a problem with the way revenue was measured.

Huron said in a previous report issued in August 2002 that many of the companies that restate their results because of accounting misstatements eventually file for bankruptcy protection, though it takes an average of almost a year after the restatement for them to do so, giving investors plenty of early warning.

Companies that are forced to restate are often those in danger of missing earnings and revenue targets. The pressure on managers to reach those goals may prompt them to be too aggressive in booking revenue—perhaps by stealing it from a future period.

> **Note**
>
> Take notice of the extent of a restatement; a few million dollars in one quarter is very different from three years of restatements that involve hundreds of millions of dollars.

Red Flag 4

Companies That Answer Criticism by Stressing Compliance with Accounting Rules

One of the most frequent responses of companies facing criticism over their financial statements is that there is no problem because "they are fully in compliance with Generally Accepted Accounting Principles [GAAP]." When you see this, don't be lulled into a false sense of security—there are an increasing number of occasions when the SEC has taken action against companies for being deceptive in their accounting even though they are not breaching the United States accounting rules, often referred to as U.S. GAAP.

For example, in May 2002, the SEC found that private schools operator Edison Schools Inc. inaccurately described aspects of its business in filings with the commission, even though the practices did not contravene GAAP. Edison had failed to disclose that a substantial portion of its reported revenues consisted of payments that it didn't receive. The money concerned was paid directly by school districts to teachers for their salaries and for other costs of operating schools run by Edison. The company consented to the SEC's issuance of an order that declared that it had violated certain securities laws through the accounting practice and ordered it not to do so again, though it didn't admit to or deny the charges.

Volcker says the problem with GAAP is that its reliance on a myriad of specifics rather than a few principles means that it "just breeds an effort by some very smart people spending all their time working out how to get around rules."

Red Flag 5

When an Auditor's Record Suggests Lax Practices or Conflicts of Interest

When an auditor like Andersen starts to get a reputation for lax and conflicted practices, it may be time to worry if a company you are investing in uses them. Before the Enron, WorldCom, and Global Crossing blow-ups, the warning signs had been there at Andersen—big accounting scandals at its clients Sunbeam, Waste Management, and the Baptist Foundation of Arizona showed that there were problems in the firm. In June 2001, for example, six months before Enron's collapse, Andersen agreed to pay a $7 million penalty, the largest the SEC ever imposed on an auditor, for faulty audits at Waste Management.

In some cases, it may be a particular regional office of an accounting firm rather than the whole organization that has a poor record, which means that it may be wrong to tar everyone with the same brush.

Red Flag 6

If an Audit Committee Hints at Internal Conflicts or Accounting Concerns

Under the new law, it will be much more important than in the past to read the annual report of a board's audit committee, which should be in the proxy statement (or annual results). The report may indicate whether there have been any clashes among management, the auditor, and the audit committee over how conservative or aggressive—which often means how close to the edges of legality—the company's accounting policies are. The audit committee members will want to protect themselves from any litigation if there has been fraud on their watch, so they are more likely to disclose any problems promptly.

Given the increasing prominence and powers of the audit committee within the board, any indications that there is a conflict with management over accounting policies might quickly be followed by the departure of the CEO, the CFO, or both.

Red Flag 7

If Management Doesn't Seem to Care Much About Internal Controls

The new Sarbanes-Oxley law also requires each annual report to include an internal control report, which will include management's assessment of the strength of internal controls and related comments from the outside auditor. Any sign of either template style treatment of this new and potentially important area of disclosure or suggestions that there could easily be a breakdown in controls may be a red flag. The example of BDO Seidman's warning to U.S. Technologies underlines this.

Remember that most of the big losses suffered by banks through rogue traders—such as the scandals that destroyed the British merchant bank Barings and more recently cost Allied Irish Bank's subsidiary Allfirst Financial Inc. $691 million in losses—resulted mainly from a breakdown in internal risk controls. At Baltimore-based Allfirst, foreign exchange trader John Rusnak managed to hide mounting losses from his bosses for years through a system of false accounting—even persuading them he had been making money and earning bonuses as a result. He pleaded guilty to bank fraud in October 2002 and received a prison term of 7-1/2 years.

Red Flag 8

If a Fraud Is Declared, Expect News to Get Grimmer As More Is Uncovered

When a company announces that it is carrying out an internal probe into its accounting or that there has been a fraud, be prepared for the news to get bleaker and bleaker over the following months.

In his book *Accounting Irregularities and Financial Fraud,* Young takes readers through the stages of a typical fraud investigation begun when a member of staff blows the whistle. He says the fraud is "probably worse than anyone thinks," and "it probably goes back further than anyone thinks."

We know this is the case from the recent spate of scandals at companies such as Enron, WorldCom, and Adelphia. Grim initial revelations are never the end of the affair. Once the forensic accountants have delved into the accounts, there are almost bound to be further nasty disclosures. At WorldCom, for example, an initial $3.8 billion alleged fraud had within a few weeks turned into $7.1 billion—and a little while later more than $9 billion.

Red Flag 9

A Warning from the New Auditor Watchdog

Critics of the accounting profession are hoping that the formation of the new Public Company Accounting Oversight Board will lead to much more rigorous policing of auditors' ethics and behavior. And while the initial controversy over who will run it has taken away some optimism, it remains the case that if it uses effectively all the powers it has been given, the new board will be able to make a real difference.

All public accounting firms will have to register with the board and be subject to its disciplinary powers. The major firms will also have to submit to annual inspections to see whether they comply with legal requirements and professional and ethical standards set by the board and the SEC. Identification of breaches can be followed by a formal investigation and disciplinary action.

The board will have the power to permanently revoke or temporarily suspend the registration of an accounting firm and to bar an individual auditor from practicing. It will be able to impose fines of up to $15 million on a firm or $750,000 on an individual for each occasion on which there has been an intentional or reckless violation of laws and standards or repeated instances of negligent conduct.

During the annual inspections, the board will review selected work by a firm, which may include audits that are the subject of litigation or some other controversy, and also test a firm's quality control system.

If an accounting firm or individual refuses to testify, provide the board with documents, or cooperate with an investigation, either the firm or person can also face the suspension or revoking of registration.

Although board hearings into disciplinary charges won't be held in public, it will be worth investors' while to keep tabs on any public announcements of subsequent action such as fines and revoking or suspension of registration. Of course, the revocation of registration for a major accounting firm would have huge consequences and is highly unlikely, but nobody would have imagined before the Enron scandal that a firm such as Andersen could disintegrate.

Red Flag 10

Beware of Accountants Who Are Promoters of the Latest Business Fad

Key figures in the accounting profession were clambering aboard what historian and journalist Kevin Phillips describes as "the carousel of fools" as it was speeding up at the height of the Internet-telecoms boom.

Rather than being the vital gatekeepers for investors by trying to prevent greedy executives from monkeying with the numbers, accountants joined the "new paradigm" mania, declaring that there was a need for a new kind of accounting for a new era. In some cases, they either turned a blind eye to management manipulation of accounts or even helped them do it.

It is too much and probably not wise to ask that accountants stick completely to what is sometimes derisively called bean counting. We need smart accountants—if only because corporate crooks can be pretty smart, too. But we don't need auditors who see their role as financial engineers helping corporate clients maneuver their way around accounting principles and rules so that their financial results will look more appealing.

It is helpful to read a book written by senior Arthur Andersen partners around the height of the stock market bubble in 2000 to understand how a firm that was once known as the conscience of the accounting industry sank to the depths of a humiliating criminal conviction, public opprobrium, and disintegration.

The book, *Cracking the Value Code: How Successful Businesses Are Creating Wealth in the New Economy*, is in itself unremarkable for the times in which it was written and published in that it declared that the new era was "different from anything we have dealt with before," and that companies all needed to "embrace a new model of how to create value."

But this wasn't coming from technology analysts, consultants, or journalists. This was coming from the high priests at Arthur Andersen, who were supposed to be safeguarding the integrity of financial statements for investors.

The authors of the book—Andersen's then managing partner of U.S. operations Steve Samek, then worldwide managing partner for strategy and planning Richard Boulton, and management consultant Barry Libert—quote approvingly from a *Fast Company* magazine article's talk of "a new breed of company," and "a new world order."

Then, there is an onslaught of criticism of the traditional accounting system, which is seen as becoming obsolete, as Samek and his co-authors argue that stock market valuations are a much better guide to the worth of companies than anything that might lurk on a balance sheet.

"Organizations are creating value in totally new ways, using assets and combinations of assets heretofore unrecognized under traditional accounting systems—and certainly unmeasured," they write.

The authors declare that "value creation—that is future value captured in the form of increased market capitalization—is how successful businesses are creating value in the New Economy."

The traditional income statement is condemned because it "categorizes as 'expenses' many of the most significant sources of value—people, for example—and overlooks much of the value derived from customer relationships and information (except for that arising from transactions during the period under review)."

The authors championed a whole series of companies whose share prices have collapsed, some of which have been at the center of accounting frauds or have faced SEC probes into alleged manipulation.

They include Lucent Technologies, Xerox, Qwest Communications, AOL Time Warner, Gap, Williams Cos., idealab!, and CMGI.

So, look for sober thinking from the accounting firms that audit companies you invest in. They are not supposed to be stock boosters, stock pickers, financial engineers, or promoters of new economic theories. There are plenty of other people who can do that.

14

Media Munchkins and Masters: Separating Puff Piece Writers from Hard Diggers

"There is no real penalty for being wrong; the journalists, the commentators, and the analysts blithely chalk up their mistakes to the market's unpredictability and quickly turn to the next day's haul of hot information. It is a mutual manipulation society that affects anyone with a direct or indirect stake in the market, which is to say nearly everyone in America."

—Howard Kurtz in *The Fortune Tellers: Inside Wall Street's Game of Money, Media and Manipulation*, 2000 (The Free Press)

News reports about the results of Qwest Communications International's results for the fourth quarter of 2000, published in January 2001, almost uniformly focused on the telecommunications company's announcement of a 44 percent increase in profits. But, any investor who relied on this information would have been sorely misled.

Journalists had fallen for the line peddled by company officials who only released selective numbers calculated on a so-called "pro forma normalized basis and excluding non-recurring items." There you have three bright red flag words: "pro forma," "normalized," and "non-recurring"—which basically means "earnings before a lot of bad stuff." Once the true picture became clear two months later, it turned out that instead of making a profit of $270 million as reported, Qwest had actually lost $116 million—an admission that the company made on page 42 of exhibit 13 in its annual financial statement filing with the SEC.

What the media should have done is hassled the company for the net earnings figure, and if it wasn't forthcoming, the media should have reported this prominently, giving the stories a skeptical edge from very early on.

It is events like this that have led to some soul searching in newsrooms since the technology stocks bubble burst.

The Wall Street Journal, for example, now tells its reporters they must start earnings stories with the net income rather than some pro forma figure, according to deputy managing editor Daniel Hertzberg. At Reuters, we stress that reporters in the United States should usually focus the story on net income, and if they don't, there has to be a good reason why not (the market's main interest is sales growth would be one). Also, we demand full explanations of any kind of pro forma measurements so that readers know exactly what has been left out.

Many news organizations are now asking analysts and money managers more often to disclose what interest they or their firms may have in a particular stock they are discussing. Regulators are now requiring Wall Street to provide such information.

And, certainly, there are more reporters focusing on accounting and being given the time to delve into company books and to cover such issues as executive pay. Still, more needs to be done in many parts of the media. Financial journalists still have enormous power to move the price of a stock or an entire market by their reporting.

Among the most critical analyses of the media's role in the technology bubble and the corporate scandals have been those in the publications of journalism schools.

"The print media's coverage of Enron's top executives was pure hagiography," writes *The Columbia Journalism Review*'s Scott Sherman in a piece published in March 2002. He accused top business magazines of "cheerleading and obsequiousness."

In an article for Harvard University's *Nieman Reports* in June 2002, *Washington Post* energy reporter Peter Behr lists the following lessons for the media from the Enron collapse:

- the need to question stories that are too good to be true

- the need to listen to contrarians, skeptics, and short sellers, while recognizing they have an axe to grind

- the need to hold companies to a more demanding standard of disclosure; and if they won't give answers, to write more stories that say so

There are still, though, some harsh lessons to be learned, according to Reuters global head of news, Stephen Jukes. "This has been a wake-up call for all of us in the media industry," he said of the criticism of the media following the bursting of the market bubble. "There is no doubt in my mind that some media organizations were swept up in the Internet boom and helped fuel a personality cult that sprang up around some of the more flamboyant CEOs."

Jukes said it is more critical than ever for journalists to maintain a questioning and critical stance toward everything they report on and to rigorously avoid conflicts of interest. "It is the duty of reporters to make sure that readers—and investors—know if there are vested interests at stake."

Marjorie Scardino, the CEO of *Financial Times* publisher Pearson, attacked the media, including the *FT*, for not working hard enough "to ferret out" accounting scandals. "We could have done a lot more digging. But business journalists often don't know a lot about business," she was quoted as saying in an interview with the *Royal Society of Arts Journal* in the United Kingdom.

With that view in mind and realizing this is far from a perfect media world, here are some key red flags for investors.

Red Flag 1

If a Top Publication Exposes Dubious Accounting or Corporate Behavior

If a reputable publication such as The Wall Street Journal or Fortune starts questioning the accounts of a company, investors should sit up and listen. It was the Journal that finally started piecing the Enron puzzle together in October 2001. About seven months earlier, Fortune's Bethany McLean wrote that the energy trader's impenetrable accounting combined with high expectations for its stock increased chances of a nasty surprise. She wrote that even a straightforward question such as "How exactly does Enron make its money?" couldn't be easily answered.

Often, those who act quickly on alarm bells rung by the media can avoid losing their shirts. Quick action could have helped investors in Belgian-based Lernout & Hauspie Speech Products, NV if they had sold immediately after reading the *Journal*'s August 8, 2000, report about the discrepancy between reported Korean sales and the comments of some identified customers who said they did no business with the computerized voice-recognition software concern. The report hurt the stock price, but it didn't sink immediately, allowing time for those who saw this as a worrying development to exit. Lernout & Hauspie eventually filed for bankruptcy in 2001 after an audit revealed that it had booked $373 million in phony revenue between 1998 and 2000.

Red Flag 2

Magazine Covers and Awards Aren't an Aid to Smart Investing

When the magazine *Business 2.0* was launched in August 2001, it stuck Enron's then CEO Jeff Skilling on the front (along with two other CEOs), and it ran a cover story about the Internet's continued impact on the economy. A day after the magazine hit the streets, Skilling resigned.

Welcome to a contrarian indicator of a company's fortunes. Some investors suggest you might be able to draw an inverse correlation between the number of magazine covers and magazine awards that an executive gets and his or her company's share price. I have yet to see the mathematical proof of this theory, but certainly the anecdotal evidence has piled up in recent years. If you were to name just about any CEO or CFO at the center of a corporate scandal in recent years, you would probably find that in happier times he or she had graced the covers of major magazines or received awards from them—usually complete with glowing profiles.

As Michael Young warns in his book *Accounting Irregularities and Financial Fraud*, rapidly expanding companies will almost inevitably have a high profile in the financial press. However, their stock prices "may reflect journalistic accolades more than business fundamentals."

My favorite indicators of possible trouble ahead are the CFO Excellence Awards that are sponsored jointly by *CFO Magazine* and the now-collapsed accounting firm Andersen. WorldCom's former CFO Scott Sullivan (at the time of writing he had pleaded not guilty to multiple fraud charges) received one in 1998, Enron's former CFO Andrew Fastow, who was charged in September 2002 with money laundering and conspiring to defraud the energy trader, was honored in 1999, and Tyco's former CFO Mark Swartz, who was charged a month before with helping to loot $600 million from the company and its shareholders, received one in 2000.

Red Flag 3

Journalists Who Fail to Ask the Hard Question

We all have a rough day from time to time, but there are some reporters who consistently fail to ask the hard questions of people whom they are interviewing. This failure becomes particularly obvious on television, but it can also show itself in uncritical profiles and stories in the printed media, too. These reporters aren't worth an investor's time of day. Instead, get to recognize and watch the reporters who always make sure that the subject of an interview is kept on his or her toes or who have a reputation for exposing accounting shenanigans and other corporate wrongdoing.

"There are good and bad writers with objectivity and lack thereof at all the big publishers," according to short seller David Tice, who said that he particularly trusts *Forbes* magazine. "Sometimes reporters write puff pieces—they just question managements, they get told some good news, and they just report it. Sometimes reporters are cynical and question, and if that guy writes a favorable piece later on, then you know you can believe it more than the guy who just writes 100 percent puff pieces."

> **Note**
>
> Take note of the bylines of those journalists who write stories about corporate shenanigans that turn out to be on the mark and those whose reports aren't borne out by subsequent events. Learn to differentiate.

Red Flag 4

Be Aware That Some Media Commentators Also Trade Stocks

Some media commentators trade the stocks that they talk about on TV shows and write about in columns. They should be viewed in the same way as any investor or analyst who has a vested interest: with a skeptical eye. Most news organizations, including Reuters, have policies forbidding their staff from trading in stocks when they are writing about them.

But some media commentators boast about being investor-journalists, saying it gives their reports an edge over dispatches by the reporter writing from the sidelines. Business news web site TheStreet.com, for example, aggressively markets the stock picking Action Alerts Plus service run by its co-founder and former hedge fund manager James Cramer, saying readers will be told within minutes what he is trading. Note that Cramer is not allowed to trade any stocks that he mentions on his CNBC television and radio shows for five days afterward.

Also be wary of conflicts at industry consultants and market research firms. Some companies will pay market-research firms to produce glowing reports about a product or a business strategy. Often, these are issued to the media as unbiased research surveys without any mention of who paid for them to be produced. Some stock newsletters also get paid to write glowing articles about companies. And, when you see money managers interviewed in the media, remember that they are unlikely to talk negatively about a stock if they own a sizeable amount of it.

Red Flag 5

Take Media Popularity Polls with More Than a Pinch of Salt

Investors shouldn't give too much credence to popularity contests run by the news media and should instead focus on surveys that are based on statistics. An important example of the former type is *Institutional Investor* magazine's annual polls of money managers to determine who they think are the best brokerage research analysts. The problem with these polls is that they turn into beauty contests, with analysts openly lobbying for votes. There is a good reason for this jockeying—in the past, coming in the top three for a sector was likely to mean higher pay and bonuses. Among the past winners in the poll was Merrill Lynch's then Internet analyst Henry Blodget, who in 2000 came top of the electronic commerce and new media sector despite a series of disastrous buy recommendations. Salomon Smith Barney's former telecommunications analyst Jack Grubman, who was at the center of 2002 investigations into allegedly tainted research, was also a previous winner.

The magazine's top editor defended the poll, which in 2002 was sponsored by Reuters Group Plc, saying it accurately reflects analyst performances. "The voters are smart enough to vote in their own economic self interest," said Michael Carroll, editor in charge. "Jack Grubman, for better or for worse, made people a lot of money in the '90s," Carroll told Reuters in October 2002.

Former SEC Chairman Richard Breeden, though, describes the *Institutional Investor*-style popularity method as "inherently wrong" and misleading because the criteria for judging analysts should be the performance of the stocks they select.

Red Flag 6

Speed Requirements Can Leave Reporters Open to Hoaxes

The race to be first with the news among wire services, the broadcast media, and newspaper dot-com web sites means that reporters can be open to manipulation. In the Qwest example that I have mentioned, no news agency journalist had the time to call the company to seek the net income number before putting some headlines out. In an ideal world, the kind of profit being reported would be defined quickly in a headline, and readers would also be told that the company hadn't disclosed its net income. If there is confusion, investors should hold off on trading until the picture clears. But that isn't how it works. Within moments of headlines being spat out onto computer terminals around the world, orders are whizzing off to traders, for whom it doesn't matter whether headlines give the full picture—provided they are making a profit.

And even worse, the hoax press release that gets through the news organizations' safeguards is an editor's worst nightmare. But in these days of sophisticated technology and crooks who know how to use it, such frauds will continue to be perpetrated and some may succeed. Among recent examples of such hoaxes, the most infamous occurred when a small press release service called Internet Wire distributed a false press release concocted by a former employee announcing that the CEO of a company, Emulex, had resigned and that the company was restating earnings. Bloomberg News, Dow Jones, and some other media groups sent out stories without realizing it was a hoax, and Emulex shares plunged. At Reuters, we didn't fall for the hoax but we certainly weren't celebrating our rivals' problems—we fully realized that we could be a victim in the future, and we reinforced our training and controls as a result. The former Internet Wire employee was trying to cover his losses on his short sales of Emulex stock by driving the price down. He pleaded guilty to fraud charges and was sentenced to 44 months in prison.

Veteran gumshoe Jules Kroll says he is surprised there aren't more hoaxes of journalists. "You get these young kids out of school, and they may have an experienced editor—maybe—but it has got to be easy to fool somebody and have it come out on the wire."

Red Flag 7

News Reports That Only Rely on Analysts Who Provide a Very Narrow View

Reporters who are dependent upon analysts from the big brokerages to help them analyze companies don't have the same credibility as those who use a wider range of sources, such as independent research firms, money managers, consultants, former employees, advertising agencies, and so on. With Wall Street's research far from ready to be given a clean bill of health, it is unfortunate that too many reporters remain overly reliant on big brokerage analysts. That dependence is likely to diminish, though, as an increasing number of brokerages are forbidding their analysts from talking to the media following the controversy over tainted research.

Note

Take note of the kinds of sources used in news reports and ask if they have an axe to grind.

Red Flag 8

Details of a News Report May Have Leaked Out Before Publication

Reporters working on background or investigative pieces about particular companies can inadvertently let the market know what they are working on. When researching a story, a reporter has to ask his or her source a series of questions, and if the line of inquiry isn't disguised enough, a source can soon start to make an educated guess that a publication is working on a piece about a company's accounting policies.

By its very nature, a story about accounting policies is more likely to be negative than positive, so the source may either sell the stock short or suggest that tack to others in the expectation that the stock will fall when the article is published. In his book, former hedge fund trader Nicholas Maier writes that for one period in the 1990s, "It seemed like all of Wall Street knew what was going to be in *BusinessWeek*." The magazine hits the newsstands on a Friday morning, but often, the stock had moved on Thursday, he said. *BusinessWeek*'s closely guarded "Inside Wall Street" column, which mainly consists of stock tips, has been at the center of a number of insider trading cases. In one, the perpetrators went as far as to pay a postal worker to get an early peek at the magazine.

15

Abstention to Follow Addiction: When Disenchantment with Low Returns Hits Home

"We live in a new age. Performance is not enough. When a trillion or so in New Economy market cap goes up in smoke. When advisers rate a stock a 'buy' and it goes bankrupt a couple of weeks later. When the system designed to provide confidence in the numbers falls apart. It changes things."

—General Electric Co. Chairman and CEO Jeffrey Immelt at the company's annual meeting on April 24, 2002

The generation that got used to the bull market of the 1990s and saw every drop in the market as an opportunity to buy stocks at lower prices is finding it hard to cope with the hangover it is suffering today.

Too many people still think the hair of the dog will get rid of their headache, but some leading investors and financial figures think that a period of abstention followed by selective drinking of only the finest wines may be in order.

"I have talked to people who are 35 or less, and while they are obviously worried, they are still convinced that the stock market goes up 10 percent a year. That's all they have seen. But if you believe that, you're a dope," said former Federal Reserve chairman Paul Volcker.

He makes young investors look at charts that show the Dow Jones Industrial Average was the same in 1982 as in 1962, and that was a period when consumer prices went up by 50 percent. "It makes no impression on them," sighs Volcker, who was credited with breaking the back of U.S. inflation in the early 1980s and containing the Third World debt crisis when it erupted in 1982.

He is not alone in asserting that many investors are too optimistic about a quick return to generous returns on stocks. "I think the biggest risk by far is that people have not come to terms with a low nominal rate of return. It is very clear that the overall equity market cannot do better than about 6 to 8 percent a year," said highly ranked value investor Bill Miller. Miller says this estimate holds "unless you believe in fairy tales about ever rising valuations."

Worse, if executive compensation—especially the excessive use of options—continues to rocket, investors will see almost half that return pocketed by management, Miller argues. He says that if investors can only get 3 to 5 percent a year in stocks and they can get 7 percent in investment grade bonds, "stock prices will be in for a long slide."

Of course, much of corporate America has not yet accepted the prospect of lower returns. Major companies, such as General Motors Corp., still assume a 9 percent annual return on their pension fund assets. Warren Buffett's Berkshire Hathaway, in contrast, assumes a more sober—and some would say realistic—6.5 percent.

John Bogle, the founder of the mutual fund behemoth Vanguard, says the problem in the 1990s was that stock prices lost their connection with the value the companies were generating through earnings growth and dividends, and that was why the day of reckoning came.

A return to much lower average returns means that the stock market is unlikely to play such a big role in the popular imagination as it did in the 1990s.

Bill Lerach, the nation's best-known securities class-action lawyer, agrees that interest may soon drop off. "I have a fairly strong feeling that we have witnessed the generational peak of the equity culture," he said. "I think that you are going to see a lot less interest in equities going forward, in part because people have been burned and they don't trust Wall Street now. And there is going to be a lot more conservative investing, a lot more debt buying, and the like. We have seen this before: When one generation gets murdered in the equity market, it tends to take a long time to correct itself."

We have already seen that retreat from the market starting to happen, reflected in sharp declines in everything from online stock transactions to the number of people watching the CNBC financial television channel. Several personal finance magazines, including *Bloomberg Personal Finance* and *Mutual Funds*, have closed.

One danger, given the disenchantment with individual stocks and many mutual funds, is that investors will seek another road to rapid riches—through the even less regulated hedge fund industry. And this possibility comes at a time when crooks, the reckless, and the incompetent threaten to make hedge funds one of the most dangerous places for all but the smartest of investors in the next few years, Wall Street experts believe.

Hedge funds, once the preserve of the Park Avenue set, are now being marketed to a much wider group of people at a time when the funds' ability to take a bet against stocks through short selling makes them particularly appealing, given investors' recent experience with a bear market. Certainly the hedge fund industry's overall performance has been tempting—with the average hedge fund gaining 10–15 percent during the bear market between 2000–2002.

New funds are springing up every day, and there are now about 6,000 in the United States, with some estimates suggesting that the amount of money pouring into hedge funds may have almost doubled to close to $600 billion since the beginning of 2000.

An almost complete absence of regulation, large minimum investment requirements, high fees, and the industry's secretive nature leave plenty of room for those with nefarious intent.

Warning of an impending disaster is John Gutfreund, the former head of Salomon Brothers. "If you want a prediction from me," he said, "the next debacle, which we are just heading into, is the proliferation of hedge funds. If you were asked to define how a hedge fund functions and how it makes money, you would be hard pressed," he said. "They are not regulated and it is just designed for sin."

The smartest investors pay private intelligence companies, such as Kroll, to check the backgrounds of hedge fund operators before they commit their money. "I think it will be one of the next areas to blow up," says founder Jules Kroll. "As more and more people go into the hedge fund business, the quality of the people doing it will deteriorate dramatically."

Kroll's firm has been asked to conduct more than 200 investigations into hedge funds, which charge much higher fees than mutual funds, since the beginning of 2000.

In the largest hedge fund fraud to date, Manhattan Investment Fund founder Michael Berger pleaded guilty to defrauding investors out of $400 million and then tried to withdraw the plea, claiming he was mentally incompetent at the time he made it. He failed to appear at his sentencing hearing in March 2002, and a warrant was issued for his arrest.

In October 2001, Florida hedge fund manager David Mobley was sentenced to more than 17 years in prison after being convicted of fraud, money laundering, and tax evasion in a scam that conned rich retirees out of $124 million. He spent the money on a lavish lifestyle and on meeting his own debts, prosecutors said.

Several other medium-sized hedge funds closed down around the end of 2002. The SEC also brought 12 hedge fund fraud cases in 2002, against five or less in each of the previous four years. But investigators fear that these problems will be modest compared with what might be ahead.

Traditionally, hedge funds demanded a minimum investment of $1 million, and the securities industry's cops left them alone because they didn't market to the mass population. But now that minimum figure has started to come down, and there are funds of hedge funds—which work like mutual funds—that offer those with much less money the chance to buy into a range of investment vehicles.

The SEC is taking more interest, though at the time of writing, it had yet to announce firm proposals, and some industry experts doubt that much will change.

Indeed, momentum in a number of corporate reforms proposed at the height of the scandals of the summer of 2002 seemed to have been lost by early the following year.

Here is a brief outline of what was (or in many cases *wasn't*) happening in early 2003.

- The regulators' $1.5 billion settlement of allegations of tainted stock research had led to some modest reforms on Wall Street, but hardly radical change. The final details of the written version of the settlement were still being haggled over in March 2003. Those details may make a big difference to the success or failure of the many class action law suits being brought against Wall Street investment banks by investors.

- New York Stock Exchange proposals for reform of listing rules to force companies to create more independently structured boards had yet to get full SEC approval. Under the original plan, companies have another two years after it gains SEC approval to meet many of the demands, so don't expect rapid change.

- The move by some companies, such as Coca-Cola Co., to expense stock options had failed to set off a stampede by others. By early 2003, only a fraction of publicly traded U.S. companies had agreed to regard stock options as a cost, and very few of those are the technology companies that are the heaviest issuers.

- Among the first moves by members of the new accounting regulator, the Public Company Accounting Oversight Board, were to vote against changing its auditor every five years, a rejection of a symbol of independent auditing, and to vote themselves salaries of $452,000 each. It was still without a new chairman by March 2003.

- By March 2003, some of the leading figures in the corporate scandals of 2001 and 2002, including Enron's former chairman Kenneth Lay and WorldCom's former CEO Bernie Ebbers, had yet to be charged with any misdemeanors—a warning to investors that there is as much gray as there is black and white in the nation's securities laws. Even if these figures are eventually charged, prosecutors are likely to have a long legal road ahead of them.

It had become clear that it would probably take another series of scandals for there to be anything more than modest and slow reforms in the boardrooms and executive suites of America.

Money Manager David Dreman says he is disturbed by the lack of real reform. "Change has been minimal, and the current administration appears to be leaning toward keeping it this way," he said in reference to the Bush government. He said that after the 1929 crash, Congress passed major legislation and some key figures—including the president of the New York Stock Exchange and a leading banker—went to jail. "In the recent bubble the public was bilked for trillions, and the investment bankers, analysts, and the rest of the circus responsible get minor fines relative to the profits they have made."

Appendix A
Tips for Handling Your Broker, Financial Adviser, or Financial Planner

A survey of more than 200 affluent investors, defined as those with more than $500,000 of investable assets, showed that 26 percent were considering changing their investment adviser in the summer of 2002 because he or she was affiliated with an investment banking firm. The study, by consulting firm Spectrem Group, also showed that two thirds of those surveyed believe there is a conflict of interest when a company acts as both investment adviser and the underwriter of securities recommended by that adviser. Add those concerns to the knowledge that a broker's main job is to get you to buy shares you don't own and sell shares you already do so that he or she can generate commissions whatever the circumstances, and you have a basis for investor distrust. With that in mind, here are some tips to consider when getting advice.

- Be clear about the differences between brokers and financial planners. Often, the major investment banks muddy the waters by calling their brokers "financial advisers." The term investment adviser, by the way, is also very loose and could apply to someone from a mega-mutual fund group such as Fidelity or a one-man-and-a-dog advisory operation. In his book *Take on the Street*, former SEC Chairman Arthur Levitt recommends investors hire a financial planner who has certification either through the Financial Planning Association (*www.fpanet.org/plannersearch*) or the National Association of Personal Financial Advisors (*www.napfa.org*). Investors should pay for the services either on an hourly basis or by flat fee for a set number of visits.

- If you have a financial adviser or broker who is affiliated with a brokerage or investment bank (either directly as an employee or through some other kind of business relationship), be careful of potential conflicts of interest. This particularly concerns any stocks or funds he or she might be recommending that have been underwritten or launched by the firm for which they work, or an affiliate. You do not want to buy just to help the broker meet a sales target for his or her firm's own products. Always ask how a financial advisor is getting rewarded and what business connections he or she has.

- When a broker or financial adviser doesn't listen to your needs and is always after selling you the next big thing, ditch him or her pronto.

- When an adviser seems to be more like a tarot card reader, watch out. If you really want someone to predict the future, you may be better off going to a carnival. An informed discussion about the way the economy and market might be heading is fine, but fortune telling is a no-no.

- Avoid an adviser who pressures you to act quickly, telling you to grab an opportunity now. You should resist, and you should probably get yourself a new adviser. Remind yourself that if it's a great company now, it should be as great in a week, in a month, or in five years. And leave the "low risk, high reward" proposals for dumber clients.

- Make sure you know how an adviser is paid; usually it is on a commission basis. For example, if an adviser recommends a money manager, ask how much is in it for him or her. Unwillingness to discuss such topics openly is a bad sign.

- Negotiate over commissions at every turn. There is almost always a range and opportunities for discount.

- Avoid buying stocks with borrowed funds. Sometimes, brokers will suggest that you buy stocks on margin with money lent to you by the firm. This is fine if the stock climbs in price, but if it declines, you can not only lose your initial investment, but you have to pay back the borrowed money, too. In a rapidly declining market, a broker may sell the shares on your behalf without even consulting you—which means you lose control over the whole process.

- Try to choose a broker or an adviser based on recommendations from friends or business associates whom you trust and who can give you a clear indication of what he or she has done for them.

- Always check out a broker or an adviser's background. You can glean a lot, including usually any disciplinary proceedings a broker has faced, by checking the National Association of Securities Dealers' web site (*www.nasdr.com*) and asking for information about the person concerned. Another place you can check out a broker or an adviser and also make a complaint is through the state securities regulators. There is a link to many of these sites on *www.sec.gov.*

- If your broker or adviser has a poor disciplinary record, you should ask for an explanation. If the answers are evasive or if you are not entirely satisfied, you should go elsewhere.

- Examine any written statements very carefully for authenticity, and do some occasional unannounced checks in person at the brokerage office. Compare and contrast written statements with any web access you have to your accounts. I am not saying any of this is guaranteed to expose fraudulent brokers, but it can only help.

- Never become a brokerage client or purchase any kind of securities investment from a cold call. Remember, there are always going to be fraudulent boiler room operations specializing in high-pressure tactics and seeking to prey on the unsuspecting.

• Oh, and if your broker tries to tell you that Wall Street really has been portrayed unfairly in recent years and is full of the scrupulously honest, that may be reason enough to drop him or her. You want somebody who knows it is a game and helps you to play it.

Note

Use web sites such as *www.stockpatrol.com* or *www.virtualgumshoe.com* to make further checks on your broker or financial adviser. Don't forget search engines such as *www.dogpile.com* can be helpful.

Appendix B
A Glossary for Investor Survival

accounting irregularities

Usually a nice way of saying fraud. Clearly, it is in the interests of some accountants and companies to make the shenanigans sound less terrifying, and it succeeds wonderfully. In his book *Accounting Irregularities and Financial Fraud,* attorney Michael R. Young writes, "Perhaps out of a belief that the word fraud was too rude for its authoritative literature, accountants have historically avoided the term fraud altogether and, instead, divided financial statement misstatements into two categories: errors and irregularities."

aggressive accounting

A form of accounting where a desired result, often higher earnings or sales, is put before prudent interpretation of accounting rules and principles. Risks turning into fraud.

bake-off

A meeting called by a company to hear final presentations from investment bankers seeking its business—often to underwrite its initial public offering. Bake-offs gained notoriety because of the way Wall Street analysts would join the meeting and make positive sounds about the stock's prospects and often indicate that they would stick a buy label on it. This was widely seen as part of an effort by analysts to win business for their investment bank. (Such meetings are also sometimes known as *beauty contests*.)

Barney deal

A company desperately in need of revenue, perhaps because it is falling short of forecasts, swaps goods or services—software has been a favorite—with a friendly company. The companies draw up two contracts and both can then book revenues. Usually, there is no business justification for the transaction. The term is named after the children's TV character Barney, a purple dinosaur who proclaims, "I love you, you love me."

big-bath charges

A big write-down of the value of assets through restructuring and other one-time charges. If aggressively done, it can in one fell swoop remove costs and artificially boost profits. It can also lead to the miraculous creation of reserves that can be surreptitiously used to bolster future earnings.

black-box accounting

A term often used for financial statements that are indecipher-able to the outsider, perhaps because of lack of disclosure or their complexity. It suggests some deliberate obfuscation on the company's part.

booster-shot reports

Positive analyst reports intended to artificially boost a company's stock price, usually just as some shares are about to be sold onto the market.

brag-a-watts

Boosting electricity trading volumes, usually through *wash trades* (see separate entry), to raise revenue rather than because anybody really wanted to buy so many megawatts to light and heat a factory or a community.

burn rate

The rate at which companies burn through available cash when they have negative cash flow. It became a major focus in 2000–2001 when it became clear that many Internet companies were going to fail and access to new capital raisings was turned off.

channel stuffing

When a company, usually a manufacturer, sends its customers products that they haven't ordered, or sends them products much earlier than they ordered them. It then books revenue and profits on the unsold merchandize. It is stuffing too many things through the distribution channel and is often used to boost short-term revenue and profits at the expense of future results.

cherry picking

A practice in which money managers, traders, and brokers allocate unprofitable trades to their clients while diverting profitable trades to their own accounts.

Chinese wall

In the New Oxford American Dictionary, "an insurmountable barrier, especially to the passage of information or communication." On much of Wall Street, it has meant nothing of the kind; it has either been ignored or regarded as a minor irritation to be stepped around.

churning

Excessive and unnecessary trading of a client's stocks portfolio by a broker or money manager who aims at generating commissions rather than improving returns.

confetti cutter

The recommended kind of shredding machine if you want to make sure that documents cannot be pieced together again by investigators. These machines shred to Security Level 5—the level favored by the Department of Defense and other federal agencies. Often retailing at more than $1,500, Level 5 shredders slice paper into 1/32 by 7/16 inch rectangular shreds. "It would take an infinite number of monkeys an infinite number of years to piece that paper together," said former State Department employee Sy DeWitt, a managing director at security risk consultants Pinkerton, in an interview with Reuters in January 2002.

corporate governance

The relationship among the forces—mainly the management, board, and shareholders—that determine the direction and performance of a company.

commission kickbacks

Investors pay much higher than normal commissions to brokers for trading shares as a kickback for the investor receiving an allocation of shares in a hot IPO or for being cut in on some other deal. Some investors paid commission rates 50–60 times normal levels during the IPO mania in 1998–2000. This was a way that the investment banks ensured they shared in the windfall profits to be made when prices soared on listing.

cookie-jar reserves

Cash that a company stashes away into reserve accounts in the good times to draw down when conditions are tougher. Often, this is done without full disclosure so that investors are hoodwinked into thinking earnings are lower than they really were in the go-go years and higher than they were in the rougher times.

creative accounting

Manipulation of a company's accounts to create a desired picture.

death spiral preferred financing

Financing that can kill off troubled companies while the financiers profit. It works like a convertible bond—only the goalposts can move so that the bond owner is entitled to convert into an increasing number of shares the lower the price goes. It gives the convertible bond owner an incentive to sell the stock to drive down its price. (The financial instruments are sometimes known as death spiral convertibles or toxic convertibles.)

Dunlapped

A term for the slash and burn, take-no-prisoners approach of Albert ("Chainsaw Al") Dunlap, who was the CEO of paper products maker Scott Paper and then of kitchen appliance manufacturer Sunbeam in the 1990s and who fired thousands of workers soon after taking over at each. Dunlap often used the term himself in interviews. The original sense was more positive, indicating that a company had been turned around with dizzying speed. However, Dunlapping lost credibility when Dunlap was fired after results started to deteriorate as questions about the company's aggressive accounting began to grow.

earnings management

Strategy in which a company seeks to manage the volatility of its earnings so that they have a smooth appearance from quarter to quarter. It is all about disguising what is happening in the real world during a particular period. Often, it means borrowing sales or profits from one quarter and putting them in another or giving an artificial impression about recurring growth through the use of asset sales, reserves, and pension fund returns.

EBITDA

Earnings Before Interest, Tax, Depreciation, and Amortization. A measurement of earnings that has been promoted by many companies as giving a better idea of performance than net profit, which includes ITDA. Companies often wrongly refer to it as cash flow. It is also open to manipulation. As Mulford and Comiskey write in their book *The Financial Numbers Game*, it "is truly a creative income statement-based measure."

financial engineering

The narrowest definition of this term is the combining or cutting up of existing financial products to make new ones. But, the term is increasingly being used to describe any complicated use of derivatives and other financial instruments as well as the use of various structures aimed at improving the look of a balance sheet.

flipping

The purchase by investors of shares at the initial public offer (IPO) price and then rapid sale at a profit once trading begins. Many top clients of major brokers flipped their shares during the Internet IPO boom.

forensic accountants

Accountants who have been specially trained to delve deep into a company's books and affairs to ferret out fraud. A cross between a detective and an auditor, they are usually called in when a company's accounts are the subject of an investigation.

friends and family allocations

Shares reserved in initial public offers for executives and other employees of the issuing company and its affiliates—plus some for others with close ties, such as customers and suppliers. During the Internet boom, some of these shares were taken by investment banks as part of an underwriting agreement and were allocated to "friends of the investment bank."

front running

The practice in which a broker or trader buys or sells a stock in full knowledge that a client has just placed a big order to buy or sell that security. The broker or trader is taking advantage of inside information from the client, who may well be put at a disadvantage if the broker's order moves the market and the final price of the original order is worse as a result.

going concern qualification

When accountants slap a "going concern qualification" onto their audit of a company's financial statements, it means they fear the business is in such poor financial condition that it could go under.

golden parachute

A large cash payment or other financial compensation guaranteed to a CEO or other executive in the event of a takeover of a company. In recent years, this term, and the term platinum parachute, have also been used loosely for large payments made to executives when they have resigned under pressure or have been fired.

laddering

The practice of encouraging investors who are allocated shares in an initial public offering to put orders in at set higher prices when the stock first trades so that it will climb up a ladder of orders. Failure to place the orders may mean that the investor concerned might not get as generous an allocation of shares in the next hot IPO.

lazy Susan

(Sometimes known as the *round tripper*.) A swap that allows two companies to boost their revenue without any real goods or services changing hands, very popular in the energy trading and telecommunications businesses in 2000–2001. Advantage: investors

think your revenue has gone up and yet it hasn't cost you more than the paperwork.

Lerached

As in "to be Lerached." A term used by Silicon Valley attorneys and companies facing class-action lawsuits for alleged securities fraud that were filed on behalf of investors by Bill Lerach, co-managing partner of the law firm Milberg Weiss Bershad Hynes & Lerach and the most prominent attorney in this line of business.

piggy backing

Same as *front running*.

proxy statement

A statement issued annually by publicly traded companies ahead of an annual meeting. It includes board nominations, voting instructions, shareholder resolutions, and important information about a board, compensation of executives, and ties between directors and the company.

pump-and-dump

This was more normally associated with Mafia-run "boiler room" brokerages, but some believe that the whole Internet and technology IPO market was one giant pump-and-dump scheme. In the classic "pump and dump," perpetrators will seize on a tiny company with very few shares on issue and a very low share price. They will buy a large number of shares and then start a promotional campaign to stir up positive interest in the stock, possibly through cold calling to investors, newsletters, messages in chat-rooms, message boards, and emails. They then sit back and watch the stock price rise as some people are duped into buying. The low number of shares available for purchase (low original issue and the manipulators own a lot) should accelerate the rise. They can then sell out at a profit and the stock will sink because there was no fundamental reason for its gains in the first place. The losers are the investors who bought the stock based on the promotional campaign by the manipulators.

rank and yank

A brutal system for assessing employees used at Enron. They were ranked every six months on a 1–5 scale, with 15 percent put in the lowest category and then given six months to improve or be fired (yanked). Corporate America has had similar systems before, at General Electric Co. for example, but these tended to be only annual measurements with fewer employees sent packing.

related-party transactions

Another name for deals with entities and individuals that are in some way affiliated with the company concerned. Examples include a contract from the CEO's privately owned aircraft company to fly the company's executives around the world. These deals create the perception that a favor was given or that a company received a worse bargain than if it had gone to a provider of the service that had no such relationship.

repricing of stock options

Often a desperate measure taken when a company's share price has dropped so far below the exercise price of its management and employee stock options that the options are next to worthless. The company reprices them or replaces them with new options.

reverse-stock-split

When a company reduces the number of shares it has on issue by swapping out a larger number for a substantially smaller number. Often companies will give shareholders 10 shares for every 100 or 200 they had originally, through a one-for-ten or one-for-twentysplit. It is often a desperate measure to lift its notional share price by a company trying to avoid delisting by an exchange, such as the New York Stock Exchange, after its share price falls below $1.

ricochet trading

A technique allegedly used by Enron and others in the California power crisis. The energy traders would buy power in California at capped prices, move it to another state, and then sell it back to California at higher uncapped prices.

roundtrip trading (or round-tripping)

See *lazy Susan*. Also sometimes called a Boomerang deal.

salting

Tampering with results during gold mining exploration by adding gold dust brought in from outside the area of drill testing. The word is derived from the most primitive form of salting—the use of a salt shaker to sprinkle gold dust onto rocks. Extensive salting of deposits in Indonesia was thought to be behind the collapse of Canadian gold mining company Bre-X in 1997.

Sarbanes-Oxley Act of 2002

The main corporate reform legislation passed by Congress in 2002 in response to the wave of scandals.

short and distort

In many ways the opposite of the pump-and-dump. In this scheme, a short seller will short a stock and then spread false rumors about its financial health or other issues. When the stock drops on the rumors, the short seller will buy back the stock at a profit. The likely losers are the company concerned and any investors who sold as the stock declined because they believed the rumors.

special-purpose entities

These are vehicles set up to allow a company to place certain assets off its balance sheet and then finance them. Because the assets are off balance sheet, there is often minimal disclosure. The problem occurs if the risk of holding those assets remains with the original company rather than the new SPE. In that case, if something goes wrong, investors are suddenly faced with liabilities they didn't know existed, which is what happened at Enron.

spiff

A trading term for a kickback or commission, which are sometimes the same thing.

spinning

A term used to describe an underwriting investment bank's allocation of some shares in a hot IPO deal for a corporate chief in the hope or expectation that the executive will return the favor by giving the investment bank some choice business.

springloading

Completing the acquisition of a company after making sure that it has delayed reporting revenue while bringing forward expenses. The idea is that the company's performance will suddenly appear to have improved under new ownership, artificially boosting the acquirer's sales, earnings, and possibly its share price.

stock options

Stock options offer the right but not the obligation to buy a stock at a set price within a particular timeframe.

tying

The case in which loans are granted to companies by banks only if the companies also agree to give the lender more lucrative investment banking business, such as underwriting for stock sales and mergers advisory work. Such quid-pro-quo arrangements became widespread in the late 1990s. Laws aimed at preventing tying were circumvented through the use of different affiliates for various transactions. A link is also very difficult to prove.

wash trading

Same as *roundtrip trading*.

Index

About the Author

Martin Howell heads up Reuters equities news coverage for the Americas out of New York and is responsible for a team of more than 120 reporters in the United States, Canada, and Latin America. He has played a major role in directing Reuters coverage of the Enron collapse and the impact of the September 11 attacks on corporate America. Before that he was one of the editors in charge of the news agency's U.S. corporate news coverage. Prior to joining Reuters, Howell, 42, worked for *Bloomberg News*, AP-Dow Jones, the *Far Eastern Economic Review,* and the *Hong Kong Standard* in the Far East. From 1980–1986 he worked for British provincial newspapers. Howell, who is British, was so desperate to become a reporter when he was 18 that he turned down the chance to study economics at the London School of Economics and instead went straight into the profession. He attended university later and has a diploma in Mandarin from the University of London's School of Oriental and African Studies. He continues to work on improving his Chinese in his spare moments. He lives in Flushing, in the New York borough of Queens, and regularly visits Martha's Vineyard in Massachusetts, where his two daughters live. Chess, backgammon, cooking Asian food, and swimming are his current pursuits, though good coffee and conversation with friends and his kids are always his top preference.